Unlocking *Dracula A.D. 1972*

ALSO BY DAVID HUCKVALE
AND FROM McFARLAND

Artificial Intelligence in the Movies: A History (2024)

The Piano on Film (2022)

*Terrors of the Flesh: The Philosophy
of Body Horror in Film* (2020)

Dirk Bogarde: Matinee Idol, Art House Star (2019)

*A Green and Pagan Land: Myth, Magic
and Landscape in British Film and Television* (2018)

Movie Magick: The Occult in Film (2018)

*Music for the Superman: Nietzsche and
the Great Composers* (2017)

*A Dark and Stormy Oeuvre: Crime, Magic and Power
in the Novels of Edward Bulwer-Lytton* (2016)

Hammer Films' Psychological Thrillers, 1950–1972 (2014)

*Poe Evermore: The Legacy in Film,
Music and Television* (2014)

*The Occult Arts of Music: An Esoteric Survey
from Pythagoras to Pop Culture* (2013)

*James Bernard, Composer to Count Dracula:
A Critical Biography* (2006; paperback 2012)

*Ancient Egypt in the Popular Imagination: Building
a Fantasy in Film, Literature, Music and Art* (2012)

*Visconti and the German Dream: Romanticism, Wagner
and the Nazi Catastrophe in Film* (2012)

*Touchstones of Gothic Horror: A Film Genealogy
of Eleven Motifs and Images* (2010)

Hammer Film Scores and the Musical Avant-Garde (2008)

Unlocking *Dracula A.D. 1972*
A Classic Horror Film in Context

DAVID HUCKVALE

McFarland & Company, Inc., Publishers
Jefferson, North Carolina

LIBRARY OF CONGRESS CATALOGING-IN-PUBLICATION DATA

Names: Huckvale, David author
Title: Unlocking Dracula A.D. 1972 : a classic horror film in context / David Huckvale.
Description: Jefferson, North Carolina : McFarland & Company, Inc., Publishers, 2025. | Includes bibliographical references and index.
Identifiers: LCCN 2025030202 | ISBN 9781476696126 paperback ∞
ISBN 9781476656090 ebook
Subjects: LCSH: Dracula A.D. 1972 (Motion picture) | Horror films—History and criticism | Dracula films—History and criticism | Chelsea (London, England)—In motion pictures | BISAC: PERFORMING ARTS / Film / Genres / Horror | LCGFT: Film criticism
Classification: LCC PN1997.D735 H83 2025 | DDC 791.43/72—dc23/eng/20250714
LC record available at https://lccn.loc.gov/2025030202

ISBN (print) 978-1-4766-9612-6
ISBN (ebook) 978-1-4766-5609-0

© 2025 David Huckvale. All rights reserved

No part of this book may be reproduced or transmitted in any form or by any means, electronic or mechanical, including photocopying or recording, or by any information storage and retrieval system, without permission in writing from the publisher.

Front cover illustration by Joshua Ryals

Printed in the United States of America

McFarland & Company, Inc., Publishers
Box 611, Jefferson, North Carolina 28640
www.mcfarlandpub.com

To Simon J. Ballard

Acknowledgments

I would like to thank Donald Fearney for his assistance and Alan Gibson's daughters, Jessica and Sarah, for their kind permission to publish his "Notes on Directing (1987)" in the appendix.

Take One Vampire—the second assistant camera clapper loader starts the prologue.

Contents

Acknowledgments	vi
Prefatory Synopsis	1
Introduction: Critics	3
One. Contemporaneity	13
Two. Camp, Kitsch and Cult	29
Three. Cause of the Conflict	41
Four. Context	52
Interlude One: Chelsea	67
Five. The Occult	78
Six. Cushing and Christopher	92
Seven. Cast and Crew	110
Eight. Cameras and Choreography	128
Interlude Two: Cars, Locations and Costumes	146
Nine. Décor and Music	151
Epilogue: Requiescat in Pace Ultima	165
Appendix: Alan Gibson's "Notes on Directing (1987)"	173
Chapter Notes	177
Bibliography	183
Index	187

Prefatory Synopsis

For those who have bought this book but have not actually seen the film it is about, a synopsis may be necessary.

In 1872, Lawrence Van Helsing (Peter Cushing) finds himself wrestling with Count Dracula (Christopher Lee) on top of a coach in Hyde Park. We never learn how this unusual situation occurred, but the upshot is that the coach crashes, and Dracula is impaled on one of the spokes of the carriage wheels. Van Helsing, severely wounded, drives the spoke firmly into the vampire's heart before expiring himself, but someone else is aware of what is going on—Dracula's unnamed disciple (played by Christopher Neame, who will later reappear as a young man called Johnny Alucard). The disciple gathers Dracula's dried blood in a glass vial and buries it in the same graveyard in which Van Helsing is later buried.

The action now moves forward a century, and we find ourselves at a party in London in 1972. Johnny Alucard and a group of swinging hippies have infiltrated an upper-class gathering where the band, Stoneground, is performing. The police are called and the hippies leave. Reconvening at a coffee bar in King's Road, Johnny suggests that they all take part in a Black Mass. One of the group is the granddaughter of a descendant of Lawrence Van Helsing. She is named Jessica (Stephanie Beacham) and her grandfather is named Lorrimer (Peter Cushing again). Lorrimer is a professor of anthropology and the occult at the University of London, and fully aware of his grandfather's death at the hands of Dracula.

After being scared by Joe Mitcham (William Ellis), who leaps from behind the gravestone of Lawrence Van Helsing at St. Bartolph's Church, Jessica attends the Black Mass, which Johnny uses to summon Dracula back from the dead. Dracula wants to have his revenge on Lorrimer by vampirizing Jessica, but his first victim turns out to be another member of the group—a girl named Laura Bellows (Caroline Munro), whose severed head and exsanguinated body are discovered the following day in the derelict graveyard. The police are alerted, and due to Laura's connection to Jessica, Inspector Murray (Michael Coles) decides to pay Lorrimer a visit to find out if he can help solve the case. When Lorrimer is informed of the condition of Laura's body, he begins to suspect that Dracula has been revived.

Meanwhile, Dracula claims his second victim—another member of the group of friends named Gaynor Keating (Marsha Hunt)—by draining her of blood. Johnny demands to be made a vampire as well, as a reward for having summoned the Count back to life. Dracula grants this request, and Johnny sets off to find his own victim, having disposed of Gaynor's body in Hyde Park.

When the police discover these new bodies, Van Helsing is summoned to Scotland Yard, where he explains the basics of vampire lore to Inspector Murray. Van Helsing has previously scooped up some holy water at a nearby church to serve as protection during the encounter with Dracula he is contemplating.

Before he can do that, however, Jessica is kidnapped by her boyfriend, Bob (Philip Miller), whom Johnny has by now turned into one of the undead as well. She is taken to the church to await Dracula's pleasure. When Van Helsing discovers what has happened, he seeks out Johnny to find out where his granddaughter has been taken. Van Helsing and Johnny fight in Johnny's flat. Johnny is overcome by the rising sun and destroyed by the clear running water of his shower. The police arrive and agree to accept Van Helsing's plan to destroy Dracula by himself. He makes his way to the church, where he discovers Jessica lying on the altar. Dracula appears, and the final combat between them begins. Van Helsing thrusts a silver-bladed dagger in the vampire's chest, but Dracula is able to will Jessica to remove it. Seemingly triumphant, Dracula chases Van Helsing outside, unaware that Van Helsing has prepared a trap—a pit filled with stakes into which Dracula tumbles after being blinded by the handy holy water Van Helsing splashes in his face. Dracula disintegrates and Jessica, startled by the dead body of her boyfriend which has been left lying in the graveyard, is comforted and led away by her grandfather.

Introduction: Critics

> The Time: Now
> The Place: King's Road, Chelsea
> The Killer: Count Dracula
> —Publicity tag for *Dracula A.D. 1972*

Hammer Films was fond of beginning its movies with introductions, either voiced or left for the audience to read by itself. Before the company forged its association with Gothic horror, *Four-Sided Triangle* (dir. Terence Fisher, 1953) opens, after the main titles, with a quotation from Ecclesiastes before James Hayter sets the scene and later faces the camera to introduce himself (or, rather, the character he's playing). *The Curse of Frankenstein* (dir. Terence Fisher, 1957) sets the scene with the title presented in a Gothic font against a suitably scarlet background. Francis De Woolf speaks the opening voice-over of *The Hound of the Baskervilles* (dir. Terence Fisher, 1959), while *The Brides of Dracula* (dir. Terence Fisher, 1960) employed an uncredited actor to intone its opening words. Andrew Kier delivered the rather clumsy mixed metaphor, written by Anthony Hinds, which opens Fisher's 1966 *Dracula: Prince of Darkness* ("the fountainhead himself perished"), and the Canadian Robert Beatty, who often narrated Hammer's trailers, spoke the only English words in *One Million Years B.C.* (dir. Don Chaffey, 1966). Rupert Davies, who plays the Monsignor in *Dracula Has Risen from the Grave* (dir. Freddie Francis, 1968), provides the voice-over after the discovery of Dracula's first atrocity. Ralph Bates explains the situation after the main titles of *Dr. Jekyll and Sister Hyde* (dir. Roy Ward Baker, 1971), while Douglas Wilmer provides the voice-over in the prologue of *The Vampire Lovers* (dir. Roy Ward Baker, 1970).

The reason I mention all these examples is by way of my own introduction to the contextualization of Alan Gibson's once much-maligned *Dracula A.D. 1972*, which also opens with a voice-over:

> The year: 1872, and the nightmare legend of Count Dracula extends its terror far beyond the mountains of Carpathia to the Victorian metropolis of London. Here in Hyde Park, the final confrontation between Lawrence Van Helsing and his arch enemy, the demon vampire, Dracula.

The voice is uncredited, as is the case with *Brides of Dracula*, but the function remains the same—to set the scene and place the film within its own historical context. All the voice-overs listed here invoke the past and provide authority, so when

David Pirie wrote of *Dracula A.D. 1972*, "it began by pretending to be a sequel to a hypothetical adventure which had taken place in 1872 (always an ominous sign),"[1] one wonders *why* such a prologue should, in itself, be regarded as "ominous." Admittedly, Hammer had, until *Scars of Dracula* (dir. Roy Ward Baker, 1970), been careful to link its Dracula sequels by connecting Dracula's previous demise with his subsequent resurrections, but that is really the only continuity between the films. And, as we have seen, the use of a voice-over was nothing new. Pirie's judgment here seems questionable, and more to do with his dislike of the film than with anything to do with the film's structure.

Pirie, writing in 1977, when *A.D. 1972* was still relatively raw and recent in his recollection, certainly didn't appreciate what its director, Alan Gibson, and screenwriter, Don Houghton, were trying to do. It is my intention in this book to argue that they succeeded remarkably well. Today, the film has been reassessed and is now a "cult classic," with many admirers, but that was not always the case. Pirie did acknowledge that the idea of updating *Dracula* was not illogical, pointing out that Stoker's 1897 *Dracula* novel was indeed set in what was then the present, "and he did everything in his book's opening section to emphasize that this formidable gentleman *was* equipped to deal with legal matters, railways time-tables, etc. His readers were then left to imagine the Count's subtle infiltration of London society," but then opines that "Hammer do[es] exactly the opposite: they bring Dracula to modern London in the first few minutes, but do everything to make it clear that this snarling and anachronistic dandy would be quite incapable of putting one foot outside the church without attracting the attention of the entre metropolis."[2] He argues that "the makers of *Dracula A.D. 1972* [a film that "invited derision at every possible juncture"[3] with "inane situations and dialogue"[4]] have not even attempted to come to terms with the starting problem of any modern Dracula, which is how to relate the vampire figure to contemporary society."[5] This argument seems somewhat specious when one considers that the majority of Hammer's previous Dracula sequels confined Dracula to his castle just as much as he is confined to St. Bartolph's Church in *A.D. 1972*, but this is something to which we will return in much more detail later.

Pirie also takes issue with Gibson's directorial style. Admittedly, in this quotation he is talking about *A.D. 1972*'s sequel, *The Satanic Rites of Dracula* (1973), but it applies equally well to the former film. He concedes that there is "some attempt to situate Dracula in truly contemporary surroundings (What better role for a modern vampire in London than a property speculator?).... But the film is betrayed by the tired, computerized, sub–*Avengers* style of Alan Gibson's direction and some atrocious interpolations."[6] Alan Frank took a similarly baleful view of Gibson's direction, which, in his view, "betrayed the anemia that had struck the Hammer Dracula."[7] In fact, as I hope to argue successfully, Gibson's approach was highly innovative and invigorating.

Unfortunately, Pirie and Frank were not the only authoritative critics to attack the film in the early years of its life. Roger Ebert wrote at the time of the film's release (December 13, 1972) that Christopher Neame's Johnny Alucard resembled Alex in Stanley Kubrick's *A Clockwork Orange* (1971):

He seems to be a symbol of the general decay at Hammer Films, which, having brought the horror film to a peak of perfection and created the first new horror superstar in years (Christopher Lee), now seems willing to follow the artistic leads of violence-come-latelies like Kubrick. Alas.[8]

Marjorie Bilbow regarded it as "a not particularly convincing attempt to bring old Drac up to date that even undemanding addicts are unlikely to find very exciting."

> The idea of Count Dracula coming to life in the present day is good and it is perfectly feasible to assume that the vogue interest in the black arts should provide him with his chance to return. The film would be much more successful if it did not make such desperate efforts to be up-to-the-minute with slang expressions that manifestly do not come naturally to the cast of the characters they are portraying, or waste so much plot time on party and disco scenes that are old-hat telly. What with music that is more bang-bang thriller than spooky, and direction that emphasizes the crime and detection element rather than the supernatural, Dracula and his activities get pushed into the background.

What Bilbow overlooks here is that the crime and detection elements were just as much to the fore in *Taste the Blood of Dracula* (dir. Peter Sasdy, 1970), which has a great deal in common with *A.D. 1972*, and are even more a largely redundant aspect of Terence Fisher's perennially praised *The Mummy* (1959). Bilbow does, however, concede that "Peter Cushing, moving serenely and sincerely through the thicket of trite dialogue and over-anxious performances, achieves moments of chilling conviction."[9]

And on the accusations go. Alan Frank accuses it of being

> an uneasy and none too effective attempt to transpose the Dracula legend from 19th-century Transylvania to the swinging Chelsea of London in 1972.[10]
>
> At the box office Dracula was now distinctly subject to the law of diminishing returns; a little fresh blood had to be injected somehow. *Dracula A.D. 1972*, a rather confining title for a tiresome piece filled with what would later have been called punk rockers, was the result.[11]

Leslie Halliwell continues: "A moment's thought would have told the producers that such a modern concept must inevitably rob the show of any period style or mystery."[12] We should, however, pause at that word "inevitably," which is as illogical and personal as Pirie's earlier use of "ominous." Why "inevitably"? It is nothing of the sort, and Halliwell's opinion again flies in the face of the contemporary settings of so many of the earlier Universal Gothic horror films. This is a question of personal *taste*, not dramaturgy.

More recently, Jonathan Rigby has hammered his own stake into the film: "Lee is required to die, to be resurrected, bite three people (one of whom is a man) and then die again, and all his scenes bar the opening one are set in a musty old church,"[13] but an unprejudiced recollection will reveal that this is actually more than the vampire was given to do in Hammer's 1958 *Dracula*, where he is not resurrected, dies only once, and similarly bites three people (Jonathan Harker, Lucy, and Mina). Though he was more peripatetic in 1958, he is in fact seen in only three locations: the castle, the undertaker's shop, and the Holmwood residence. Finally, no one, surely, could argue with the visual excellence of the church set in *A.D. 1972*.

Alas, it was not only the professional critics who were discontented with

Gibson's film. Its star, Christopher Lee, was also very unhappy with the way things had developed:

> I have become totally disenchanted with the way a great character has progressively deteriorated. That's why I will not do it any more. *Dracula A.D. 1972* was as far as you could go. It was getting away from Bram Stoker's book. It wasn't valid. The first one which I made in 1958 was the best. Of course it was the best! It was the closest to the book! I haven't seen any of them except that one, because it was the only good one. There's no more interest or fascination left in Dracula the way he has been portrayed on the screen—which is a tragedy, because he is a great and heroic character.[14]

He signed off with words that he never retracted: "At the age of fifty, I took the firm decision to Draculate no more." The deciding factors were *Dracula A.D. 1972* and *The Satanic Rites of Dracula*.[15] Forever afterward, he referred to Dracula as "That Character," but of course there were many other reasons for his avoidance of the role that had propelled him to international stardom, his complex and uncomfortable relation with Hammer itself being one, his ambition to break free from Gothic horror being another.

By 2007, Sinclair McKay was much more sympathetic, admitting that *A.D. 1972* was "one of my favourite Hammers. This preference can't be explained, it just is, that's all. Against all odds, it's an insanely cheering (and hypnotically watchable) production. Not because it's 'so bad, it's good'—but because, I suppose, that no matter how illogical and naff it all is, there is tremendously good humour running through it. Plus also a sigh-inducing nostalgia for the day when the King's Road wasn't a upper-glitzy high street for impossibly rich people but a faintly tatty parade for gormless teenagers."[16] He also defines the film as "a masterpiece of kitsch," with its depiction of "what older people imagined fashionable London looked like." Finally, he identifies where the "inadvertent charm" of the film really lies: "the *hilarious* depiction of groovy young people (and that 'young' is qualified)."[17]

There are certain aspects of this with which one can also take issue. What constitutes "kitsch" (which contemporary parlance refers to as "cheesiness") largely depends on one's own aesthetic preferences. "Kitsch" is, after all, a term of abuse, meaning "rubbish" in German, but it is of course quite possible to identify all of Hammer's horror films as peddling different degrees of kitsch, which term applies I think to *A.D. 1972*'s immediate predecessor, *Scars of Dracula*, considerably more. Christopher Lee certainly thought that film "truly feeble":

> It was a story with Dracula popped in almost as an afterthought. Even the Hammer make-up for once was tepid. It's one thing to look like death warmed up, quite another to look unhealthy. I was a pantomime figure. Everything was over the top, especially the giant bat whose electrically motored wings flapped with slow deliberation as if it were doing morning exercises.[18]

Kitsch is mostly about technique: how well or badly a style is imitated, to what extent the historical model has been manipulated or misunderstood. If *A.D. 1972* is kitsch, it is so in the ways it misunderstands its own contemporaneity; but many things once regarded with reverence, having fallen out of fashion, are now also called kitsch. *A.D. 1972* is now regarded with great affection by an increasing number of horror fans, not just due to the power of nostalgia, but also because the very considerable merits of the film itself, not least Alan Gibson's once much-derided but in fact inspired direction.

With regard to MacKay's view that the groovy young people of *A.D. 1972* are "*hilarious*," Simon J. Ballard has perceptively pointed out, "Here are a group of entitled people from privileged backgrounds (look who Jessica's granddaddy is!) who are trying in vain to capture the hippy dream during the fag-end of its life post–Manson, hence their awkward attempts at trying to sound right on, man. We see Anna wearing hip gear and driving a sports car, we hear Greg's plummy accent. … They don't seem authentic because quite simply they aren't, with the exception I think of Gaynor." Ballard also observes that far from deserving the laughter at Johnny Alucard's line about attending a "Jazz Spectacular," "There were such things back then, and that is what they were called."[19]

The film still has its online critics: "Simon T" obviously loathes it, but obviously doesn't think much of Hammer's other Draculas either:

> A stake through the heart for Hammer's cash cow. This woeful late entry in the tired and tacky Dracula series really is awful. Peter Cushing and Christopher Lee phone in their contributions in a vain attempt to distance themselves from the deeply boring "groovy" seventies setting. Michael Kitchen at least looks uncomfortable as a refugee from *Hair*. Awful music, cheap production values, and very very slow. Abby Wysmal.[20]

My purpose here is not to defend the film simply because I like it, but I would go so far as to say that *Dracula A.D. 1972* and its sequel are Hammer's most interesting Dracula films, and the ones that in fact most successfully adopt the approach of Bram Stoker's novel. Hammer's Dracula franchise started out as a one-off adaptation of the original novel. Jimmy Sangster's highly commendable compression of the plot inevitably jettisoned many expensive (and not so expensive) things. There was obviously no shipwreck, and hence no transfer of the action to Victorian London. Instead, everything takes place in a nonspecific middle–European environment, in which Dracula's castle isn't too far away from the residence of the Holmwood family, which he infiltrates. Bernard Robinson's authentically cluttered sets do, however, give a strong impression of Victorian England, as do the very proper British accents of the cast; but by keeping the action ostensibly "abroad," Sangster set up a precedent that didn't change until *Taste the Blood of Dracula*. This middle–Europeanization profoundly affected the purpose of Stoker's story, which is largely about the contamination of England by dangerous "foreign" forces. Dracula can be regarded as a Semitic, anarchist, even syphilitic enemy, which the upstanding representatives of Queen Victoria's Empire repel and ultimately destroy. In Hammer's Dracula plots, which eschew Stoker's contrast and conflict between home and abroad, Dracula becomes increasingly satanic, which he certainly isn't in Stoker's book. All that Lee's Dracula has in common with Stoker's unattractive but thoroughly up-to-date vampire is the sexual threat he poses. The increasingly theological context of the Hammer Draculas, especially within a fairytale setting, ignores the deeper political and sociological implications of Stoker's text. This is in no way a criticism of the 1958 *Dracula* in its own right, which is, as Lee rightly opined, "a fine film," but it reorganizes the material and significantly changes its meaning.

This approach continued with the sequels. As the title suggests, *Dracula: Prince of Darkness* made Dracula the truly satanic figure that he remained up to and including *The Satanic Rites of Dracula*, in which he was also a Bond villain and a property developer. Hammer's fairytale approach reached its peak in *Dracula Has Risen from the Grave*, which firmly grafted the character onto the world of the Brothers Grimm. Visually stylish, thanks to Freddie Francis's previous experience as a cinematographer, Dracula has even less to do here, but he does have one spectacular coup, in which he removes the stake that has been thrust into his heart by an atheist. Lee was worried by this interpolation, unaware at the time that he would be even more concerned by what Hammer later imposed on his famous role. Of course, *Dracula* is a profoundly Christian allegory, but *Dracula Has Risen from the Grave* employs

Lord of Misrule—Christopher Lee in *Taste the Blood of Dracula* (dir. Peter Sasdy, 1970).

a much greater array of inverted Christian symbolism, announcing its theological credentials in the title even before the film itself gets going. Dracula is even presented as a parody of Christ: He desecrates churches, robs graves, attacks the daughter of a Roman Catholic priest, and ultimately is impaled on a crucifix weeping tears of blood.

Taste the Blood of Dracula turned its back on middle–Europe and plunged the story back into Stoker's original Victorian context. It was originally designed as a film in which only Dracula's blood was to play a part, blood that transforms Ralph Bates's Lord Courtley into the predatory vampire required. However, the film's American backers required Christopher Lee to resume his famous role, and so Dracula was popped back into the story at the expense of Courtley, who actually metamorphoses into his satanic master. This was an unfortunate contingency, as Dracula has less to do now than ever before, merely counting off the victims of his revenge. These are the three Victorian hypocrites who beat Courtley to death after a particularly effective satanic ceremony in a deserted church. Why Dracula should be so concerned about the death of Courtley (whom he calls his "servant") when that death facilitated his resurrection is one of the lame absurdities forced onto the plot by the sudden change of heart from its original conception. However, the film has much to recommend it on other levels, the most significant of which is the genuinely English, Victorian setting. This brings the general mood much more into alignment with Stoker's novel, and provides Peter Sasdy with many opportunities to explore Victorian sexual hypocrisy.

A close look at the plot reveals its similarity to *Dracula A.D. 1972*. In fact, one could go so far as to say that Gibson's film is an updated remake of the former. What do we have in *Taste the Blood of Dracula*? A group of middle-aged thrill seekers, bored by the pursuit of sexual perversions in a brothel, are invited by a disciple of Dracula (Lord Courtley) to attend a satanic ceremony in a deserted church. (A couple of publicity stills show Lee's Dracula standing before an altar decked with black candles and decorated with satanic imagery that is very similar to the imagery in the main titles of *The Devil Rides Out* [dir. Terence Fisher, 1968], which itself was derived from Éliphas Lévi's famous book, *Transcendental Magic: Its Doctrine and Ritual*). Dracula's dried blood is mixed with Courtley's own liquid variety. The resulting froth gurgles up in and spills over three ceremonial goblets. The men refuse to drink, so Courtley does that for them. After the three men beat him to death, he transforms into the Count, who then sets about vampirizing the repressed middle-class children of the three men involved in the ceremony, and then gets them to murder their parents.

Compare all that with what happens in *Dracula A.D. 1972*: a group of middle-class hippies, bored with the "tired scene" of partying and snogging girls under tables, are invited by a disciple of Dracula (Johnny Alucard) to attend a Black Mass in a deconsecrated church. Dracula's dried blood is poured into a goblet and mixed with Alucard's. Foaming glutinously, it spills over the breasts of Caroline Munro's Laura Bellows, after which the hippies run away, leaving Laura to be vampirized by the revived Count.

There are even more similarities. Because both films are set in London (admittedly in different eras), the police are inevitably involved once Dracula starts piling up dead bodies. The policeman in *Taste the Blood of Dracula* is played by a scarf-swathed Michael Ripper, while the copper in *A.D. 1972* is Michael Coles's Inspector Murray of Scotland Yard; the former's scholarly Jonathon Secker (John Carson) equates to the latter's academic Van Helsing.

The much criticized decision to keep the Count confined to the ruined church in *Dracula A.D. 1972* never seems to have bothered fans of *Taste*, which similarly restrains him. In fact, he only strays outside in one brief scene on the grounds of the Harcourt's respectable Victorian villa prior to infiltrating it (which latter we don't actually see). While Courtley turns into Dracula, Alucard demands to be turned into a vampire in his own right, but the parallel is clear to see. The transformation of the children into vampires in *Taste* (hugely effective in the scene involving Martin Jarvis as Jeremy Secker, who smiles slowly at his horrified father before revealing his fresh-grown fangs) is also paralleled by the vampirization of Philip Miller's Bob, the boyfriend of Stephanie Beacham's Jessica Van Helsing in *A.D. 1972*.

As with Hammer's *The Mummy*, the element of detection is technically necessary (if there's a murder, the police are inevitably involved), but as we know who the culprit is in all three cases, the police are really rather redundant figures. Michael Coles, however, is the most convincing of Hammer's coppers, and as we shall see, the way in which Gibson skillfully choreographs the police procedural aspects of Coles's interaction with Cushing's Van Helsing (the film's natural hero) makes for much more compelling viewing. In both films, Dracula is tracked down to his deconsecrated church and destroyed there: overcome by the religious iconography of the church in *Taste*, induced by hypnagogic flashbacks of how it looked in its former glory (again, rather unconvincing); in *A.D. 1972*, impaled on wooden stakes in the moldering graveyard from which he emerged.

Wikipedia usefully describes a cult film as attracting a "dedicated, passionate fanbase which forms an elaborate subculture, members of which engage in repeated viewings, dialogue-quoting, and audience participation. Inclusive definitions allow for major studio productions, especially box-office bombs while exclusive definitions focus more on obscure, transgressive films shunned by the mainstream." When a film becomes a "cult," something different is happening from mere nostalgia, though it is of course related. A cult is also related to the idea of religion, which is a response to a need for meaning, a yearning for security, a return to a lost paradise; but whereas nostalgia attracts a broad church, a cult seems usually to appeal to the more specific experiences of a particular generation. *Casablanca* appeals to a broad church, and those who watch it now indulge in nostalgia or are merely interested in film history; *Dracula A.D. 1972*, however, is a cult film, and thus satisfies a melancholy need.

Friedrich Nietzsche was no friend of nostalgia. For him, humanity's inability to live in the moment was a problem:

> Consider the cattle, grazing as they pass you by: they do not know what is meant by yesterday or today, they leap about, eat, rest, digest, leap about again, and so from morn till night and from day to day, fettered to the moment and its pleasure or displeasure, and thus neither melancholy nor bored. This is a hard sight for man to see, for, though he thinks himself better than the animals because he is human, he cannot help envying them their happiness—what

they have, a life neither bored nor painful, is precisely what he wants, yet he cannot have it because he refuses to be an animal. … The man says "I remember" and envies the animal, who at once forgets and for whom every moment really dies, sinks back into night and fog and is extinguished forever. The animal thus lives *unhistorically*: for it is contained in the present.[21]

Our general inability to live in the present is made more painful if we feel that the past was somehow better, more familiar, and more secure. As Susan Sontag points out, "photographs actively promote nostalgia."

> Photography is an elegiac art, a twilight art. Most subjects photographed are, just by being photographed, touched with pathos. An ugly or grotesque subject may be moving because it has been dignified by the attention of the photography. A beautiful subject can be the object of rueful feelings, because it has aged or decayed or no longer exists. All photographs are *memento mori*. To take a photograph is to participate in another person's (or thing's) mortality, vulnerability, mutability.[22]

This melancholy applies even more to a cult film, in which ghosts walk through locations we might still be able to visit, and thus allow us to engage in a kind of cinematic séance, in which we are able to stand where actors, now much older if not already dead, once stood, and hope to summon a time we can now only vaguely remember. Vagueness is an essential aspect of this kind of "cultish" nostalgia, as the writer Richard Littler explained in Bob Fisher's seminal article on "Hauntology" in *The Fortean Times*:

> What makes nostalgia work is information that's missing. You have to have enormous gaps in your memory to create that strange mood. And if it's available to you online, in High Definition, then you lose that sense of dreaminess.

That half-remembered past is what makes a cult different from mere nostalgic appreciation. It is thus generational: one must have a personal connection with the period inhabited by the film, but one that is sufficiently distanced by time to create that yearning quality—that longing for "lost things." Littler discusses this with regard to why there was such an interest in the occult in the 1970s:

> In 1967, you have *Sgt. Pepper* and *Magical Mystery Tour*, both of which were about that particular generation harking back to the generation of their parents and grandparents. So there was a lot of Victoriana…. *Sgt. Pepper* is a Music Hall act, essentially what they did was to look back, and mix it with a modern sensibility. Which, at that point, was psychedelia, so you have all this history clashing together in the same artistic artefacts. And if you're harking back to Victoriana, it's inevitable that you're going to hit the Spiritualist Movement, so you're going to have Séances and ectoplasm and that filtered through … to things like [the children's TV series] *The Ghosts of Motley Hall* and *Rentaghost*.

That mood changed in Britain when the culture changed. Littler identifies the notorious nuclear war drama, *Threads*, around 1984 as the watershed, after which "the culture turns to money."[23]

This perhaps helps explain why *Dracula A.D. 1972*, which was so negatively received at the time of its release, subsequently became an icon of yearning for the generation that grew up in the era in which it was first released. In many ways, that generation's love of the film in 2024 has much in common with a yearning for the securities of home, which we feel most powerfully in childhood. The psychologist Adam Phillips discusses the idea of "home" in *Patience (After Sebald)*, Grant Gee's

2012 film about the apotheosis of psycho-geography that is W.G. Sebald's *The Rings of Saturn*:

> I think Sebald knew that only children had homes, that adults don't have homes, and that there's something childish in the best sense (and the worst sense) about the idea of home.

He argues that our fantasies about "home" are "to do with safety," a controllable environment, a kind of security in terms of invasions, and it's a bit like this is a toy that he's placed on the map of his books, as if to say "wouldn't it be nice if it could ever be like this?" but actually it's the opposite. We're not on an island. "We're interconnected, and we're interconnected in ways that are horrifying to us very often."

Might it be possible to see *Dracula A.D. 1972* as one of those comforting "homes," vaguely remembered, not quite as it really was but so much better than the sense of relative homelessness we might feel now? Could that help to explain its popularity now, apart from the equally important fact that it's such a well-made film?

ONE

CONTEMPORANEITY

> "Do old ideas rest easy in an open mind?"
> —Van Helsing in *Dracula A.D. 1972*

LIKE MANY OTHER DIE-HARD fans of Hammer's period approach to *Dracula*, Christopher Lee was at first "aghast" at the thought of setting a Dracula story in the present day, but he had the good sense to realize that "the Victorian period was arbitrary, the accident of Stoker's having lived at that time, and that after all Lon Chaney Jr. as Count Alucard had erupted into a jazz ballroom. All the same, the hippie idiom used was already out of date when then film was made and the programme at large felt wrong to me." We will return to the contentious subject of the hippie idiom later, but that and other things aside, Lee conceded that *Dracula A.D. 1972* "had certain things in its favour."[1] He was fully aware that his own interpretation of the role for Hammer was rather different from Stoker's conception. Obviously, Stoker's Dracula is in league with the Devil, and is distinctly unholy, but he is not himself a devil; certainly not *the* Devil. Stoker's vampire was once a human being and now is not, but is still subject to practical considerations and activities. As is well known, he consults Bradshaw's Railway Guide, deals with solicitors, and even transfers his money to Coutts and Co., the Queen's bankers, no less. He is observed making the beds and laying the table in his castle; once settled in London, he even helps the carters carry his boxes of earth into his Piccadilly and Carfax residences. When the vampire hunters penetrate the former, they even discover Dracula's toiletries:

> There was also a clothes brush, a brush and comb, and a jug and basin—the latter containing dirty water which was reddened as if with blood. Last of all was a little heap of keys of all sorts and sizes, probably those belonging to the other houses.[2]

But one simply cannot conceive of Lee or Lugosi washing, shaving, and wiping the blood from their lips, despite the fact that Lee insisted that Dracula must be "a believable, acceptable human, though ab-human in the literal sense of the word. I think that he must be acceptable, he must be a man of great nobility, a man of great philosophy, a man of great stillness and a man who is obviously completely irresistible."[3] Lee managed to convey this in 1958, but his Draculas became increasingly less human and more satanic with each sequel. Far from being an otherworldly figure, Stoker's Dracula is a very worldly one, but the origin of Hammer's distinctly Miltonic presentation of Dracula as Satan himself can be traced back to what Van Helsing says about him in the novel. "He learned his secrets in the Scholomance amongst the mountains over Lake Hermanstadt, where the Devil claims the tenth scholar as his due."[4] Stoker gleaned this information from Emily Gerard's 1885 article, "Transylvanian Superstitions," in *The Nineteenth Century* magazine:

> As I am on the subject of thunderstorms, I may as well here mention the Scholomance, or school supposed to exist somewhere in the heart of the mountains, and where all the secrets of nature, the language of animals, and all imaginable magic spells and charms are taught by the devil in person. Only ten scholars are admitted at a time, and when the course of learning has expired and nine of them are released to return to their homes, the tenth scholar is detained by the devil as payment, and mounted upon an Ismeju (dragon) he becomes henceforward the devil's aide-de-camp, and assists him in "making the weather," that is to say, preparing the thunderbolts.
>
> A small lake, immeasurably deep, lying high up among the mountains to the south of Hermanstadt, is supposed to be the cauldron where is brewed the thunder, and in fair weather the dragon sleeps beneath the waters. Roumenian peasants anxiously warn the traveller to beware of throwing a stone into this lake lest it should wake the dragon and provoke a thunderstorm. It is, however, no mere superstition that in summer there occur almost daily thunderstorms at this spot, about the hour of midday, and numerous cairns of stones round the shores attest the fact that many people have here found their death by lightning. On this account the place is shunned, and no Roumenians will venture to rest here at the hour of noon.[5]

Stoker even copied Gerard's misspelling of "Hermanstadt," the correct orthography being "Hermannstadt."

Because the cinematic representations of *Dracula* have so dominated our idea about what Stoker's novel is like, it is illuminating to approach the novel not as a Gothic romance but rather as a "sensation novel," in the manner of Wilkie Collins, whose often epistolary style Stoker adopted to heighten the realism and immediacy of his story. The "sensation novel" grafted elements of the Gothic onto stories set in contemporary society. In his introduction to Collins's collection of *Sensation Stories*, Peter Haining describes the genre Collins largely created by himself as consisting of "dramatic plots that revolved around hidden secrets, bloody crimes, villainous schemes and clever detective work, all occurring in everyday settings."[6] Though omitting overt supernaturalism, Collins's style and techniques are central to Stoker's approach. The most obvious parallel is Stoker's ubiquitous use of journals, letters, newspaper reports, and even telegrams, which Collins had begun to incorporate in his first "sensation novel," *Basil*, published in 1852. While nowhere near as famous as his later novels, *The Woman in White* and *The Moonstone*, *Basil* is a useful work to compare with *Dracula*. Early on in the plot, Collins refers to London pubs as "drink-vampyres that suck the life of London."[7] This description sums up the method of "sensation" writing: to evoke but not strictly employ the supernatural for dramatic effect. The villain of the piece, Robert Mannion, could well be a vampire from the way Collins describes him. He is beautiful, with a perfectly symmetrical face, which never reveals his emotions.

A key scene in the plot occurs when the eponymous Basil is invited to Mannion's home during a thunderstorm. After an uneasy conversation, Basil departs as lighting illuminates Mannion's face with a "hideously livid hue," giving "a spectral look of ghastliness and distortion to his features, that he absolutely seemed to be glaring and grinning on me like a fiend, in the one instant of its duration."[8] Also, Mannion has an extraordinarily cold hand, like Dracula: "it was so deadly cold it literally chilled mine for the moment."[9] (Dracula's hand is described as "cold as ice—more like the hand of a dead than a living man."[10]) In a dream, Basil's unfaithful wife and Mannion, her seducer, are described as monstrous iniquities incarnate in monstrous forms, "sporting talons and wearing veils" made of "one hideous network of twining worms."[11] Like Dracula, Mannion is motivated by revenge, wishing to destroy Basil's family to redress past injustices perpetrated by Basil's aristocratic father. The mother of Basil's wife is described as a living corpse: "her arms hung close at her side, like the arms of a corpse; the natural paleness of her face had turned to an earthy hue."[12] The impression is vampiric rather than "merely" deranged. After Basil beats Mannion to the ground, disfiguring him in the process, the two enemies have a final confrontation in which Collins seems to be evoking Frankenstein and his creation in Mary Shelley's novel:

> The first sight of that appalling face, with its ghastly discolouration of sickness, its hideous deformity of feature, its fierce and changeless malignity of expression glaring full on me in the piercing noonday sunshine—glaring with the same unearthly look of fury and triumph which I had seen flashing through the flashing lightning, when I parted from him in the storm—struck me speechless where I stood and never left me since.[13]

Mannion, like Frankenstein's Creature, threatens, "Go where you will, this face of mine shall never be turned away from you,"[14] and his ultimate demise is rather like that of Dracula in Hammer's *Dracula: Prince of Darkness*, in which the vampire is drowned by falling through the ice of his castle's moat:

> I heard a scream so shrill, so horribly unlike any human cry, that it seemed to silence the very thundering of the water. The spray fell. For one instant, I saw two livid and bloody hands tossed up against the black walls of the hole, as he dropped into it. Then the waves roared again fiercely in their hidden depths.[15]

Compare that passage with the way John Burke described the final scene of *Dracula: Prince of Darkness* in his novelization of the film:

> The vampire let out a vengeful howl and raised his claws towards the two on the bridge. Then he fell, groped for support that wasn't there, and plunged into the water. Up to his armpits, he managed for a few seconds to cling to the ice. Then another fragment came away and slowly, remorselessly, he was sucked down.[16]

I mention all these details to demonstrate the many Gothic elements in Collins's otherwise "contemporary," non-supernatural tale. Stoker's approach merely supernaturalizes the context. Far from being a Gothic romance in the tradition of Ann Radcliffe, still less sharing the Grimms' fairytale approach of Hammer's *Dracula Has Risen from the Grave*, Stoker's text is a contemporary thriller, the pace and texture of which has far more in common with *Dracula A.D. 1972* and its sequel *The Satanic Rites of Dracula* than any of the earlier films in Hammer's Dracula cycle.

It is a measure of just how influential Hammer's period approach to vampires was that so much criticism was made when the company placed its Dracula in the present day. This, however, had been the normal practice in vampire films before Hammer's arrival on the scene. The Bela Lugosi *Dracula*, directed by Tod Browning in 1931, is set in the period in which it was made, as was *Dracula's Daughter* (dir. Lambert Hillyer, 1936) and *Son of Dracula* (dir. Robert Siodmak, 1943). Even more up-to-date was Lew Landers's 1943 *Return of the Vampire*, which was Lugosi's second vampire film. (It is often regarded as the third, but in Tod Browning's 1935 *Mark of the Vampire* Lugosi actually plays a mortal actor who is pretending to be an immortal vampire.) *Return of the Vampire* intriguingly foreshadows many of aspects of *Dracula A.D. 1972*, which critics of Houghton's approach should have remembered before questioning the validity of placing the undead in a contemporary setting. The first comparison is that in both films, the vampires in question die twice. In *Return of the Vampire*, the Dracula figure is named Dr. Armand Tesla (Universal refused Columbia Pictures the right to use the Dracula name). In the prologue, set in 1918, Tesla is pierced through the heart with a metal spike by Gilbert Emery's Professor Saunders, assisted by Lady Jane Ainsley (Frieda Inescourt). Twenty-three years later, he is revived during the London Blitz. His body is disinterred from its tomb by an explosion, and the rod is removed from his heart by two comedy gravediggers who seem to have strayed from a modern-dress production of *Hamlet*. We also have a policeman from Scotland Yard—in fact rather more than a mere policeman: a chief commissioner, no less (Miles Mander). Like Inspector Murray's, his office has a venetian blind, but he takes rather more persuading to believe in vampires than his successor. "I may be crazy," he eventually admits, just as Murray tells Van Helsing, "If any of my superiors had been listening to what you've just said, they'd have you certified. If they thought I was going to notice of it, they'd have me certified."

The scenes of bombs being dropped by the Luftwaffe are actually the most horrifying aspect of the film; Tesla's werewolf assistant, Andreas (Matt Willis), is meant to be disturbing but is actually rather cuddly. Nonetheless, his role equates to Johnny Alucard's as disciple of the master; a title which, again like Alucard, is exactly what Andreas calls Tesla. *Return of the Vampire* is arguably even more up-to-date than *A.D. 1972* with regard to its portrayal of women, for in Lady Jane Ainsley we have a formidable female scientist on whom Tesla also vows to have his revenge. (In *The Satanic Rites of Dracula*, Houghton upgraded Jessica Van Helsing from being a casual browser of occult volumes to being, in the words of her grandfather, "a true scientist. Sometimes I think she knows more about my work than I do myself.")

Unlike *A.D. 1972*, *Return of the Vampire* cannot resist a shot of Big Ben to assure the audience that they really are in London, but what *A.D. 1972* lacks in that location, it fully makes up for with shots of Battersea Power Station and evocative parts of Chelsea. Another comparison between the two films is the similarity of the bombed-out ruins of St. Mathias's church in *Return*, where Tesla has set up residence, and the derelict graveyard of St. Bartolph's church in *A.D. 1972*, where Dracula spends his daylight hours. When Tesla is staked for the second time, his demise occurs, like Dracula's, amid this ecclesiastic rubble. We are also shown Tesla decomposing, an effect that had been discreetly overlooked in the 1931 *Dracula*. Thus does *Return of the Vampire* point the way toward Hammer's many magnificent disintegrations of Dracula.

Return of the Vampire is also adventurous with regard to its integration of Tesla into contemporary society. While Christopher Lee's Dracula in *A.D. 1972* broods on his own, confined to the interior of St. Bartolph's, Tesla cleverly decides to impersonate a refugee from Nazi Germany, one Dr. Bruckner, who has escaped from a concentration camp and has been invited to a reception by Lady Jane. ("I feel we're doing a good thing for humanity, by helping a fellow scientist escape the Nazi yoke," she explains.) But before the genuine Bruckner can introduce himself, Tesla orders Andreas to murder him, leaving the field clear for Tesla to infiltrate Lady Jane's home under a false identity. Consequently, Lugosi has a considerable amount of dialogue—far more than Lee's satanic Dracula ever had, and he also has an opportunity to exude old-world charm. While not as disapproving as Lally Bowers's outraged matron in *A.D. 1972*, Lady Jane certainly lives in comparable upper-class splendor. A large fireplace, each similarly adorned with garniture, commands the room, along with ginger jars, oil paintings, and a grand piano beneath a magnificent chandelier.

Just as Dracula hypnotizes Jessica in *A.D. 1972*, commanding her to remove the silver-bladed dagger Van Helsing has thrust into his heart in the film's climax, so too does Tesla hypnotize Professor Saunders's granddaughter, Nicki (Nina Foch). How intriguing that Nicki is his *granddaughter*!

Return of the Vampire also has fight scenes comparable to the struggle between Johnny and Van Helsing when Andreas, in wolf form, attacks two policemen. Finally, when Tesla replies to Lady Jane with, "You are a very brilliant woman, but a very foolish one, to pit your strength against mine," he adapts the same source from Stoker's novel, which Lee incorporated into his dialogue just before the final confrontation with Van Helsing: "You would pit your brains against mine, against me who has commanded nations."

John Carradine's two interpretations of Dracula in Erle C. Kenton's *House of Frankenstein* (1944) and *House of Dracula* (1945) weren't period dramas either. Though *House of Dracula* is set in a magnificently Gothic castle, it is filled with modern scientific instruments and telephones. Carradine's Count is also the opposite of Lee's satanic Dracula. He is presented as the tragic victim of a disease from which he desperately wants to be cured.

Italy's first horror film, *I Vampiri* (dir. Riccardo Freda, 1957), was also set in what was then the present; despite its swirling mist, horse-drawn carriages, and Lugosi-like attire of Germán Robles's Conde Lavud, the Mexican vampire film, *El Vampiro* (dir. Fernando Méndez, 1957) is also set in 1957. (Like *Dracula A.D. 1972*, it too has a short but very atmospheric prologue set in the 19th century; along with its dénouement it also has quite a lot in common with the end of *Dracula A.D. 1972*, the hero arriving on the scene just as Lavud is about to bite the heroine, who lies prone on an ottoman.) Paul Landres's *The Return of Dracula* (1958), with Francis Lederer as the vampire, opens with a blaring statement of the medieval "Dies irae" chant played by full orchestra, but the action of the film was firmly situated in the 1950s. Made in the same year that Hammer released its first *Dracula* film, this modest black and white film, with Lederer's excellently judged performance, also foreshadows what Hammer would latter achieve in *A.D. 1972*. It begins almost like a gangster film, but in an East European cemetery in which modern vampire hunters aim to dispatch Dracula in his tomb. They are too late. Like Count Alucard in *Son of Dracula*, Lederer's Dracula sets sail for America in search of new "opportunities," but unlike Lon

Chaney's Count, he sensibly wears a normal lounge suit and tie, the only concession to a cape being his overcoat, which he wears over the shoulder, allowing the sleeves to swing, cape-like, behind him. Arriving in Carleton, California, he integrates himself into the family of the man he has killed on the journey to his new home. In this, he anticipates Don Houghton's original idea that Dracula should stay with Johnny Alucard, a roommate situation that, in the event, never happened. Lederer's Count does, however, settle down with the Mayberry family, the members of which indulge in the kind of gossipy domesticity Stoker was careful to include in his novel to create the required sense of normality with which to contrast and contextualize the supernatural.

The Return of Dracula also foreshadows A.D. 1972's Jessica and Bob in Rachel Mayberry (Norma Eberhardt), the daughter of the family, and her boyfriend, Tim (Ray Stricklyn), but there are very few traditional Gothic images in the Lederer film. The most strikingly "Gothic" moment is the shot in which we see Lederer rise from his smoke-wreathed coffin. Like A.D. 1972, there are contemporary cops, a scholarly vampire hunter and even a Halloween mask, worn by Rachel's younger brother, which terrifies her in the same way Joe Mitcham's prank in St. Bartolph's Churchyard terrifies Jessica and Bob. The Return of Dracula even shares a line of Van Helsing's dialogue in A.D. 1972, when Gage Clarke's Reverend Whitfield says "No, no! You must be mistaken!"

Modern Dracula settings continued when Carradine appeared (as a butler rather than a vampire) in Al Adamson's quasi horror-comedy, *Blood of Dracula's Castle* (1969), which, though it takes place in a real castle in California (Shea's Castle), is similarly contemporary in style. Other modern-dress vampire films that predated A.D. 1972 include Carl Dreyer's *Vampyr* (1932) and Roger Vadim's *Et mourir de plaisir* (1960), both of which were based on J. Sheridan Le Fanu's "Carmilla"), along with Jean Rollin's series of sex-vampire extravaganzas, *Le viol du vampire* (1968), *La vampire nue* (1970), *Le frisson des vampires* (1971), and *Requiem pour un vampire* (1971).

Far more than Max Schreck's cabbage-eared monstrosity in F.W. Murnau's *Nosferatu* (1922), it was Lugosi's performance that set the template for future misinterpretations of Dracula, only one of which (directed, not very well, by Jess Franco in 1970) gave Christopher Lee's splendid Count the long mustache specified by Stoker. Even the most faithful dramatization of the novel, directed by Philip Saville for the BBC in 1976, with Louis Jordan as the Count, presents him as a clean-shaven Latin lover. The image of Christopher Lee in the role has become so pervasive that the Folio Society edition of the novel has illustrations by Abigail Rover, which similarly strip Dracula of his facial hair, and even bases the final image of him turning to dust on a still of Lee himself. The transformation of Dracula from his unappealing and rather odiferous original in the book into a clean-shaven Lothario presaged the stripping away of the contemporary setting, which is so vital to the punch and momentum of Stoker's original. Admittedly, a novel set in the Victorian period requires, if one is being faithful, a Victorian setting, but Hammer's settings became increasingly unreal until *Taste the Blood of Dracula*, thereafter reverting to the banality of a fake nowhere land in *Scars of Dracula*. While *Taste the Blood of Dracula* returned Dracula to the Victorian urban environment of London, Dracula himself was even more "popped in" than before, for reasons already explained.

In the novel, Dracula is not just a sexual threat but also a political and racial one. He is the feared "Other." He refers to himself as being the heir to a "conquering race,"[17] but he is both a barbarian and a decadent, for he is also a degenerate. He has hairs on the back of his hand, which reminded Leonard Wolf of the boy's entrapment game "in which one boy says, 'If you masturbate, you'll grow hair on your palms,' and watches to see which of his listeners looks guiltily down at his hands."[18] Wolf then goes on to quote Claude François Lallemand's belief that habitual masturbators "have a dank, moist, cold hand, very characteristic of vital exhaustion."[19] This is reminiscent of Mannion's cold hand in Collins's *Basil*. Stoker's description of the blood-gorged vampire lying torpid in his coffin during the day is a powerful metaphor of the onanist's penile tumescence:

> There lay the Count, but looking as if his youth had been half renewed, for the white hair and moustache were changed to dark iron-grey; the cheeks were fuller, and the white skin seemed ruby-red underneath; the mouth was redder than ever, for on the lips were gouts of blood, which trickled from the corners of the mouth and ran over the chin and neck. Even the deep, burning eyes seemed set amongst swollen flesh, for the lids and pouches underneath were bloated. It seemed as if the whole awful creature were simply gorged with blood; he lay like a filthy leech, exhausted with his repletion.[20]

In the 19th century, masturbation was a sure sign of moral degeneration, which was just as dangerous as a vampire's kiss. For an anti-Semite, like Stoker's contemporary, the composer Richard Wagner, Jewish blood was the equivalent of a vampire's dangerous fluid. Just as, for Wagner, Jewish blood corrupts the genetically "superior" blood of Aryans, so does Dracula's vampiric blood contaminate, even if it does not completely destroy. Wagner, like many other anti-Semites of his time, equated the degenerate habit of masturbation with Jews. For him, there was also something "unpleasantly incongruous"[21] about them, just as there is about Dracula. Wagner depicts Jews in a similar way to Stoker. In his infamous anti-Semitic tract, "Das Judenthum in Musik," cultured Jews are described as sophisticated men about town, rather like Dracula. Just as Wagner regarded Jews as a threat to the strength and vigor of the German *Volk*, Van Helsing and his band of amateur vampire hunters are true moral patriots, cleansing England of an enemy invader. There is indeed an overt trace of anti-Semitism in Stoker's novel, which suggests that Stoker (though a long way from the fanaticism of Wagner) was nonetheless very much a man of his time. The passage occurs in Chapter 26, when Van Helsing, Dr. Seward, and Jonathan Harker are trying to track down Dracula's movement. Their investigations lead them to an individual named Immanuel Hildesheim, whom Stoker describes as "a Hebrew of rather the Adelphi Theatre type, with a nose like a sheep, and a fez. His arguments were pointed with specie—we doing the punctuation—and with a little bargaining he told us what he knew."[22]

This idea of the racial and political threat of Dracula is largely lost in film adaptations. Sex predominates, naturally enough, but Hammer took an increasingly theological approach. With each successive Draculation, Lee's Count became increasingly satanic, culminating in *The Satanic Rites of Dracula*, in which the Count has a truly satanic agenda to destroy humanity.

While the presentation of Dracula himself in *A.D. 1972* was an impressively far cry from Stoker, the attempt to restore the contemporary urgency of the novel was very much in the spirit of sensation fiction. It is instructive to explore just how Stoker created his own highly "modern" context. The idea of having a solicitor's clerk visit Dracula in Transylvania is slightly forced. We later learn that Dracula is quite able to arrange the purchase of his Piccadilly residence by himself, but Stoker needed to find a way of taking the reader to Dracula's traditionally Gothic environment, which he would then contrast with Victorian London. Thus the opening chapters of the novel equate rather well with the prologue of *Dracula A.D. 1972*, which, as we shall see, rather magnificently upstages all of Hammer's previous confrontations between Dracula and his various slayers. The interior of St. Bartolph's church, in the graveyard of which he later makes his spectacular reappearance, also stands in for Castle Dracula itself. Both church and graveyard are splendidly Gothic studio creations, echoing not only Stoker's description of the environs of the Westenra Tomb in *Dracula*, but perhaps even more the earlier Gothic writing of Stoker's compatriot, Charles Maturin, in *Melmoth the Wanderer*.

> **MATURIN:** Isidora, sinking on a grave for rest, wrapped her veil around her, as if its folds could exclude even thought. In a few moments, gasping for air, she withdrew it; but as he eye encountered only tombstones and crosses, and that dark and sepulchral vegetation that loves to shoot its roots , and trail its unlovely verdure amid the joints of gravestones, she closed it again, and sat shuddering and alone.[23]
>
> **STOKER:** Never did tombs look so ghastly white; never did cypress, or yew, or juniper so seem the embodiment of funereal gloom; never did tree or grass wave or rustle so ominously; never did bough creak so mysteriously; and never did the far-away howling of dogs send such a woeful presage through the night.[24]

The rest of the film, as with most of the remainder of the novel, is a contemporary affair, resembling a detective story rather more than a Gothic romance. Unlike *A.D. 1972*, the police play virtually no part in the proceedings, Van Helsing being the Sherlock Holmes of the affair, though Stoker does have "a patrol of horse police going their usual suburban round,"[25] again anchoring the proceedings in the everyday world of "modern" London.

Indeed, Stoker takes immense trouble to fill his evocation of Victorian London with as many telling details as he can. Mina, who starts off as an assistant schoolmistress, learns shorthand, as does Jonathan (whose journal is "stenographic"). She also uses a typewriter, and compares her own journal with the columns of lady journalists. Her friend Lucy is indeed a forerunner of the kind of hippies we encounter in *A.D. 1972*—particularly Caroline Munro's Laura. Lucy uses slang, admittedly presented in respectable inverted commas. This is considered rather "racy." She refers to dressing as "a bore," explaining, "That is slang, again."[26] In *A.D. 1972*, Janet Key's Anna also says, "It was all rather a bore." Similarly, Johnny Alucard describes the party he and his friends leave at the beginning of the film as "a tired scene." Other slang expressions pepper Stoker's text later on, such as the Americanisms: "taken no chances" and "blowing my trumpet."[27] But slang soon loses its bloom, and the criticisms made of the slang in *A.D. 1972* could well be applied to Stoker's novel. Like the presumably rather promiscuous Laura, Lucy, who describes herself as a "horrid flirt,"[28] has three boyfriends, all of whom propose to her. "Why can't they let a girl marry three men, or as man as want her?" she complains. (Stoker thus echoes the three vampire women who fight over Harker in an earlier chapter set in the castle.) Quincy P. Morris also speaks slang of the American variety, which Stoker would have known at first hand from his visits to America with Sir Henry Irving when he went on tour with the Lyceum Theatre company. Complementing Harker's shorthand, Dr. Seward records his journal on a phonograph, an innovation retained in Hammer's 1958 adaptation, where it of course looks antiquated, but which was the Victorian equivalent of an iPhone when the novel was first published. Later, Mina will transcribe these phonographic records on a typewriter: the ultimate in Victorian modernity.

Stoker's text is peppered with details that are unnecessary to the actual plot but which help to create the illusion of everyday reality. Newspaper cuttings from various publications such as the *Pall Mall Gazette* and *Westminster Gazette* report key developments. In Whitby, the local paper that reports the storm in which Dracula arrives on board the *Demeter* speaks of "day-trippers." The "Board of Trade" is involved with the investigation into the ill-fated ship. There is talk of the "New Woman," who began to emerge in the 1890s, foreshadowing the women's liberation movement of the 1960s, and who was perceived as such a threat to male dominance. Indeed, the sexualization of women by the vampire's kiss is largely a metaphor of this anxiety. Train and railways stations, such as the great London termini of King's Cross, Paddington, and Fenchurch Street, all make their appearance throughout the novel—for if anything spoke of modernity to the Victorians, it was the immense growth of the railways. Mina lists quite a few precise train times in a letter to Van Helsing, which reports that Jonathan "leaves by the 6.25 tonight from Launceston and will be here at 10.18…. Will you, therefore, instead of lunching with us please come to breakfast at eight o'clock, if this be not too early. You can get away, if you are in a hurry, by the 10.30 train, which will bring you to Paddington by 2.35."[29] Similarly, in *A.D. 1972*, Johnny claims to have taken Laura (who is actually dead) to meet the 10.44 train from Victoria to Ramsgate.

Stoker also makes much of money and financial transactions. Dracula's clothes are stuffed with coins and banknotes. Seward takes chloral to aid sleep (he even writes out the formula: $C_2HCl_3OH_2O$)—and so is a drug user not unlike the "spaced-out teenagers" to whom Michael Coles's Inspector Murray refers in *A.D. 1972*.

There are telegrams, death certificates, and a whole paragraph of legal jargon with regard to Mrs. Westenra's will, which add nothing much to the plot but further help root the fantastic in the prosaic. The president of the Incorporated Law Society is mentioned—even Disraeli slips in. It is Stoker's skill in providing inconsequential details at key moments of the plot that help suspend the reader's disbelief. When Harker, for example, observes Dracula walking down Piccadilly, the Count is seen watching "a beautiful girl, in a big cartwheel hat, sitting in a victoria, outside Guiliano's."[30] This is the Victorian equivalent of Johnny Alucard, by then a vampire himself, watching Marjorie Baines (Glenda Allen) in a laundromat before pursuing and attacking her in *A.D. 1972*. Like Collins, Stoker makes sure we realize his characters have to eat, so there is constant mention of dining and breakfasting. Harker takes tea on one occasion in an "Aerated Bread Co." restaurant,[31] while Van Helsing and Seward dine at Jack Straw's Castle pub prior to their investigation of Lucy's coffin. Stoker also describes "a little crowd of bicyclists"[32] gathered at the pub—a small detail that creates even more verisimilitude. And when Van Helsing and the others attempt to break into Dracula's Piccadilly quarters, Stoker spends half a page describing the laborious work of the locksmith who has been employed to effect an entry.

The collation of the "evidence," which is "fantastic," is typed up and filed in a very modern, matter-of-fact manner, in true sensation-novel style. The vampire hunters refer to themselves as a "board of committee." Stoker also spends a great deal of time with very precise descriptions of the progress of Dracula's boxes of earth, naming the carters involved, having day-books and letter-books consulted.

Tracking down Dracula takes up the final third of the novel, and it is a classic chase in the manner of Collins's *The Moonstone*, with which it has much structurally in common, not least the shared epistolary technique. Like the vampire hunters, Collins's hero in *The Moonstone* finds himself in various seedy parts of London in pursuit of the individual whom he believes to be the thief of the eponymous jewel:

> Well, sir, the cab went from Lombard Street to the Tower Wharf. The sailor with the black beard got out, and spoke to the steward of the Rotterdam steamboat, which was to start next morning. ... The sailor went on, till he got to Shore Lane, leading into Lower Thames Street. There he stopped before a public-house, under the sign of "The Wheel of Fortune," and after examining the place outside, went in.[33]

Similarly, Harker, in *Dracula*, visits Bethnal Green and Walworth during the course of his investigations into Dracula's coffins, two of which have been deposited respectively in Mile End New Town and Bermondsey. There is talk of "a new-fangled ware-us," which is in fact "a new 'cold storage' building,"[34] and it is here that Harker discovers how very hands-on Dracula has been, helping the carters to carry the boxes of earth into his Piccadilly and Carfax residences. Harker writes his diary on the train, not in the quiet seclusion of a library, as would have been the case in a more old-fashioned Gothic novel. Lord Godalming, once the fiancé of the ill-fated Lucy, even stokes up a steam launch himself. Dracula's character is also subjected to thoroughly "up-to-date" scientific analysis by Van Helsing, who classifies the Count as "a criminal and of criminal type. Nordau and Lombroso would so classify him, and *qua* criminal he is of imperfectly formed mind."[35] (Max Nordau authored a study of degeneracy the two years before *Dracula* was published, which was dedicated to the criminologist and phrenologist, Cesare Lombroso. Dracula is therefore a scientifically validated vampire.)

Given all this contemporaneity, it does at least seem illogical to object to the 1970s setting of *Dracula A.D. 1972*, especially as the bare outline of its plot merely updates that of *Taste the Blood of Dracula*, which is so often regarded as one of the best of Hammer's *Dracula* sequels, but of course Hammer's fans at the time had grown used to the period settings of the studio's Gothic films, which themselves were part of a general fascination with Victoriana in the postwar period, particularly in Britain. At a time when modernistic ideas in architecture were demolishing so many churches and so much civic infrastructure, architects with no time for the blackened and decaying legacy of what had survived the Second World War planned a brave new world of streamlined efficiency, but the process of rejection had started before the war, as Kenneth Clarke observed in the 1949 introduction to his study of *The Gothic Revival*, first published in 1928:

> A generation influenced by the poetical insight of Mr. [John] Betjeman will find it hard to believe in the state of feeling towards nineteenth-century architecture which prevailed in 1927. In Oxford it was universally believed that Ruskin had built Keble [College], and that it was the ugliest building in the world. ... This was the atmosphere in which I wrote the short chapter which follows, called Introduction, with its assumption that the whole Revival produced practically nothing which the "sensitive eye" (a favourite feature of the 1920s) could rest on without pain. By the time I reached the epilogue I had changed my ground.[36]

John Betjeman had lamented the destruction of Victoriana in the 1930s, but it was postwar that his voice began to make a difference and ultimately led to the salvation of Giles Gilbert Scott's Gothic masterpiece, St. Pancras Station. As he wrote in a radio piece in 1950:

> If you say you like Victorian architecture today you are considered affected or ignorant. Victorian, so far as most people are concerned, is another word for jerry-built, ugly, over-decorated, hypocritical and all that goes with what is known as "bad taste." I cannot understand why people take this attitude to Victorian building.[37]

He went on to lament the attitude that "it is the Victorians who destroyed England with their ugly buildings."

> The Victorians did not string the sky with wires and turn old villages into Canadian lumber camps with forests of upright poles. The Victorians did not plant cathedral cities and old country towns with lamp-posts of concrete that look like boa constrictors leaning over with corpse lights in their mouths. ... The Victorians did not ruin market squares with flashy façades of chain stores—particularly tailoring establishments—whose black glass and glittering vulgarity have no reference to the old brick houses above them. The Victorians did not construct huge building estates on the outskirts of towns, far from shops and with inadequate bus services. No, all this glorious work was done by our own age, not by the Victorians.[38]

While the immediate postwar optimism of the late '50s—embodied in Harold Macmillan's famous phrase, "You've never had it so good"—embraced modernization, Betjeman embodied the residual misgivings about what was being lost. This, linked with a satirical approach to the outmoded behaviors and opinions of Victorian society, led to the Victoriana craze of the 1960s, epitomized by the elaborate 19th-century military costumes worn by the Beatles' incarnation as Sgt. Pepper's Lonely Hearts Club Band. This dichotomy was also discussed in Michelangelo Antonioni's *Blow-Up* (1966), his seminal analysis of the spirit of the 1960s. An early sequence in the film has the photographer, Thomas (David Hemmings), enter an antique shop filled with Victoriana. The unnamed owner of the shop is played by Susan Brodrick, who would later appear as a chambermaid in Hammer's *Countess Dracula* (dir. Peter Sasdy, 1971) and as the prim and proper Susan Spencer in Roy Ward Baker's *Dr. Jekyll and Sister Hyde*. Thomas is the epitome of then contemporary "swinging" London: He photographs doss-house inmates by night in the name of art, and makes glamour shots for fashion magazines for cash by day; he wears white jeans and a louche green velvet jacket, and drives around in a sports car.

Derelict Splendor—Don Mingaye's set for St. Bartolph's Church in *Dracula A.D. 1972* (dir. Alan Gibson, 1972). Clockwise from left: William Ellis as Joe Mitchum, Caroline Munro as Laura Bellows, Philip "Pip" Miller as Bob Tarrant, Stephanie Beeham as Jessica Van Helsing, Janet Key as Anna Bryant, Michael Kitchen as Greg Puller, and Marsha Hunt (back to the camera) as Gaynor Keating.

The antique shop, by contrast, is the epitome of outmoded Victorian clutter: Parian busts, glass domes, old dresses, pictures, and an antiquated camera—just the kind of environment, indeed, that characterizes the curio shop of Weller (Roy Kinnear) in *Taste the Blood of Dracula*. (Weller possesses Dracula's dried blood, ring, and clasp.) The antique shop owner in *Blow-Up* is "fed up with antiques" and wants to try something new, a conflict that symbolizes the tension between the Victorian past and the "white heat" of modernity that was propelling the country forward. Perhaps symbolic of that process is the giant airplane propeller Thomas buys from her.

Dracula A.D. 1972, made only five years later, definitely reflects this dichotomy; indeed, it is central to the film's overall theme. The prologue set in 1872 reminds us of Hammer's traditional Victorian style and setting before we are thrust into the chilly environment of concrete underpasses and London traffic in 1972. The contrasts continue with the opening party scene, in which the rock group Stoneground performs amid the elegant good taste of an upper-class London home. That chinless wonder, Charles (Michael Daly), has invited the group to entertain his superannuated guests is an absurd conceit, but Don Houghton obviously wanted as graphic a representation of the generation gap as possible. Electric guitars and the Carnaby Street clothing of Johnny Alucard and his hippie chums thus clash with the dinner jackets and evening gowns of the pensionable party guests as they cluster around the gilt picture frames, damask wallpaper, silk lampshades, and Adam-esque architecture.

As Sinclair McKay observed,[39] a very similar situation opens a comedy film made in the same year that *A.D. 1972* was released. This was the feature film spin-off of the popular British television sitcom, *Father, Dear Father* (dir. William G. Stewart), starring Patrick Cargill as Patrick Glover, the sympathetic and indulgent father of two teenage daughters. Like Jessica Van Helsing, these girls, Anna (Natasha Pyne) and Karen (Ann Holloway), are polite and well brought up. They too could easily say, like Jessica, "the full extent of my wild ways is half a pint of lager now and again." Glover is similarly as bewildered and affectionate as Cushing's Van Helsing. The whole point of the comedy is the generation gap, and the film starts with a "groovy" party in Glover's elegantly appointed London home. The décor is very similar to the home of Charles's parents in *A.D. 1972*. Instead of the considerably raunchier music of Stoneground, the teenage friends of Anna and Karen dance to the music of Waldo de los Ríos, whose pop version of Mozart's 40th Symphony—"Mozart 40"—reached the top ten in 1971. He later released a whole album of similar tracks on the album *Mozart in the Seventies*.

The teenagers of *Father, Dear Father* are better behaved than the Alucard gang (one of them, played by Richard O'Sullivan, calls Glover "Sir," while Anna stops a guest drinking whisky from a decanter: "Don't touch that!" she shouts. "It's Daddy's!"), so this kind of pop music played on an LP is perhaps more appropriate than inviting Stoneground into the living room, but it was no less popular at the time. Disturbed by his daughter's early morning disco, Glover goes downstairs to put a stop to it:

"This noise has gone on long enough," he insists. "I'm going to put my foot down." Upon which he steps in a plate of spaghetti. Anna greets him.

"Hello, Daddy. Nice to see you getting 'with it.'" She introduces him to one of the guests: "Daddy, this is Dumbo. He's a Laughing Chamberpot."

"A what?"

"It's a group. Like Mantovani."

"Do you realize it's three o'clock in the morning? What are the neighbors going to think with all this boogie-woogie blaring out."

"Boogie what?"

"Boogie! Music! I mean, don't misunderstand me. I like to see you having fun." (He interrupts Karen, who is kissing a boy.) "Karen! Will you stop talking while I'm snogging!—Nobody can say that I'm square."

All this might seem hopelessly dated now—far more so, in fact, than *A.D. 1972*—but it was, like the Dracula film, just as much a product of its time.

Other intriguing parallels between the two films continue. A policeman turns up, explaining, "We've just had a complaint phoned in about the noise of your party." In fact, as we later learn, Glover has called the police himself. Over breakfast the following morning, we learn that a china figurine has been smashed, a breakage that also happens in *A.D. 1972*. (Johnny Alucard deliberately smashes a porcelain figure at Charles's party.)

"But it was on top of a bookcase!" Glover protests.

"So was Richard," Karen replies.

Glover is also appalled at finding a bra left lying around.

"Celia wanted to burn it," Anna explains, "She suddenly decided to join the Women's Lib."

To which Karen adds, "Good job she didn't burn her own. It would have been the great fire of London all over again." She also argues that her father thinks "we'll get pregnant if we sit on a warm bus seat."

Compared with all this, *Dracula A.D. 1972* seems almost like reportage. An intriguing amount of British horror films begin with or contain party scenes. Some have period settings, like the parties in *The Ghoul* (dir. Freddie Francis, 1975), located in the roaring 1920s, or Roger Corman's British-made *The Masque of the Red Death* (1964), which goes further back into an unspecified medieval period. But the majority are set in the 1960s, the golden era of party-going (Corman would update things three years later in *The Trip*, in which Peter Fonda experiences LSD). Alan Gibson's *Goodbye Gemini* (1970) is based on Jenni Hall's 1964 novel, *Ask Agamemnon*, which explored the sleazy underbelly of '60s party culture. Like *A.D. 1972*, *Goodbye Gemini* also features a swinging party, but on this occasion it is set on board a houseboat, where there was obviously much less room to dance and no room at all for a live band, so the music (specially composed in the manner of Burt Bacharach by Christopher Gunning) was supposedly played on records. Nonetheless, quite a lot of guests manage to fit in, and Gibson articulates the confined space with considerable panache. The previous year, Michael Armstrong's *The Haunted House of Horror* also used a party to propel the action forward. In *Goodbye Gemini* the party introduces Jacki and Julian (Judy Geeson and Martin Potter) to the corrupt Clive (Alexis Kanner); in *The Haunted House of Horror*, a group of teenagers, thoroughly bored by what Johnny Alucard would later call "a tired scene," leave their boring party to explore the supposedly haunted house of the title, but the murders that subsequently occur there turn out to be committed by a deranged member of their own group.

Parties, where alcohol and drugs are consumed and sex so often take place, are suitably Dionysian affairs to unleash the irrational forces that propel the plots of horror films. *The Curse of the Crimson Altar*, which was released in America under the title *The Crimson Cult* in a double bill alongside *The Haunted House of Horror* in 1970, also features a very hedonistic party to celebrate the annual "burning" ceremony in honor of a witch named Lavinia. The first thing we see is a rather bored woman having her bosom adorned with blue paint. Director Vernon Sewell obviously had great fun shooting naked legs, champagne being poured over other female bosoms, collapsed drunks in corners, couples smoking various substances, bare-chested men, a party game that ends in a cat fight, and some clumsy groping, all culminating in a mock battle between two teenage girls with paint brushes as swords and artist palettes for shields, raised on the shoulders of two hearty men. All this is designed to get us in the mood for the distinctly sadomasochistic hallucinations featuring Barbara Steele's Lavinia later on.

A party proved to be a similar kind of catalyst in Robert Hartford-Davis's *Corruption* (1968). Whereas *The Curse of the Crimson Altar* places the trendy party in the antique environment of Craxted Lodge (in fact W.S. Gilbert's old home, Grim's

Dyke in Middlesex), *Corruption* plunges Sir John Rowan, the somewhat staid plastic surgeon played by Peter Cushing, into the sleazy "grooviness" of a party held by a fashion photographer named Mike Orme (Anthony Booth). Sir John's much younger fiancée, Lynn (Sue Lloyd) is a fashion model and has asked him to come along to celebrate her latest shoot with Orme. Out of his depth in this rowdy "swinging" environment, an accident caused by an altercation between Rowan and Orme, after Orme insists Lynn take off her clothes, causes a floodlight to fall on Lynn's face, hideously deforming her. Here again, it is a party—in which two men pretend to throw a girl over a balcony, blue satin shirts and red PVC bodices rub up against Union Jack boater hats and face-painted bimbos, all suffused in cigarette smoke and pop music—which creates the mood of misrule required to initiate a catastrophe, which in turn sets the rest of the film in motion.

While not exactly a horror film, Michelangelo Antonioni's *Blow-Up* (1966) foreshadowed all these later "horror" parties by using a party scene not only to create the mood of the time but also to parallel its amoral hedonism with the unexplained murder, which Thomas, the fashion photographer, thinks he has photographed. As Terence Towles Canote observes:

> This party sequence in many respects seems somewhat cold and detached, with an underlying tone of menace about it. Although there can be little doubt that Thomas has attended such parties before, in this instance he seems very much a fish out of water....
>
> Most of the Sixties party scenes in these films have an ominousness about them, a sense that something is not quite right. This is particularly true of the psychedelic Sixties party scenes, most of which can be downright disturbing. What is more, many of the Sixties party scenes end disastrously. After dropping acid in a cemetery in *Easy Rider*, Wyatt, Billy, and the prostitutes know only fear and despair. The final party in *Beyond the Valley of the Dolls* ends even more disastrously. The message behind such films, even ones that seem to favour the counterculture of the time such as *Easy Rider* seems to be obvious: it is not wise to stray too far from traditional morality or catastrophe will ensue.[40]

Blow-Up captures the '60s party scene when it was actually happening. By the time *A.D. 1972* came along, that particular scene was over, but, as *Father, Dear Father* demonstrates, *A.D. 1972* wasn't as out of touch with reality as many people think. Indeed, much of the film accurately reflects the imagery of the time. We see Alucard, dressed in black, driving a sports car like Hemmings's Thomas in *Blow-Up*. (Neame later recalled that it was "a Triumph Stag, which was the latest car of the time."[41]) His flat is stylishly modern (the color scheme is suitably black-and-blood-red against white walls with purple drapes), but he also displays an antique grandfather clock and a Tiffany lamp. Modern London is also contrasted with the elaborately traditional interiors of Van Helsing's home (to which we will be returning in much more detail later). Most significant of all is the contrast between the dereliction of St. Bartolph's Church and the cranes, rubble, and rickety fences that surround it. It is here that Dracula returns from the past—and in Hammer's terms, that past is specifically Victorian. The interior of the church is one of Hammer's most convincingly realistic Gothic sets. By the time of *The Satanic Rites of Dracula*, made the following year, St. Bartolph's has been demolished and a high-rise tower block has been built in its place in which D.D. Denham, aka Dracula, sets up his headquarters.

The fate of St. Bartolph's was shared by a great many Victorian churches in British cities during the 1960s and '70s. Liverpool was no exception. John Cunningham and Arthur Hill Holme's Holy Trinity Church in Birkenhead was closed in 1974, one year after *The Satanic Rites* was released. Its demolition two years later coincided with Hammer's last horrific hurrah—the very loose but equally brilliant adaptation of Dennis Wheatley's *To the Devil a Daughter* (dir. Peter Sykes, 1976). Significantly, the 15th-century church used in that film had already been deconsecrated, and it became a private residence subsequent to its appearance in the film. (Intriguingly, it was dedicated to St. Botolph, who unlike St. Bartolph is a recognized saint. St. Bartolph is entirely fictional.) While the Grade II listed St. Botolph's survives, nothing remains of Liverpool's Holy Trinity, which has now been replaced by unremarkable business premises and storage units, which lack even the corporate phallic power of D.D. Denham's development. Even before the 1960s, similar acts of architectural vandalism were visited on churches that had survived Hitler's Luftwaffe. Charles Barry's St. Matthew's Church in Manchester, for example, was demolished between 1951 and '52, during a period that led to John Betjeman's formation of the Victorian Society in 1958, which attempted to preserve the increasingly endangered architectural legacy of the 19th century. Alas, St. Matthew's was replaced by another '60s office block, while St. Anne's in Mansfield and St. Mary Major in Exeter followed in 1971. In 1974, Richard Norman Shaw's Holy Trinity Church in Bingley, Yorkshire, suffered the wrecking ball, followed in 1979 by Charles Augustin Busby's St. Mary's Church in Leeds—Busby is of interest because his father was the composer Thomas Busby, who wrote music for the first English Gothic melodrama (Thomas Holcroft's 1802 *A Tale of Mystery*), which foreshadowed the horror films and horror film scoring that were yet to come.

Dracula A.D. 1972 thus reflects what was happening in the real world at the time, but also firmly roots its modernity in Hammer's own Gothic past. Nowhere is this more apparent than in the brief appearance of James Bernard's famous "Dra-Cu-La" theme at the outset, which serves as an unofficial fanfare for Hammer Films itself. That it accompanies the Warner Bros. logo is neither here nor there. It announces a Hammer film, with all that this implies, thus setting up expectations, which it will challenge but ultimately confirm.

Two

CAMP, KITSCH AND CULT

> "Hey, you've even got taste."
> —Gaynor in *Dracula A.D. 1972*

SINCLAIR MCKAY'S DESCRIPTION OF *Dracula A.D. 1972* as a masterpiece of kitsch is worth exploring in more detail. Is it really any more kitsch than Hammer's earlier Dracula pictures? Could it, in fact, be far less? To begin with, what exactly do we mean by "kitsch"? One way of defining it is to say that it misunderstands, misrepresents, and then commercially exploits the historical models it tries to imitate. Ultimately, it is unwilling to engage with reality. It is a poseur, and like all poseurs, it fundamentally hides its emptiness behind a borrowed style. King Ludwig II's Bavarian castles might thus be classified as kitsch in that they attempt to recreate the past, but in terms of a contemporary fantasy of it. Ludwig dreamed of being a medieval king, but had no real political power of his own. In this respect, it is highly appropriate (though obviously never intended by Ludwig himself) that the mighty throne room in Neuschwanstein Castle has everything to represent the divine right of kings except a throne, for Ludwig was deposed before the throne could be installed. Walt Disney World's Cinderella's Castle, itself based on Neuschwanstein (and the chief logo of Disney films), is thus doubly kitsch: a copy of a copy, consecrated to a commercialized fantasy.

However, an equally important aspect of kitsch is that it takes itself entirely seriously. So too did Hammer.

Escaping into a fantasy might suggest a lack of confidence in dealing with the present, and that great iconoclast, Friedrich Nietzsche, was very much aware of the dangers of this sort of historicism:

> The oversaturation of an age with history seems to me to be hostile and dangerous to life ... [it] weakens the personality ... it disrupts the instincts of a people, and hinders the individual no less than the whole in the attainment of maturity ... it leads an age into a dangerous mood of irony in regard to itself and subsequently into the even more dangerous mood of cynicism.[1]

Kitsch magnifies its models. It gilds the lily. Kitsch revives the past in an attempt to escape uncomfortable truths about the present. Hence the world's most highly paid pianist, Liberace, was doubly kitsch, as he based his act on an already kitsch impression of 19th-century virtuoso pianists such as Liszt and Chopin. Liberace was strongly influenced by Charles Vidor's Chopin biopic, *A Song to Remember* (1945), which gave him the idea of using a candelabra as a kitsch accessory. Because kitsch resurrects what is dead and attempts to bring it back to life, it was highly apt that Liberace was cast as a mortician in Tony Richardson's 1965 film adaptation of Evelyn Waugh's satire of the Hollywood funeral business, *The Loved One*. The grotesque resurrection of Liszt that was Liberace has a similar effect to that of Boris Karloff's Frankenstein's Monster, for Liberace was nothing if not a reanimated assemblage of long-dead cultural body parts. He played boogie-woogie on a rococo piano while wearing a pantomimic fantasy of period dress and flashing his teeth like a benevolent vampire.

Perhaps the whole idea of vampires is kitsch. As *The Loved One* explores with such mordant wit, death is the ultimate manifestation of kitsch, along with its paraphernalia (the sentimentalized overstatements of funeral parlors and the theatricality of mourning rituals). Knowledge of our mortality, it could be argued, makes our entire lives kitsch, for all our aims, ideals and efforts are proved futile in the end. The rictus grin of Death laughs at everything, especially good taste. Hitler became the modern godfather of kitsch, investing political platitudes with the glamour of style. Nazism was a triumph of surface theatricality, illusion and imitation over whatever might once have been authentic, all in the name of a grotesque cult of death. *Kitsch* and *Kunst* (art) became interchangeable terms in Nazi Germany. Kitsch is the king of a counterfeit kingdom that promises everything for a price but is fundamentally bankrupt.

All these criteria suggest that Hammer's previous Dracula films, set in a fairy-tale world or amid resurrected Victoriana, are far more kitsch than *Dracula A.D. 1972*. Of course, looking at the early 1970s from our own perspective, it is easy to think of this film as being a kitsch misunderstanding of that particular decade, but perhaps it is we who are the kitsch offenders here, misunderstanding the period in which the film was set. Could the kitschiness of that film have been imposed on it by our own "unhealthy" obsession with the past, and the misunderstanding caused by *nostalgia*? Could this be why the film has now attracted a cult following?

Of course, *Dracula A.D. 1972* has no pretensions toward profundity. It is quite honest about what it is trying to do. It has very little to say about the human condition but it does reflect many other things. As Sontag pointed out in her essay about the "the imagination of disaster":

> Ours is indeed an age of extremity. For we live under continual threat of two equally fearful, but seemingly opposed, destinies: unremitting banality and inconceivable terror. It is fantasy, served out in large rations by the popular arts, which allows most people to cope with these twin specters. For one job that fantasy can do is to lift us out of the unbearably humdrum and to distract us from terrors—real or anticipate—by an escape into exotic, dangerous situations, which have last-minute happy endings. But another of the things that fantasy can do is to normalize what is psychologically unbearable, thereby inuring us to it. In one case, fantasy beautifies the world. In the other, it neutralizes it.[2]

Sontag is also illuminating with regard to the many ways in which kitsch is related to "camp," which she defines as emphasizing "texture, sensuous surface, and style at the expense of content." She continues, "All Camp objects, and persons, contain a large element of artifice.... Camp is a vision of the world in terms of style—but a particular kind of style. It is the love of the exaggerated.... Camp sees everything in quotation marks. ... It is the farthest extension, in sensibility, of the metaphor of life as theater. ... Pure Camp is always naïve. Camp which knows itself to be Camp ('camping') is usually less satisfying. ... In naïve, or pure, Camp, the essential element is seriousness, a seriousness that fails."[3]

How far may we apply these criteria to *Dracula A.D. 1972* more than to its predecessors? Of course, personal taste makes such judgments unstable (Google actually classifies the film as "Horror/Comedy"), but in terms of comparison we can safely say that *A.D. 1972* is far less camp and kitschy than *Scars of Dracula*'s flimsy castle sets, lazy historicism, stilted dialogue, obviously artificial bat, and comedy scenes featuring Bob Todd, which would be more at home in a *Carry On* film. Roy Ward Baker's attempt at seriousness in *Scars* disastrously fails, and is hence an example of naïve camp. Lee described himself as being unintentionally "a pantomime figure," but he was also aware of how much the presentation of Dracula had become increasingly a victim of "camping"—camp which knows itself to be camp. In 1958, for his first appearance as the Count, he agreed to wear a cape (which Stoker's vampire doesn't), but, crucially, one that was "black on both sides."

> My sticking point came when the suggestion was mooted of evening dress with an Order, which struck me as unlikely in a castle in the middle of Transylvania. Stylisation is all very well, but if it goes over the top you're left with camp. In the end I was allowed to wear a black suit with cravat and pearl tiepin. We held out against ruby tiepins and cuff links, and scarlet lining to the cloak, until the sequel.[4]

When that first sequel, *Dracula: Prince of Dracula*, appeared, the Count was sufficiently demonized to lose his tongue altogether, which hardly stops wagging in the novel. The Count in *Dracula: Prince of Darkness* had no lines at all, and became a mute monolith of menace rather than an insidious infiltrator—in other words, he became *stylized*. Another observation from Sontag is illuminating here:

> "Stylization" in a work of art, as distinct from style, reflects the ambivalence (affection contradicted by contempt, obsession contradicted by irony) toward the subject-matter. This ambivalence is handled by maintaining, through the rhetorical overlay that is stylization, a special distance from the subject.[5]

It was, ironically, the urbane, apparent normality of Dracula in 1958, stripped as it was of Bela Lugosi's extreme artificiality, which made the film so unusual at the time. Lee recalled how during the midnight screening of the film in New York, the previously rowdy audience were utterly silenced by "the ordinary conversational tone" of the Count, which "switched them off like a knob being turned on the radio. From then on there was only direct reaction. The Count tamed them."[6] The ritual that resurrects the vampire in *Dracula: Prince of Darkness* is no less elaborate and exaggerated than the Black Mass over which Johnny Alucard presides in *A.D. 1972*. Philip Latham, as Dracula's faithful retainer, Klove, is actually far more disturbing than Dracula himself, and he performs the ceremony with unsettlingly pedantic precision. There is also far more blood involved than in St. Bartolph's Church, Klove having an entire corpse to drain into Dracula's sarcophagus.

Dracula Has Risen from the Grave has rather more visual stylization, thanks to Freddie Francis's colored light filters applied to the edge of the frame during the vampiric episodes, the effect of which emphasizes the film's already fairytale setting. Though the production takes itself seriously, the publicity suggested that camp was creeping around the peripheries: a poster depicting a virginal female neck wearing a sticking plaster announced, "Dracula Has Risen from the Grave—obviously." The publicity for *Taste the Blood of Dracula* continued this trend with its tag line of "Drink a Pint of Blood a Day" echoing the Milk Marketing Board's advertisements of the time. Costume dramas have a tendency toward exaggeration. One can get away with extravagances in period fantasies that contemporary naturalism prohibits. It is doubtful that one could contain the highly stylized interior of the Chateau Meinster in *The Brides of Dracula* (dir. Terence Fisher, 1960), with its gigantic griffins, if the film had been set in the period in which it was made. Stylization and naturalism usually don't mix, as John Badham's 1976 production of *Dracula* demonstrated. Derived from the 1973 Nantucket Stage Company's theatrical production starring Frank Langella, which was designed in very stylized terms by Edward Gorey, Universal decided on location work and realistic settings for the film, with the exception of Carfax Abbey. There, spiders' webs are presented symbolically, and in Arcimboldo style, skeletal faces peer out from architectural details. The result is indubitably camp and sits uneasily with the naturalism of the rest of the film.

The two American International Count Yorga films starring Robert Quarry, which suggested the new direction in which Hammer subsequently took its Dracula series, mixed naturalism and camp stylization rather more successfully. Originally planned as pornographic exploitation films, it was Quarry who persuaded the producers to take the subject more seriously. In *Count Yorga, Vampire* and *The Return of Count Yorga*, both directed by Bob Kelljan in 1970 and 1971, characters living in modern Los Angeles are confronted with the Bulgarian menace of Quarry's Yorga, who wears red velvet jackets, bow ties and Dracula-esque capes, which complement his ironic, detached persona. The contrast might not work had Quarry failed to negotiate the tension between camp and genuine menace. Kelljan also punctuates the action with bouts of brutal vampire violence. The effect is consequently surreal, and what might so easily have turned into comedy is utterly undercut by shock tactics, in which the vivid imagery of dreams suddenly bursts into reality.

A rather good example of this successfully negotiated problem can be found by comparing the opening of *Count Yorga, Vampire* with Stan Dragoti's 1979 *Dracula* satire, *Love at First Bite*. Both films have to find a way of transitioning the old European count to modern-day America, and they achieve this in similar ways. Count Yorga, who arrives in his coffin on board ship, is carried to his new residence in Los Angeles by an undead servant, Brudah, who has the coffin placed on the back of a suitably red pickup truck. *Love at First Bite* has Arte Johnson's Renfield do much the same thing but with his rather more comical yellow VW Beetle. If one removes the jazzy music that accompanies this, one is left with a similar impression to the opening of *Count Yorga*, which uses no music, relying instead of the sounds of the Port of Los Angeles, before a sinister narration explains something of vampire lore.

Quarry turns from an urbane, somewhat anachronistic poseur to a deadly demon, who runs, fangs bared, toward the camera and his victims with arms outstretched, accompanied by a disturbing sustained note. The film depends upon

Hammer's previous notoriety to make its ironic effect, most notably in a scene in *The Return of Count Yorga*, when the vampire watches Hammer's *The Vampire Lovers* (dir. Roy Ward Baker, 1970) on television. One simply cannot imagine Lee's Dracula pulling off one-liners like Yorga's comment to a boy pianist strumming rock chords in *The Return of Count Yorga*, who asks, "Do you like this sort of music?" to which Yorga replies, in devastating deadpan, "Only when played well." Yorga is quite aware of his own camp detachment from the time in which he lives, but simultaneously regards the modern world as far more unreal than his own reality, as it fails to accept that "there are such things." The modern world laughs at monsters and vampires, as the Halloween costumes worn by guests at the orphanage in *The Return of Count Yorga* (one of which is a crude representation of Dracula) clearly demonstrate. Yorga observes this, again with an ironic detachment that Lee's Dracula would find impossible. One of the reasons for this is that Lee's Dracula is satanic, whereas Yorga is "merely" a vampire with no pretensions of Miltonic grandeur. Though he shares Lee's stillness and piercing gaze, he is able to exchange relatively normal dialogue with the other characters, move among them, and be accepted by them, which Lee was only ever allowed to attempt in the very brief but equally impressive opening scenes of the 1958 *Dracula* and in a fake Russian accent in *The Satanic Rites of Dracula*. Echoing Dracula's welcoming speech to Jonathan Harker, Yorga addresses his next potential victim, Cynthia (Mariette Hartley), in *The Return*:

"I am Count Yorga,"
"Count Yorga? You mean a real Count?"
"Yes."
"Oh, how marvelous. Then, that isn't a costume?"
"No."
"Oh, forgive me, that was thoughtless."
"Not at all."
"Yes it was. I'm Cynthia Nelson."
"How do you do?"
"How were you able to get here with the bridge out?"
"I flew."
"No, really."
"I recently acquired the old gateway mansion."

When Yorga communicates using sign language with a deaf woman named Jennifer, Cynthia asks how he managed to learn it. Yorga replies:

"When you've lived as long as I, you gather a bit of knowledge along the way."

Back in the cellar of his mansion, he enjoys sitting on a throne upholstered in purple silk, marshaling his undead female slaves who will soon attack Cynthia's family in their own living room. The juxtaposition of Quarry's camp irony with uncompromising violence is truly unnerving in a way that no Hammer film ever quite managed to match. This murder scene is, of course, an obvious reference to the infamous killings, in 1969, by three members of Charles Manson's "family," who entered the home of Hollywood actress Sharon Tate, murdering her and four others. (A further macabre aspect of this atrocity was that Tate had previously starred in two horror films—J. Lee Thompson's *Eye of the Devil* in 1966 and her husband Roman

Polanski's *The Dance of the Vampires* in 1967.) Manson, who had been involved in acts of criminality since he set his school on fire at age nine, had already served multiple prison sentences for theft and armed robbery by the time he set himself up as a guru after dabbling with Scientology. He believed his various "followers" were reincarnations of primitive Christians, whom he set about brainwashing into total submission to his demented demands by means of LSD, hypnosis, and unconventional sex. His "family" was eventually based at the Spahn Ranch in Los Angeles, an old film and TV set once used for Westerns, where Manson preached apocalyptic race war. Before they set out to commit the Tate murders, he ordered his perpetrators to "totally destroy" everyone and be "as gruesome as you can." Once inside Tate's home, Charles "Tex" Watson, a drug dealer under Manson's influence, announced that he was the devil "and I'm here to do the devil's business," before he and another member of the "family," Susan Atkins, tied up Tate and her former boyfriend, hairstylist Jay Sebring, with a nylon cord around their necks. When Sebring protested at the pregnant Tate's treatment, Watson shot him. Tate then pleaded to be allowed to live long enough to give birth to her child but was stabbed 16 times by both Watkins and Atkins and then hanged by the nylon cord. This utterly horrific crime was only one of several committed that night.

The uncompromising home invasion and slaughter scene in *The Return of Count Yorga* is, significantly, played without a note of music, which lack adds immensely to its "realism." In this respect it resembles the violent struggle between Paul Newman's Professor Armstrong and Wolfgang Kieling's Gromek in Hitchcock's *Torn Curtain* (1966), which is made all the more disturbing without the cue Bernard Herrmann originally scored for it. In an interview with Bryan Forbes at the British Film Institute in 1969, Hitchcock stated that his aim in that scene was to demonstrate how difficult it is to kill a man: "It is a messy business. It is a horrible business, and it should be a deterrent, because it's not all that easy. They usually show the killings on screen as very simple—a gunshot and 'bang!' you're dead, but if you don't have a gun or can't use a gun it just shows you what a horrible, awful thing it is to kill someone."[7] Music always reminds us that we are watching a movie. Removing it can remove that reassurance. (Don Sharp's *The Kiss of the Vampire*, made for Hammer in 1963, also ends with a similar kind of mass slaughter, also without music—though on that occasion it is bats who attack the vampires, and hence the violence is made doubly "unreal.")

The equivalent shock scene in the first Count Yorga film concerns the corrupted Erica (Judy Lang), who is discovered feeding on the blood of a mutilated kitten. Hammer, of course, used plenty of blood but never indulged in anything quite as bestial as this, and even at his most ravenous, Lee's Dracula only ever sported a dribble of blood on his lips and cheeks. Erica's mouth, however, is positively smeared with blood like an infant after messily eating a strawberry ice cream. Such graphically disturbing imagery deliberately contrasts with the film's often self-consciously absurd dialogue, such as that between Hayes and his friend Michael:

"How would you feel 'bout driving wooden stake through someone's heart?"
"Marvelous."
"That's good, because I think you and I are going to have to kill Count Yorga."

"What! You gotta be joking."
"No, I mean it. Listen...."
"No, you've gotta listen to me for a change."

Another way in which the Yorga films differ from Hammer's vampire epics is their ironic, pessimistic endings. Both films end with the death of Yorga, but at the end of the first one, the sole survivor is attacked by his now undead girlfriend, while at the end of *The Return*, the vampire hunter, Dr. Hayes, by then already undead himself, attacks the woman he was previously trying to save. Hammer always took more optimistic approach, restoring the status quo at the end without exception.

The idea of a Gothic vampire living in the here and now provided Hammer with the idea it needed to escape from the dead end of *Scars of Dracula*, but their vampire was not yet ready fully to integrate himself into society, let alone to be ironic. That would happen in the sequel, but here, Dracula stays put within the Gothic environs of St. Bartolph's Church. As we have seen, this has been viewed by unsympathetic critics as a missed opportunity, but it is a confinement that differs little from what we observe in *Taste the Blood of Dracula*. Houghton's original draft of the screenplay of *A.D. 1972* has Dracula sharing Johnny's Chelsea flat,[8] but this was considered inappropriate and was cut. So too were the appearance of monster movie posters on the walls of the Cavern Club Coffee Bar (itself a reference to the Liverpool club where the Beatles began their career), along with specific reference to Hammer's *Lust for a Vampire*, which Bob (Philip Miller) suggests Jessica might like to go to see in the cinema. These details were obviously direct references to Count Yorga watching *The Vampire Lovers* on TV, but were obviously thought to undermine the realism that was being sought. Being self-referential can backfire awkwardly, as it does when Mark Eden's character says the spooky house in which he finds himself in *The Curse of the Crimson Altar* is the kind of place where you might bump into Boris Karloff (who was indeed starring in that film, but not as himself). This kind of thing is the equivalent of an actor suddenly breaking the fourth wall and addressing the camera. The conceit works in *Count Yorga*, however, because of Quarry's already ironic and knowing presentation of the vampire.

There is really only one intentionally ironic line in *A.D. 1972*, which occurs when Johnny invites Marsha Hunt's Gloria to his flat. "Come in for a bite," he suggests with a sly smile, as he gets out of the car. Otherwise, the script refuses to ironize itself. True, the embroidered monogram "D" on the altar cloth on the church in *A.D. 1972* conforms to Sontag's definition of camp (and anyone else's definition of kitsch for that matter), and Gibson would have been well advised to have removed it; also, Van Helsing's laborious demonstration that "Alucard" is "Dracula" spelled backward is redundant for all but the most impervious of audiences, and is consequently absurd, but the film is indeed far less camp than any of Hammer's previous vampire films. However, its serious approach to itself did not necessarily apply to the way in which it was promoted, with American trailers being more fang-in-cheek than British ones. British audiences were enticed by Bill Mitchell, who lent his trans–Atlantic baritone, much used in voice-overs at the time, to a fairly straightforward trailer, but one American alternative relished the line "Welcome back, Drac," while another, which was attached to some U.S. theatrical releases of the film and

Publicity Stunt—the poster for *Horroritual*.

called *Horroritual*, confronted the viewer with the actor Barry Atwater in Halloween Dracula makeup, rising from a cobweb-strewn sarcophagus. In a fake–Lugosi accent, he swears the audience into the Count Dracula Society:

> Raise your left hand. No, no—your *left* hand. Now repeat after me: "I do hereby swear, aver and depose that I will herein after assist in all the efforts of the Count Dracula Society so long as they remain consistent with the loyalties of a good American, and in sign whereof I will receive all privileges thereto, so help me Christopher Lee."

We can reasonably assume that Christopher Lee would have deemed all this "fatuous," as indeed it is. Thunder rumbles, the vampire laughs and signs off with: "Now! Now! You are one of *us*!" Significantly, the trailer ends with James Bernard's famous "Dra-Cu-La" theme. This helps to brand the film, of course, but the trailer rather misses the point.

Straddling these two promotional approaches is a short featurette, *Prince of Terror*, featuring another trans–Atlantic narration, though this time the approach is more dignified, despite its somewhat knowing tone. Lee and Cushing appear out of role, beaming happily and apparently having a good time during rehearsals for the opening party scene of the film.

The narrator explains that the thrill-seeking youths are "led by Johnny Alucard—what is it about that name?" Well, Van Helsing will, of course, laboriously demonstrate that later, if anyone is still in doubt. Lee is then shown inserting his fangs prior to a take, and smiling mischievously at the makeup girl as he does so. The narrator then continues:

> Little wonder that this genuinely scholarly and mild-mannered gentleman, fluent in eight languages, deriving his descent from one of the oldest Italian noble families, has been crowned "Prince of Terror." He defers graciously to Boris Karloff as king.

We now know that in latter years Lee increasingly resented

Party Guests—Marsha Hunt and Peter Cushing in a promotional photograph for *Dracula A.D. 1972* (dir. Alan Gibson, 1972).

such a moniker, insisting that he was neither the prince nor the king of horror, but what *Prince of Terror* wishes to impart, in its playful way, is dignity, authority, and pedigree:

> At home in London, with his actress wife, Birgit, and eight-year-old daughter, Christina, the aura of monstrosity is much diminished. Here, the scholar comes to the fore [we see Lee pull down a hardback copy of Lotte H. Eisner's classic study of German films, *The Haunted Screen*], but are not even these lucubrations ever so slightly tainted with that major preoccupation?

The vocabulary here is obviously designed to impress: "Aura," "diminished," and "lucubration." Few people in 1972 would have used "lucubration" in everyday parlance. "Slightly tainted with that major preoccupation"? Again, formality is to the fore, but a *knowing* formality—and hence a mild satire. The scene then changes to the cast and crew on location. Lee sweeps back his widow's peak against the breeze:

> Even the prince must be up and out at the crack of frosty dawn for another meeting with the unrelenting Van Helsing and his ubiquitous stake. It's enough to give a vampire heartburn.

"The crack of frosty dawn" is just one adjective more than necessary to avoid being mannered and consequently camp, especially as it doesn't actually look that frosty in Aldenham Country Park, close by Elstree Studios, where the prologue sequence is here shown being rehearsed: Alan Gibson demonstrates how he wants Lee to be impaled with the spoke from a carriage wheel. Lee raises his eyebrows as he (perhaps reluctantly) accepts what he is being asked to do. The impression is that he is above such nonsense, but, being a professional, he delivers exactly what's wanted.

All this is, of course, deeply self-referential. Such a promo reel would never have been made for Hammer's original 1958 *Dracula*, but by 1972, Hammer's way with Dracula was too well known to resist comparisons with his former incarnations. And this raises the question of *A.D. 1972*'s status as a cult film. Umberto Eco has some very useful things to say about what makes a cult movie:

> The work must be loved, obviously, but this is not enough. It must provide a completely furnished world so that its fans can quote characters and episodes as if they were aspects of the fan's private sectarian world, a world about which one can make up quizzes and play trivia games so that the adepts of the sect recognize through each other a shared experience. Naturally all these elements (characters and episodes) must have some archetypical appeal, as we shall see. One can ask and answer questions about the various subway stations of New York or Paris only if these spots have become or have been assumed as mythical areas and such names as Canarsie Line or Vincennes-Neuilly stand not only for physical places but become the catalyzers of collective memories.[9]

Retrospection and comparison with previous films are essential aspects of cult status. Like *Casablanca*, which Eco uses as an example, *Dracula A.D. 1972* "carries a sense of déjà vu to such a degree that the addressee is ready to see in it what happened after it as well."

> It is not until *To Have and to Have Not* that Bogey plays the role of the Hemingway hero, but here he appears "already" loaded with Hemingwayesque connotations simply because Rick fought in Spain. Peter Lorre trails reminiscences of Fritz Lang, Conrad Veidt's German officer emanates a faint whiff of *The Cabinet of Dr. Caligari*. He is not a ruthless technological Nazi; he is a nocturnal and diabolical Caesar.[10]

Eco also suggests that a cult movie must allow the spectator to "break, dislocate, unhinge it so that one can remember only parts of it, irrespective of their original relationship with the whole"[11]—in other words, it must to some extent be formulaic—an assembly of well-known, generally understood components. Clichés, in fact. Eco calls them "stereotyped situations derived from preceding textual tradition and recorded by our encyclopedia, such as, for example, the standard duel between the sheriff and the bad guy or the narrative situation in which the hero fights the villain and wins, or more macroscopic textual situations, such as the story of the *vierge souillée* or the classic recognition scene."[12] One might say that an important aspect of a cult movie is that it should contain as many stereotypes as it can, and be firmly part of a genre. Whether the film is good or bad is, by contrast, irrelevant to its cult status, but it should not be general in its appeal. A cult film appeals to a particular group of people, whereas a James Bond film appeals to tastes across the board as well as Bond fanatics. Peter Cushing had a rather more straightforward analysis of the stereotypes necessary for making a cult film, which he explained while making a film that was neither good enough or bad enough to become a cult itself, despite the clichés on which it was constructed (*The Legend of the Werewolf* [dir. Freddie Francis, 1975]).

> Well, you see, for eighteen years these pictures have been popular and the mass of people who go the pictures, it's rather like those who buy their favourite brand of chocolates; they know that when they open the box they'll find the coconut creams and the truffles and that sort of thing, and they know when they see this kind of film they'll get what they're looking for. And so they're catered for by the scriptwriters.[13]

As S.S. Prawer observes:

> The tone, timbre, and resonance of an actor's voice, his habitual cadences and verbal gestures, the play of his features, the movements of his hands and body, become familiar to us and make us watch for variations as well as repetitions. The aura of his previous performances enters, as we have seen, into our conception of his personality—and so, very often, does what we know or surmise of his off-screen life and personality.[14]

By 1972, audiences had come to know what to expect from Hammer's Dracula films: how Lee would look, how Cushing would emote, what methods would be used to dispatch the vampire, that there would be a final struggle, that a young woman would be placed in danger, that good would triumph over evil, and that there would be blood and erotic evocations. As Eco also says, "Two clichés make us laugh but a hundred clichés move us because we sense dimly that the clichés are talking among themselves, celebrating a reunion."[15] And that is what fans of a cult movie do among themselves: they celebrate a reunion with what they love—often with like-minded people who feel the same way. Eco believes that "the extreme of banality allows us to catch a glimpse of the Sublime."[16] It is unfair (and incorrect) to call *A.D. 1972* banal, but it is true that it is much more a study in style than content. There is, after all, no new content here, as we have already observed in our comparison of it with *Taste the Blood of Dracula*. The film's most intriguing quality is how it manages to update an old idea.

In the case of *Dracula A.D. 1972*, Lee and Cushing's previous incarnations as Dracula and Van Helsing inform and direct our expectations of and response to the film. At the time of the film's release, those interpretations had always been set in the past, so the contemporaneity was a considerable shock. With the passing of time, however, a patina of familiarity has built up around what had originally been a much more raw and, for many, alienating experience. Nostalgia is a kind of beeswax. *A.D. 1972* has now become a period piece, lovingly polished. Though Cushing had played Van Helsing only twice before, his performance here is not only more nuanced than in the past, but it is also profoundly retrospective. Playing his own grandfather, he floods the screen with memories of his past association with Hammer, while subsequently presenting us with a completely convincing modern character. Lee's Dracula is quite literally a reincarnation of his past roles, but with even more charisma. Both actors in fact look more convincing and authoritative than they do in any other of their Hammer film appearances. Greater age, experience, and, as Lee himself observed, improved makeup made them look better than ever, but it is their aura of former association that crowns the film, just as their joint guest appearance in the otherwise undistinguished Sammy Davis Jr. vehicle *One More Time* (dir. Jerry Lewis, 1970) suggested far more than the few seconds of screen time they were given as Dracula and Baron Frankenstein.

Three

Cause of the Conflict

> "I have returned to destroy the House of Van Helsing
> forever—the old through the young."
> —Dracula in *Dracula A.D. 1972*

THE MOST SUSTAINED APPLICATION OF a revenge plot in modern literature is probably Alexandre Dumas's *The Count of Monte Cristo* (1844). Imprisoned for 14 years, the victim of a conspiracy of false pretenses, the hero, Edmond Dantès, requires the punishment of his enemies to fit their crimes; hence, a duel is far too straightforward a method:

> "Oh, yes," replied the count; "understand me, I would fight a duel for a trifle, for an insult, for a blow; and the more so that, thanks to my skill in all bodily exercises, and the indifference to danger I have gradually acquired, I should be almost certain to kill my man. Oh, I would fight for such a cause; but in return for a slow, profound, eternal torture, I would give back the same, were it possible; an eye for an eye, a tooth for a tooth, as the Orientalists say,—our masters in everything,—those favored creatures who have formed for themselves a life of dreams and a paradise of realities."[1]

The novel charts the planning and execution of Dantès' complex revenge, leading to his triumph:

> "I am he whom you dishonoured—I am he whose betrothed you prostituted—I am he upon whom you trampled that you might raise yourself to fortune—I am he whose father you condemned to die of hunger—I am he whom you also condemned to starvation, and who yet forgives you, because he hopes to be forgiven—I am Edmond Dantès!" Danglars uttered a cry, and fell prostrate. "Rise," said the count, "your life is safe; the same good fortune has not happened to your accomplices—one is mad, the other dead."[2]

Dumas's novel is an exotic adventure, and we can sympathize with the vengeance of its wronged hero, but revenge is also a very popular device in horror films where such sympathy is not always so appropriate. It motivates Bela Lugosi's Vitus Werdegast in *The Black Cat* (dir. Edgar J. Ulmer, 1934), who flays his enemy, Hjalmar Poelzig (Boris Karloff), while Poelzig is still alive. Thus does Werdegast avenge Poelzig's treachery in stealing both his wife and daughter from him, along with having been responsible for the slaughter of thousands of Werdegast's countrymen during the First World War. The Creature from the Black Lagoon took its revenge for having been shot and left for dead in its first film by abducting the leading lady, Lori Nelson, in *Revenge of the Creature* in 1955 (dir. Jack Arnold). A rather different Creature appeared in Terence Fisher's *The Revenge of Frankenstein* (1958), in which Peter Cushing's Baron aims to prove his critics wrong by creating a perfect human. Unfortunately, what starts out looking perfect soon ends up as a degenerate cannibal.

Witches often have revenge on their persecutors by coming back from the dead, a state of affairs Mario Bava mixed with vampirism in *Black Sunday/The Mask of Satan* (1960). Minus the vampirism, a supposed witch also made a vengeful comeback in *The Woman Who Came Back* (dir. Walter Colmes, 1945), while the spirit of a male warlock possessed Vincent Price's Charles Dexter Ward in Roger Corman's *The Haunted Palace* (1966). Similar things happened in John Moxey's *City of the Dead* (1960) and Don Sharp's *Witchcraft* (1964). The word "revenge" itself was deemed powerful enough to help sell *The Vengeance of She* (dir. Cliff Owen, 1968), which isn't, in fact, about revenge at all. Vincent Price in *The Abominable Dr. Phibes* (dir. Robert Fuest, 1971) and his Edward Lionheart in *Theatre of Blood* (dir. Douglas Hickox, 1973) then sent up the whole idea of revenge tragedy; in the case of the latter, the specifically Shakespearean variety. Phibes gets his own back on the doctors who failed to save his beloved wife on the operating table, while Lionheart rewrites the Bard to obtain (literally in one case) his pound of flesh from the critics who failed to honor him with a Critics' Circle Award.

Dracula A.D. 1972, like most of Hammer's *Dracula* sequels, is also a revenge drama. Unlike the Elizabethan revenge dramas, from which these Dracula films can claim a distant descent, they are not tragedies, as the principal heroes survive, but Dracula's motivation has much in common with the somewhat flimsy justifications that motivate traditional revenge tragedy. That is largely neither here nor there; what both Hammer's Dracula films and Elizabethan revenge tragedy are really concerned with is the manner in which the revenge is enacted.

Stoker's *Dracula* novel is not strictly speaking a revenge story, despite the fact that it contains one of the lines that Christopher Lee interpolated into *The Satanic Rites of Dracula*, where it in fact has much more relevance. Stoker's line for Dracula is "My revenge is just begun! I spread it over centuries, and time is on my side," which Lee modifies to "My revenge has spread over centuries, and has just begun!" Even in this modified form it sits uneasily, from a stylistic point of view, with the rest of the script, much like the quotation from Stoker's *The Jewel of Seven Stars*, which Valerie Leon's Margaret Fuchs also slightly modifies in Seth Holt's *Blood from the Mummy's Tomb* ("A land where love was not base, but a divine possession of the soul!"[3]). In fact, the word "revenge" appears only twice in the whole of Stoker's novel, the first occasion being in Chapter 15, where it is used only rhetorically by Van Helsing, and not with regard to Dracula. Lord Ruthven, the villain of John Polidori's 1819 tale, "The Vampyre," which became a melodrama by J.R. Planché the following year, and an opera with music by Heinrich Marschner the year after that, is motivated more by lust than revenge. James Malcolm Rymer's Victorian penny dreadful, *Varney the Vampire*, which was one of Stoker's inspirations, mentions the word rather more (mostly from the point of view of Varney's victims). Varney admits in a conversation with his accomplice, Robert Marchdale:

"I feel some desire of revenge against those dastards who by hundreds have hunted me, burnt down my mansion, and sought my destruction."—"That I do not wonder at."

"I would fain leave among them a legacy of fear. Such fear as shall haunt them and their children for years to come. I would wish that the name of Varney, the vampire, should be a sound of terror for generations."—"It will be so."[4]

Stoker's Dracula is motivated far more by the will to power than by revenge. He wishes to invigorate himself with fresh blood and extend his empire of the undead. Based more closely on the novel than any other Hammer *Dracula* film, the studio's first attempt in 1958 followed this line. Here, Dracula is after blood, pure and simple. Neither does revenge play a role in the first sequel, *Dracula: Prince of Darkness*, where the vampire seems only to be interested in his pursuit of the film's two female leads (Suzan Farmer and Barbara Shelley). It is only in the third film in the series, *Dracula Has Risen from the Grave*, that a revenge plot appears, alongside an increased theological element. Having been drowned in the icy waters of his castle moat at the end *of Dracula: Prince of Darkness*, the Count has good reason to be vengeful. However, the ones responsible for his demise (principally Andrew Keir's renegade priest Father Shandor), don't feature in John Elder's screenplay, so a new nemesis and a new motivation for Dracula had to be found. The problem is solved by Rupert Davies's monsignor, who performs an exorcism and then fixes a large crucifix to the door of Castle Dracula. Meanwhile, his cowardly assistant priest (Ewan Hooper) bangs his head on a boulder during a storm. When blood from the wound reaches the submerged body of Dracula, the vampire is reanimated, and is immediately outraged by this intrusion on his property ("Who has done this thing?" he shouts in the operatic manner in which Lee would have excelled had he become the opera singer he always wanted to be). Dracula vows to have his revenge on the monsignor by turning his daughter (Veronica Carlson) into an undead bride.

Such a weak motivation obviously required extra elements to spice things up— hence the idea of an atheist staking the vampire midway through the film, only for Dracula to survive, because the atheist can't pray. There's also an interesting reference to Auschwitz when the dead body of Barbara Ewing's barmaid, Zena, is disposed of in the ovens of the subterranean bakery below the pub in which Dracula has taken up temporary residence.

Revenge also drives the action of *Taste the Blood of Dracula*, but in this case the basis for it is even weaker, for reasons explained above. Rather than avenging any personal slight, this time Dracula is annoyed merely because three elderly men have killed Lord Courtley. "They have destroyed my servant," he announces. "They will be destroyed." Thereafter, all he has to do is compel the various offspring of his enemies to kill their own parents, before vampirizing some of them as well, his dialogue being merely numerical for the most part. He growls, "The first," "The second," "The third," until he can claim, "Now my revenge is complete." No wonder Christopher Lee became so disenchanted with the way in which "that character" was being treated. *Scars of Dracula* refrained from revenge and replaced it with mere punishment—Dracula branding Patrick Troughton's Klove with a red-hot saber for disobeying orders. In this failed attempt to return to the mood of Stoker's novel, poisoned soup was the closest things got to the fabled dish that is best served cold. (Jenny Hanley's heroine is, however, prevented from sipping a bowl of this dubious potage even as she raises a spoonful of it to her lips.)

After such disappointments, *Dracula A.D. 1972* in fact offered Lee much more than had been on placed on the coffin lid before. Although Dracula's motivation was again revenge, he at least had a real reason for it, as we see Van Helsing Senior destroy him in the prologue. Abducting Van Helsing's granddaughter is the kind of thing that the vampire, Lord Ruthven, relishes in Planché's melodrama. Ruthven, like Dracula, is, in Lee's words, "irresistible to women and, presumably, as far as men are concerned, unstoppable."[5] Ruthven must marry the virginal Lady Margaret before the setting of the moon if he is to avoid destruction, and he very nearly succeeds:

> **RUTHVEN:** She's mine! My prey is in my clutch,—the choicest, crowning victim!—Ha! revive, my bride.
> **LADY MARGARET:** Where am I? Where is my father? ... How wild a fancy seized him, that you were dead.[6]

But Ruthven's motivation is not so much revenge as survival. Conversely, when Van Helsing realizes that Jessica has become Dracula's victim, he exclaims: "This is his revenge, a revenge stretching over the years: a diabolical vendetta against the kin of Lawrence Van Helsing, my grandfather. He wants to sate his hatred in this way, by making my granddaughter into the creature he is, by making her into one of the living dead: a vampire."

Lee also has more lines in *A.D. 1972* and its sequel than he had in previous Draculas, and as well as looking better than he ever did before, he also has much more to do. Though Dracula claimed his revenge was complete in *Taste the Blood of Dracula*, that privilege was more nearly achieved in *The Satanic Rites of Dracula*, where he plans not only to end his own existence but also, as Van Helsing puts it, "to bring down whole universe with him. The ultimate revenge: Thousands dying of the plague, and like the shadow of death itself, one figure scything its way through the terror and anguish: Count Dracula. It is the Biblical prophecy of Armageddon."

Revenge plots are all very much alike, and are the simplest way of creating the conflict that is essential to all drama. It is an ancient device. Aeschylus's *Oresteia* trilogy is motivated by the desire of Electra and her brother Orestes to avenge the murder of their father, Agamemnon, by Clytemnestra. Orestes then murders her, after which Orestes is pursued by the Furies, before a final resolution; but the cause of that tragedy has a long lineage stretching back long before the plays begin. The origin story concerns Zeus's son, Tantalus, who slays his own son, Pelops, and then feeds his flesh to the gods to test their omnipotence. The gods bring Pelops back to life, and his wife, Hippodamia, gives birth to a son, Atreus. The original crime of Tantalus thus sets the series of murders and revenges in motion, which follow one another like a domino race. The idea of a distant crime that has consequences much later is particularly relevant to *Dracula A.D. 1972*, which is particularly concerned with how the past events affect the present. Not only does the plot revolve around the relation between what happened in 1872 and the vengeance sought by Dracula in 1972, but there are also other resonances from this film's place in Hammer's Dracula history. If Hammer had made this film as the first in its series as *Dracula A.D. 1958*, its effect would be very different, as it would not be able to be self-referential, as *A.D.*

1972 so obviously is. Not only is *A.D. 1972* diagetically retrospective, it is also non-diagetically aware of the films that preceded it. Van Helsing points out early on, somewhat in the manner of a Greek tragedy, how his family "has a tradition of research into the occult. To us it has been a serious, lifelong study." That the old conflict with Dracula is still very much in his thoughts is demonstrated by Cushing's marvelous scene, immediately after Jessica leaves him, in which he seems almost psychically aware of the trouble that is brewing. He half removes his grandfather's book on *The Legend of Dracula, the Vampire*, and then glances at the woodcut of Dracula's fangs-bared features before touching his forehead with both hands, as though fighting off some psychic intrusion from the past. After another glance at the woodcut, he looks at the portrait of his grandfather, which stares out from the past; and the is very much impacting the present here. We find the same device in Greek tragedy with the oft-employed figure of the seer.

Later, Van Helsing points out to Inspector Murray, "My grandfather died fighting a vampire. The most terrible, the most dangerous vampire of all time, but before that, he collected proof, positive proof. Oh no, there was nothing ludicrous about it. He was a scientist. His evidence was conclusive. There is evil in this world. There are dark, awful things. Occasionally, we get a glimpse of them. But there are dark corners and horrors impossible to imagine—even in our worst nightmares. There is a Satan." We will discuss Cushing's immaculate performance of these lines later, but what is important to realize here is the contextualization of the plot of *A.D. 1972* in the past—the past of the film's own narrative, and Cushing's past as an interpreter of Van Helsing in the 1958 *Dracula* and *Brides of Dracula* (in which Dracula himself is absent). There is a similar nostalgic reference to his past performances as Frankenstein in Hammer's last Frankenstein film, *Frankenstein and the Monster from Hell* (dir. Terence Fisher, 1974), in which he says, "I haven't felt so elated in my life, not since ... well, that was a long time ago." It is also significant that Van Helsing refers to Satan in his dialogue with Murray, as Dracula is by now very much a stand-in for the Prince of Hell.

Cushing recalled, "In *Dracula A.D. 1972* I played my own father—or was it my grandfather?—in a flash-back sequence, but whoever I was, I conked out after a ferocious encounter with Christopher Lee's stupendous Dracula."[7] But he wasn't the only member of the cast to play his own ancestor. Christopher Neame plays both Johnny Alucard and whatever the unnamed ancestor is called in the Victorian prologue. Johnny has inherited Dracula's dried blood and Dracula's ring, which he proudly puts on his finger when contemplating the Black Mass he has arranged. Further echoes of the past resonate here, as the ring is in fact a replica of the original one worn by Bela Lugosi in *Abbot and Costello Meet Frankenstein* (dir. Charles Barton, 1948) subsequent to John Carradine's Dracula wearing it in *House of Frankenstein* (dir. Erle C. Kenton, 1944) and then *House of Dracula* (dir. Erle C. Kenton, 1945). The ring was then given to legendary fan collector Forrest J. Ackerman, who had several copies made, one of which he gave to Christopher Lee, who wore it in all the Dracula films from *Dracula Has Risen from the Grave* onwards. It is indeed a shot of this ring that fills the screen at the end of *The Satanic Rites of Dracula*, providing a fitting epitaph to Hammer's Dracula cycle.[8]

A.D. 1972's preoccupation with the past is almost as strong as its desperate attempt to be up-to-date. The prologue firmly roots what follows in historical events, of which the audience is continually reminded. St. Bartolph's Church, which we see intact and in rural surroundings during the prologue, is derelict by 1972, deconsecrated and in the midst of urban sprawl. When the teenagers visit the church for their Black Mass, Jessica discovers her grandfather's gravestone, with its Latin inscription: "Requiescat in Pace Ultima"—"Rest in Final Peace." "Why '*final*'?" she asks, which Don Houghton leaves the audience to answer for themselves. The hope of the Victorian mourners was, of course, that Van Helsing Senior would not become a vampire himself; this suggests that his family were quite aware of his researches into the occult. As Van Helsing Junior later points out, vampire hunting runs in the family. The Latin R.I.P.U. ends the film too. Van Helsing repeats it to Jessica and it is then superimposed over the final shot, in the same scarlet Gothic font that introduced the main titles. This suggests that the evils of the past have now been canceled out, and that the domino effect has been stopped. Similarly, the final play of the *Oresteia* trilogy, *The Eumenides*, ends the cycle of individual vengeance with the reestablishment of law and order. No one knew at the time that a sequel would require Lee's Dracula to be resurrected one final time.

Greek tragedy always placed violent acts off-stage, and only reported bloody deeds. (Richard Strauss and Hugo von Hofmannsthal's operatic rendition of *Elektra* in 1904 revels in bloodshed in a very un–Greek, rather more Hammery way.) Long after ancient Greece, however, Elizabethan drama took up the revenge theme and turned it into a veritable genre, beginning with *The Spanish Tragedy*, written at the end of the 16th century by Thomas Kyd, which probably influenced the most famous example of revenge tragedy that is Shakespeare's *Hamlet*. (Laurence Olivier's 1948 film adaptation also featured Peter Cushing as Osric and purportedly a brief walk-on appearance by Christopher Lee as one of the courtiers at Elsinore.) The sticking point in *Hamlet* is that Hamlet himself takes far too long to take his revenge on King Claudius for the murder of Hamlet's father. Hamlet says he is "very proud, revengeful, ambitious," but also realizes that he needs to "spur my dull revenge." In the end, he does strike, and the stage is littered with corpses like the end of Hammer's *Vampire Circus* (dir. Robert Young, 1972), which, of course, is a very distant descendant of this kind of thing.

In *Vampire Circus*, Count Mitterhaus (Robert Tayman) decrees, after having been staked through the heart, that "the town of Stetl will die. Your children will die to give me back my life." And thus it transpires. In *The Spanish Tragedy*, as J.R. Mulryn puts it, the ghost of Andrea "seeks revenge for his death in battle at the hands of Balthazar; Bel-Imperia looks for vengeance for Andrea's, her lover's death; Balthazar and Lorenzo seek revenge on Horatio for winning Bel-Imperia's love; Hieronimo pursues vengeance for the murder, by Lorenzo and Balthazar of his son Horatio."[9] As one might expect, hanging, stabbing, poisoning, and suicide pile up the bodies:

> *Andrea:* Ay, now my hopes have end in their effects,
> When blood and sorrow finish my desires:
> Horatio murdered in his father's bower,
> Vild Serberine by Pedringano slain,

> False Pedringano hanged by quaint device,
> Fair Isabella by herself misdone,
> Prince Balthazar by Bel-imperia stabbed,
> The Duke of Castile and his wicked son
> Both done to death by old Hieronimo,
> And good Hieronimo slain by himself:
> Ay, there were spectacles to please my soul.[10]

The ghost of Andrea in *The Spanish Tragedy* delights in revenge, which is also personified on stage alongside him throughout the play:

> Then, sweet Revenge do this at my request;
> Let me be judge, and doom them to unrest:
> ….
> Hang Balthazar about Chimera's neck,
> And let him there bewail his bloody love,
> ….
> Let Serberine go roll the fatal stone,
> And take from Sisyphus his endless moan;
> False Pedringano for his treachery,
> Let him be dragged through boiling Acheron,
> And there live, dying still in endless flames,
> Blaspheming gods and all their holy names.[11]

Dracula's vindictiveness is surely a paltry thing beside such corrosive vitriol.

Suicide, rape, and poison play their parts in Thomas Middleton's *The Revenger's Tragedy* (1606). Vindice keeps the skull of his betrothed, Gloriana, who was poisoned by the Duke, as a gruesome memento mori:

> My study's ornament, thou shell of death,
> Once the bright face of my betrothed lady,
> When life and beauty naturally fill'd out
> These ragged imperfections;
> When two heaven-pointed diamonds were set
> In those unsightly rings—then 'twas a face
> So far beyond the artificial shine
> Of any woman's bought complexion,
> That the uprightest man (if such there be,
> That sin but seven times a day) broke custom,
> And made up eight with looking after her.[12]

Later, in a scene that borders on necrophilia, he anoints the skull with poison and fixes it to an effigy of the Duke's lover:

> Look you, brother,
> I have not fashion'd this only for show
> And useless property; no, it shall bear a part
> E'en in its own revenge.
> This very skull,
> Whose mistress the duke poison'd with this drug,
> The mortal curse of the earth shall be reveng'd
> In the like strain, and kiss his lips to death.
> As much as the dumb thing can, he shall feel:
> What fails in poison, we'll supply in steel.[13]

The idea of a kiss of death certainly relates this scene to Dracula.

In John Webster's *The Duchess of Malfi* (1613/14), the Gothic horror is raised to a truly grisly height. The Duchess, who has been forbidden by her two brothers, Ferdinand and the Cardinal, to marry her steward, Antonio, attempts to elope with him, but is pursued and captured with her children by him. Antonio manages to escape, only to be accidentally killed at the end; but before that, Ferdinand, who is a depraved madman, presents the Duchess with a severed dead man's hand, which she is persuaded to believe is Antonio's. She is then shown lifelike figures of Antonio and her children, which have been made to look like corpses. Believing this trickery, she resolves to die.

Ferdinand arranges a group of madmen to "serenade" her, further to unnerve her in her imprisonment. Intriguingly, it was the "dismal kind of song" Webster has them sing that James Bernard eventually set to music for a BBC radio production of the play in 1954, prior to his becoming Hammer's house composer. Indeed, he used the melody he had composed for Webster's madmen for the main theme of *The Curse of Frankenstein*:

> O let us howl, some heavy note,
> Some deadly-doggèd howl,
> Sounding as from the threat'ning throat,
> Of beasts and fatal fowl.[14]

Soon after this grotesque scene, two executioners appear with a coffin, cords, and a bell and proceed to strangle the Duchess on Ferdinand's orders, overseen by his servant, Bosola, who adds a macabre and highly existentialist commentary to the act:

> Hark, now every thing is still,
> The screech owl and the whistler shrill
> Call upon our dame, aloud,
> And bid her quickly don her shroud.
> Much you had of land and rent,
> Your length in clay's now competent.
> A long war disturbed your mind;
> Here your perfect peace is signed.
> Of what is't fools make such vain keeping?
> Sin their conception, their birth, weeping:
> Their life, a general mist of error,
> Their death, a hideous storm of terror.[15]

The Duchess survives long enough to be told that the figures she thought were her children were fake, but in the end, Bosola, horrified by what he has been forced to do, avenges the Duchess by killing Ferdinand and the Cardinal and ending up being killed himself.

> Revenge!—for the Duchess of Malfi, murdered
> By th'Aragonia brethren; for Antonio,
> Slain by this hand; for lustful Julia,
> Poisoned by this man; and lastly, for myself,
> That was an actor in the main of all.[16]

Hammer's Dracula films belong to this tradition, their visual poetry substituting for the linguistic poetry in the plays. In both the Elizabethan tragedies and the Dracula films, revenge is merely the excuse for the presentation of violence. It is how such violence is executed that forms the main focus of interest. And one must not forget that the Elizabethan revenge tragedies were originally performed in what we would now call "modern-dress" productions. There was no historicism in the Elizabethan theater. Even *Hamlet*, which was already an old story in Shakespeare's day, would have been performed in the here and now. *Dracula A.D. 1972* is, of course, not the profound meditation of the human condition that *Hamlet* is, but it shares much in common with the plays that inspired Shakespeare's most famous play.

While we are on the subject of *Hamlet*, it is worthwhile recapitulating a subject mentioned earlier with regard to what Umberto Eco has to say about *Hamlet*'s relation to cult films, like *Casablanca*—or, in our case, *Dracula AD. 1972*. Eco confesses that he is "tempted to read *Casablanca* as T.S. Eliot read *Hamlet*, attributing its fascination not to the fact that it was a successful work (actually he considered it one of Shakespeare's less fortunate efforts) but to the imperfection of its composition."

> [Eliot] viewed *Hamlet* as the result of an unsuccessful fusion of several earlier versions of the story, and so the puzzling ambiguity of the main character was due to the author's difficulty in putting together different topoi. So both public and critics find *Hamlet* beautiful because it is interesting, but believe it is interesting because it is beautiful.[17]

These ambiguities in the plot of *Hamlet* might find parallels with gaps and inconsistencies in *Dracula A.D. 1972*—things for which there are "no psychological reason[s]." Eco believed that Michael Curtiz, the director of *Casablanca*, "was simply quoting, unconsciously, similar situations in other movies and trying to provide a reasonably complete repetition of them."[18] A cult movie "should display not one central idea but many. It should not reveal a coherent philosophy of composition. It must live on, and because of, its glorious ricketiness."[19] Of course, one may find ricketiness even in great masterpieces. Richard Wagner's epic *Ring* cycle, which was to a considerable extent inspired by Aeschylus's *Oresteia*, revolves around the cursed Ring of the Nibelung. The only way to avoid world catastrophe in that work is for the ring to be returned to the Rhine Daughters from whom it was stolen, but even though this happens right at the end, the world still ends. In a famous letter to his friend August Röckel, Wagner wrote: "Above all, I am struck by your question why, since the Rhinegold is returned to the Rhine, the gods nevertheless perish.... I believe that, at a good performance, even the most naïve spectator will be left in no doubt on that point. It must be said, however, that the gods' downfall is not the result of points in a contract ... no, the necessity of this downfall arises from our innermost feelings."[20] Well, Wagner has something of a cult following too.

While they don't detract from the pleasures of the film, the plot of *Dracula A.D. 1972* does have a certain ricketiness. To begin with, why does Johnny Alucard's Victorian ancestor make Dracula wait one hundred years to have his revenge? Of course, Don Houghton needed a way to contrast the old with the new, and this seemed a good enough device, but it is indeed rickety. We have already observed how unlikely a rock group successfully entertaining a group of superannuated partygoers in evening dress would be, even without the disruption caused by Johnny and his friends. At the other end of the film, one does wonder why Van Helsing bothers to pay Johnny Alucard a visit to find out where Jessica has been taken, when the obvious place to find her is in St. Bartolph's Church. Van Helsing realizes that Dracula will be returning there, so what better place to keep his victim until the appointed hour? During the film, why doesn't Dracula simply pay Van Helsing a visit at home, where he could bite Jessica and kill his nemesis at the same time? He could easily find out where he lives. Also, it does seem to be rather a coincidence that Janet Key's Anna, who knows where Johnny lives, happens to be driving past Van Helsing just as he is desperately searching for Johnny.

None of these inconsistencies detract from the overall sweep of the film under Alan Gibson's direction, however. The plot is, after all, nowhere near as important as Peter Cushing's intense and utterly serious performance of Van Helsing, opposite the majestic and compelling Dracula of Christopher Lee. The latter here reaches the peak of his satanic development of the character, which began in *Dracula: Prince of Darkness*. One might think that the apogee was reached in *The Satanic Rites of Dracula*, but his greater interaction with Van Helsing in that film (even adopting a fake Russian accent at one stage), brings him closer to his original portrayal in the 1958 *Dracula*. In other words, he is more human because he is more socially integrated. In *Dracula A.D. 1972*, he is majestically apart. He has his servant, Johnny, but otherwise stands alone in St. Bartolph's Church, biding his time, rather like Satan in Dante's *Inferno*—"The Emperor of the kingdom dolorous."[21] Having emerged from the mist of his resurrection in the middle of the film, he extends his hand, suggesting that he expects Johnny to kiss his ring like a satanic Pope. The camera angle, peering up at his towering form from the ground, suggests Milton's line, "High on a throne of Royal State," on which Satan sits in *Paradise Lost*. Indeed, there is much of Milton's Satan in Lee's interpretation of Dracula. Revenge motivates them both:

> What though the field be lost?
> All is not lost; the unconquerable Will,
> And study of revenge, immortal hate,
> And courage never to submit or yield,
> And what is else not to be overcome;
> That glory never shall His wrath or might
> Extort from me: to bow and sue for grace
> With suppliant knee, and deify His power.[22]

Dracula also has an "unconquerable Will." His first words in *A.D. 1972* are, "It was my Will."

His hatred is also immortal, surviving his physical destruction at the beginning of the film. He may have missed the opportunity to destroy Lawrence Van Helsing's son, but the grandson (Lorrimer) will do nicely, once he's corrupted Jessica. He has also missed his chance with Lorrimer's son (Jessica's unnamed father), who is presumably dead by the time the film starts. (Cushing looked rather too old to play Jessica's father as originally intended. Grief over the death of his wife, Helen, had aged him, but also invested him with an increased intensity and melancholy, which the contemporary setting made even more compelling.)

In *Paradise Lost*, it is actually Beelzebub who suggests an attack on the newly created species of humanity as the best way of enjoying revenge on God:

> Seduce them to our party, that their God
> May prove their foe, and with repenting hand

"It was my will!"—Christopher Lee as Dracula in *Dracula A.D. 1972*.

> Abolish his own works. This would surpass
> Common revenge, and interrupt His joy
> In our Confusion, and our Joy upraise
> In His disturbance; when His darling Sons
> Hurled headlong to partake with us, shall curse
> Their frail Originals, and faded bliss,
> Faded so soon.[23]

Dracula similarly exacts his revenge on Van Helsing (who stands in for God here). Indeed, the scene toward the end of the film in which Jessica, hypnotized, stands behind Dracula (having pulled the knife from his chest that Van Helsing has thrust into it), is comparable to Eve's plucking of the apple from the Tree of Knowledge in the garden of Eden. Dracula, like the serpent, persuades her to disobey Van Helsing's desperate plea, "Jessica! Don't go near him! In God's name, don't touch him!" But she does, and removes the dagger, which appears to have had as little effect on him as the stake in *Dracula Has Risen from the Grave*, when the young atheist, who has thrust in his heart, refuses to pray. (Intriguingly, Planché's aforementioned 1820 vampire play has a very similar line: "Touch him not, Margaret! Fly the demon's grasp!"[24])

Ultimately, however, Dracula loses, so it's hardly surprising that in his final incarnation for Hammer, after having been turned to dust, drowned, impaled, overcome by Christian iconography, and struck by lightning in previous films, he wants to destroy humanity as a whole, not just Van Helsing. Despite his being rather more "human" in that film, the scope of his revenge is fully the equal of Satan's.

Four

CONTEXT

> "This *is* London. This is the *twentieth* century"
> —Inspector Murray, *Dracula A.D. 1972*

DRACULA A.D. 1972 CONFRONTS MANY modern anxieties: class conflict, permissive society, disaffected youth, fears about sexually transmitted diseases (for which vampirism is surely a metaphor), rape, murder, mutilation, and kidnapping. *The Satanic Rites of Dracula* even went on to embrace Armageddon by germ warfare.

However, the past really is a foreign country, where they do indeed do things differently. I was eleven in 1972. In terms of its own vampire films, Hammer was 14. The company had made five Dracula epics by that time, and British society had changed immensely since 1958, when Hammer's first Dracula film appeared. At that time, the mood in Britain was rather more optimistic than it had become by 1972. In 1957, the year of Hammer's Gothic launch with *The Curse of Frankenstein*, British prime minister Harold Macmillan assured everyone that they'd "never had it so good." He boasted, "Go around the country, go to the industrial towns, go to the farms and you will see a state of prosperity such as we have never had in my lifetime—nor indeed in the history of this country." Macmillan argued that increased steel, coal, and motorcar production had increased wages, exports, and investments. The Second World War had ended only 13 years before, but what Harold Wilson, the Labour prime minister, would call "the white heat of change" in 1963 seemed already to be under way. Landmark events that pointed toward the culture of the 1960s had already taken place by 1958. The BBC Radiophonic Workshop, later to create one of the most famous pieces of television music in Delia Derbyshire's realization of Ron Grainer's *Doctor Who* theme, was opened that year; the philosopher Bertrand Russell founded the Campaign for Nuclear Disarmament; construction of the M1 motorway had begun; Shelagh Delaney's "kitchen sink" working-class drama, *A Taste of Honey*, premiered on May 7; parking meters were installed for the first time; debutantes were no longer presented at court; Cliff Richard, the English Elvis, had his first hit record with "Move It"; the much-loved BBC children's TV show, *Blue Peter*, was first aired on October 16, while in November, Earl's Court hosted the world's first exhibition of computers.

Amid all this excitement, Hammer's *Dracula* burst onto the scene, in full color, with a sexually athletic vampire count in the shape of Christopher Lee, opposed by the already well-known Peter Cushing, who had risen to fame through the new medium of television. Apparently bloody and violent, with a strong aroma of illicit sexuality and sonorous, thrillingly visceral music by James Bernard, *Dracula* appalled the establishment, but it had immense appeal for its youthful target audience. In fact, the blood and violence were employed very sparingly, and much was left to the imagination of the audience, but Terence Fisher's approach paved the way for far greater gore to come. Set in a Victorian past that would soon be so trendily collected and lamented amid its simultaneous destruction, the film also catered to an appetite for nostalgia redolent of lost securities and lost certainties, while salivating at the prospect of the greater social and sexual freedoms. The way in which the film was promoted was similarly titillating, stirring up expectations, which perhaps made the experience of the film feel more shocking than it actually was. As Peter Hutchings observed with regard to the original film poster for *Dracula*:

> There is a physicality to the image, with Dracula's hand powerfully grasping the woman's shoulder (and resting very near her left breast) which was uncommon in previous *Dracula* films where the physical business of blood-letting occurred offscreen and where onscreen the Count usually contented himself with giving people a nasty stare. This physicality is underlined by a certain aggression apparent in the image's composition—not only in Dracula leaning out towards us but the woman also seems to be almost falling out of the poster.[1]

This expectation of sexual violence developed with successive Dracula films, and the *Dracula A.D. 1972* poster features three images of threatened women, all glowered over by an enraged Dracula. The American poster went even further, adding, "The Count is back, with an eye for London's hotpants ... and a taste for everything." Significantly, the German release retitled it as *Dracula Jagt Mini-Mädchens* ("Dracula Hunts Mini-Girls").

The explosion of pop music in the 1960s, epitomized by the Beatles, along with the hippie movement in America with its promise of peace and love, suggested there was even more cause for optimism. S.S. Prawer nicely encapsulates the mood of the time as being "orientated towards 'youth,' 'vitality,' 'creativity,' 'energy,' 'originality,' 'life,' and 'excitement.'"

> An England in which "classless," "unstuffy," "straightforward," "toughly professional," "down to earth," "skeptical," "aware," and "irreverent" were accepted terms of praise, in which the "satire industry" flourished, in which sexual activity was discussed and exhibited with a frankness never known before; the England of the Beatles and Carnaby Street boutiques; the England of miniskirts and eclectic modes of dress that drew freely on the discarded fashions of the Victorian and the Edwardians; the England of "swinging London," which saw itself as "the entertainment capital of the world"—but also the England of anti-nuclear demonstrations, Aldermaston marches, Vietnam protests, and Cold War consciousness as well as that of race-riots, the Kray and Richardson gangs, the Profumo and Devonshire sex-scandals, the Great Train Robbery, and the Moors Murders.[2]

Affluent, increasingly permissive young people were steadily rejecting the socials norms of their parents. Women were becoming increasingly liberated, epitomized by Julie Christie in John Schlesinger's *Darling* (1965), whose character had "a quality of independence, a stylishness which didn't depend on being looked at by a man, but required men to look at her, which was a quite different way of going about things, so, although she didn't in fact represent economically or even morally a different sort of woman, she somehow *looked* different from the Rank girls in particular, who had been used before." Christie explained that the desire of her character in that film was to prove that "there was nothing that you couldn't do—that includes sexual—was absolutely true in real life."[3]

> Here was a woman who didn't want to get married, didn't want to have children like those other kitchen-sink heroines; no, Darling wanted to have *everything*. Of course at the time, this was seen as greedy promiscuity and she had to be punished for it. But there was an element of possibility for women, of a new way of living, which is why the film was such a success.[4]

For Michael Caine, his role in *Alfie* (dir. Lewis Gilbert, 1966) typified "the attitude of a lot of men in the '60s. There had always been tremendous morality, you know. I mean, to put it quite frankly, you could never get laid. I came from South London, which was like living in Sicily without the sunshine or the pasta. I mean, you only had to look at a girl twice and the brothers came round to kick the daylights out of you. You had to get married. I mean it was real shotgun wedding time; and then suddenly the '60s came, you know, and girls all burned their bras, after everybody had spent ten years trying to work out how to undo the clips, and, wow! And so Alfie was there, and Alfie was archetypal of that, and his attitude was rather the same as the start of the women's liberation movement, where they said, 'we're going to go out and have sex. We don't care about romance anymore. We're going to have sex with whom *we* want to do it, and we don't care,' well, that's how the men were, except they did it first."[5]

Robert Murphy put it more succinctly:

> [Alfie's] characteristics—an almost psychopathic vulgarity which links women, clothes and cars as commodities to be flaunted to prove to the world that he has achieved success without the privileges of birth or education—could be tentatively identified with the working-class actors, photographers and pop stars who were supposed to inhabit Swinging London.[6]

London became the focus of everything that was new. Michelangelo Antonioni came to London in 1966 to film *Blow-Up*, his rumination on the illusion and reality that were the '60s, for exactly that reason: "I could have made it in New York or in Paris—but not in Rome—because the film is the story of a fashion photographer, and in Rome they are not as important as they are in London. I think London right now is the city which offers exactly the right background for a story of this kind." Antonioni perceived a freedom and "turmoil" in '60s London, which made it livelier than anywhere else.[7]

Robert Murphy illuminatingly points out that even the year of peak output of Gothic horror, 1965, also represented the beginning of a change in the way Hammer purveyed their horror products:

> Hammer's horror films had been so popular in the late 50s because they seemed to bring excitement and colour into a dull, conformist society. By the mid–60s, in the wake of the "new wave" and the "youth revolution," things had changed. What had once been repressed and unspoken could now be represented openly. Films like *Alfie* and *Blow-Up* made Fisher's fairytale world look increasingly tame. *Dracula: Prince of Darkness* went some way to accommodate the new climate with its throat-cutting ceremony and the staking/raping of Barbara Shelley. But the forces of good represented by Father Sandor are complacently confident in the face of the puny threat represented by Dracula, and the film's moral outlook is conservatively conventional.[8]

Roman Polanski points out that the '60s "was a time of great expectations—of great aspirations, you know. In this atmosphere there were so many young people beginning, doing interesting things. There was a general atmosphere of admiration of young talent, with a fashion photographer recruited from the cockney crowd. It was a time of the triumph of the lower class. It was a time where people in jeans started driving Rolls Royces." Richard Lester adds, "throughout the '60s we had been questioning all our old certainties—about war, class, sexuality, race and got caught up in the revolution that had ricocheted around the world. In the 1960s the specter of another, possibly final war had begun to haunt us. The Cuban Missile Crisis and accelerating arms race brought many thousands onto the streets campaigning for nuclear disarmament."[9]

Homosexuality was also emerging from the shadows, considerably helped by Basil Dearden's *Victim* (1961), starring Dirk Bogarde as a homosexual barrister, which played a significant part in the 1967 reform of the law. As Antony Nicholls's Lord Fullbrook says in that film:

> Of course youth must be protected, we all agree about that, but that doesn't mean that consenting males in private should be pilloried by an antiquated law and made meat for blackmail.

However, the Manson murders of 1969 confirmed doubts about the sustainability and reality of all this optimism, along with the growing recognition that human beings hadn't really changed. Many people now argued that permissiveness had merely released the violence that social restraints had formerly kept under control. The student riots of 1968 were reflected in Lindsay Anderson's satire of the underlying viciousness of the British public school system. *If*—the title refers to Rudyard Kipling's poem advocating old-fashioned upper-class grit and fortitude—expressed Anderson's desire to be free from all institutions and authorities. At the end of the film, two boys from a traditional public school, along with a girl they have befriended, massacre the masters and guests with machine gun fire as they leave the school's prize giving ceremony.

Events soon caught up with the unleashed violence depicted in Anderson's film. The aggressive entrepreneurial capitalism that would later come to characterize Margaret Thatcher's monetarist policies later in the decade was initiated when Richard Branson formed his Virgin company in February 1970. Earlier, in January, Karl Marx's grave in Highgate Cemetery was vandalized, suggesting a symbolic defeat of social idealism. In April, Paul McCartney left the Beatles—another symbolic reminder that the 1960s were now over—and by the end of the year he had filed a lawsuit against his former colleagues. Much more significantly, unprecedented acts of violence began to characterize the news. The IRA was to dominate this development in the U.K. In July, the British Army found itself in open combat on the streets of Belfast. Three civilians and ten soldiers were killed. Later in the month, two canisters of tear gas were thrown in the House of Lords, and on September 9, the PLO initiated the first ever hijack of a British plane (BOAC Flight 775).

The relaxed censorship of the time gave *The Sun* newspaper the opportunity to launch its infamous topless Page Three Girl feature in November—indicative of the new permissiveness that Hammer would also be keen to exploit in their Karnstein vampire films.

Violence and social unrest increased in 1971. The Post Office experienced its first ever strike in January just as the country was being introduced to decimal currency. Unemployment reached a postwar high in April, while in May, the far-left terrorist Angry Brigade detonated a bomb in that quintessentially '60s Kensington store, Biba. The Irish troubles continued with the British government interning hundreds of terrorist suspects without trial, which led to more rioting and 20 further deaths. By September, the death toll of the so-called "Troubles" had reached 100.

This was the state of the United Kingdom when *Dracula A.D. 1972* started shooting in September. In October, the BBC screened Jeremy Sandford's television play, *Edna the Inebriate Woman*, which caused considerable social and political debate about homelessness and addiction. Later that month, the Angry Brigade set off another bomb, this time in the revolving restaurant at the top of the Post Office Tower in London, which effectively closed the tower to the public for good.

By this time, the hippie dream of peace and love, along with the slang that expressed it, was well and truly over. Though *Dracula A.D. 1972* has been much criticized for being out of touch with regard to that, it does in fact reflect what was happening in society at the time. After all, modernity and optimism in this film fail. Many of the young people in it are killed. Their culture is thus seen to be dangerous and destructive, and it is left to the old-fashioned Van Helsing to remove the evil and restore the old order. The "mausoleum," which is how his granddaughter describes his home, turns out, in the end, to be a place of life and salvation, in contrast to the wayward new ideas of the permissive society. Of course, there is tension in that too; part of that permissiveness was a fascination with Van Helsing's shared interest in the occult, which is itself retrogressive. The difference is that Van Helsing takes the occult very seriously—even to the point of occupying a chair in occult sciences at the University of London—whereas Jessica and her friends are only attracted to it "for kicks." Straddling the two is trendy, satanic Johnny Alucard, who might be viewed as embodying the age itself, looking both back and forward, like the hippies before him, and coming to a similarly sticky end. Johnny's defeat by Van Helsing is a mirror image of the Manson murders, which finished off the hippie dream. Depending on one's viewpoint this is either a good or a bad thing. Robert Irwin, in his novel *Satan Wants Me*, sees it as lamentable. The hippies who dabble in the occult in his story aren't in any real danger from the Devil, as Irwin doesn't believe the Devil exists, but he regards the disintegration of '60s idealism as a real evil:

> Everybody sold out. I lived through years of the Great Betrayal and Sell-Out of the hippy dream. We were going to change things. We were going to set free the hearts and minds of our generation—and not just our generation. "Insanity is hereditary. You get it from your kids." People would cease to own people. There would have been a gentler, more generous and more colourful world. There was a lot of energy about. By the end of the sixties, we should have been witnessing the ultimate transformation of humanity. As Nietzsche put it, "Man is a bridge, not a goal."
>
> But we lost. The old bankers, generals, policemen and professors prevailed. And I am they. They, the men in suits, who every morning walk across Waterloo Bridge, heading for the City are no better than criminals. The Juggernaut rolls on. First we lost the battle and then our souls.[10]

In terms of *Dracula A.D. 1972*, it is the superannuated guests at chinless Charles's party who ultimately win. The forces of law and order eject Alucard and his friends from their living room at the beginning of the film, while the triumph of Van Helsing and all he stands for at the end is the final blow to permissive hippie culture. When Jessica returned in the form of Joanna Lumley for *The Satanic Rites of Dracula*, she has become a reformed character. No longer is she part of a group of thrill-seeking hippies, she now wears a sensible Laura Ashley dress, demurely serves coffee to the police, and is her grandfather's "right hand." As the professor observes, "sometimes I think she knows more about my work than I do myself. There's little sense in trying to keep secrets from her. She has an ingrained curiosity: the hallmark of a true scientist."

Sinclair McKay observes that Britain in the early 1970s, with its "soot-encrusted buildings standing in litter-strewn city centres" and "grey pre-cast concrete council blocks and office skyscrapers," was "an even weirder hybrid than it had been through the previous decade":

> Left-wing agitprop and maxi-skirts jostled in close proximity to the slightly flared pinstripe suits of the rapacious property developers. The Conservatives under Edward Heath were in, as indeed were cravats and tie-dyed T-shirts. ... Britain, heavily unionised, was experiencing further industrial unrest.... The cost of living rose inexorably.....
> As for most of the British film industry, the game was almost up. The Yanks had gone home; Rank, once the towering titan, was foundering desperately and had gone into business with EMI.[11]

When *Dracula A.D. 1972* began filming in 1971, British film and television were dominated by horror, crime, and suspense, which often reflected the prevailing misogyny and racism of the time. On January 26, 1971, Thames Television screened an episode of the series *Shadows of Fear*. Entitled "The Death Watcher," it starred John Neville as a crazed researcher into the paranormal who attempts to drown a female academic (Judy Parfitt) to prove his theories about life after death. The underlying implication of the drama is that this intelligent woman is a danger to herself, who should have listened to the wise counsel of her husband and stayed at home. Many viewers at the time would have been reminded of the real-life case of the murderer John Christie, as advance publicity of Richard Fleischer's *10 Rillington Place* had already been in the news (it was released at the end of January). Starring Richard Attenborough as the serial killer, it begins in the last year of the Second World War with Christie asphyxiating Muriel Eady before strangling her and then having sex with her dead body. When he buries Eady's corpse in his back garden, he uncovers one of his previous victims; but that was only the beginning in Fleischer's grisly reconstruction of Christie's other murders, which included infanticide, along with an infamous miscarriage of justice resulting in the wrong man being hanged.

Though based on a true story, Fleischer's film has much in common with the kind of horrors in which Hammer would continue to specialize until the stagnation of the company in the mid–1970s. It also stars Judy Geeson, who would go on to star in Hammer's *Fear in the Night* (dir. Jimmy Sangster, 1972). The role of her sister is played by Isobel Black, who had already appeared in Hammer's *The Kiss of the Vampire*, and would go on to appear in *Twins of Evil* (dir.

John Hough, 1971). John Hurt plays Geeson's husband (Hurt would play opposite Peter Cushing in *The Ghoul*, directed by Freddie Francis for Hammer's rival company, Tyburn, in 1975), and the burial of various corpses in Christie's back garden is also similar to what happens in *Frankenstein Must Be Destroyed* (dir. Terence Fisher, 1969). *10 Rillington Place*, which was filmed on authentic locations, also features crumbling, Victorian terraced housing, with what at first sight looks like a Victorian church at the end of Rillington Place itself. This is in fact a tower that formed part of the Western Iron Works, which like the street itself has long since been demolished. (The street was redeveloped and renamed Ruston Close shortly after the film was made. Ironically, Grenfell Tower, which suffered a catastrophic fire in 2017, stands close by.) The impression of a church tower along with the general air of postwar dilapidation and dereliction does, however, bear comparison with the environment of St. Bartolph's Church in *Dracula A.D. 1972*.

The subject of *10 Rillington Place* was also shared by *The Night Digger* (dir. Alasdair Reid), which was released in May 1971. Here, Nicholas Clay plays an impotent serial killer, Billy Jarvis, who similarly buries his young female victims, but in his case they disappear beneath the concrete of a new motorway. He ingratiates himself into the home of a blind matriarch (Pamela Brown) and her adopted daughter, played by Patricia Neal, whose real-life husband, Roald Dahl, also wrote the screenplay. Billy and his new family live amid the dilapidated splendor of Oakley Court, which gives the film the quality of the Hammer thrillers that had been previously filmed there. By this time, however, Oakley Court, conveniently situated opposite Bray Studios, had ceased to be Hammer films' preferred stately location. The company was now operating out of Shepperton Studios, having left Oakley Court in considerable need of renovation, especially with regard to the collapsing greenhouses adjoining it. The window drapes with their distinctive bobble fringing, seen in so many earlier Hammer thrillers, were still intact, however, along with what looks like authentic dust and grime. This was all perfect for *The Night Digger*'s claustrophobic mood of entrapment and corruption, in which Neal's Maura Prince struggles against her dominating mother while falling for the charms of the perverted Billy. Director Reid, doubtless aware of the association of Oakley Court with Hammer, did his best to film the place from less familiar angles, but we nonetheless encounter the famous griffins by the front door, which had served as the entrance to Chateau Meinster in *The Brides of Dracula* (1960), among other fantasy locations in Hammer's back catalog. *The Night Digger* also foreshadows the scene in *The Satanic Rites of Dracula* when motorcycle heavies pursue Valerie van Ost in her Mini car. Exactly the same thing happens when Billy chases Brigit Forsyth's district nurse in her Mini.

The year of 1971 also saw the release of Robert Fuest's *The Abominable Dr. Phibes*, which brought Vincent Price to London for a highly camp revenge drama about a very different kind of serial killer. Disfigured by a car accident caused by a precipitant hurry to the bedside of his dying wife, Victoria, Phibes subjects the seven surgeons he holds responsible for her death to bizarre versions of the Seven Plagues of Egypt. Victoria's perfectly preserved corpse was played by Caroline Munro, who, of course, went on to play the eventually decapitated Laura in *Dracula A.D. 1972*. The film also featured Highgate Cemetery, which, as we shall see later, also has a tenuous connection to Alan Gibson's film.

Blood from the Mummy's Tomb, Hammer's fascinating but ill-fated adaptation of Bram Stoker's novel, *The Jewel of Seven Stars*, also appeared in 1971, as did Tigon's *Blood on Satan's Claw* (dir. Piers Haggard). The former concerns the reincarnation of an ancient Egyptian queen in what was then the present day; the latter, the corruption of a group of 17th-century children by the Devil. *Burke and Hare* (dir. Vernon Sewell, 1972) explored the grisly careers of the infamous murderers and corpse traders, while Stanley Kubrick's 1972 adaptation of Anthony Burgess's novel *A Clockwork Orange* placed ultra-violence in a futuristic context, but one sufficiently familiar to apply directly to contemporary concerns about juvenile delinquency and social collapse.

Hammer continued to pour out Gothic fantasy. Peter Sasdy's *Countess Dracula* (1971) addressed the historical serial killer Countess Elisabeth Nádasdy, played by Ingrid Pitt, who rejuvenates herself with virgin's blood. Instead of the seedy urban decay of *10 Rillington Place*, Sasdy was able to indulge in the grandiose castle sets reused from Charles Jarrott's *Anne of a Thousand Days* (1969). This was unintentionally appropriate, considering that Henry VIII, whom Richard Burton played in that film, worked his way through six wives, beheading two of them in the process. Lesley-Anne Down played Nádasdy's daughter, Ilona, who is abducted and abused by a gamekeeper. He has strict instructions to keep Ilona away from the castle so that the rejuvenated Countess can pursue her love affair with a handsome young officer (Sandor Elès). Down played a similar kind of role as the victim of a murderous pedophile in Sydney Hayers's 1971 police drama *Assault* (U.S. title: *In the Devil's Garden*). Much is made here of electricity pylons, which ultimately kill the culprit, foreshadowing the 1979 public information film, *Play Safe*. That graphic warning against entering electricity substations traumatized a whole generation of British children with the line: "Never try to get toys back by yourself, otherwise you may not get to play with them again." Alfred Hitchcock's *Frenzy* (also from 1971) features a blowsy big-band score by Eric Rogers. The same contemporary idiom would be required from Mike Vickers for *Dracula A.D. 1972*, but Vickers's approach was much more accomplished and innovative.

Also witnessed in 1971 was the release of the surreal and highly stylized adaptation of Aldous Huxley's *The Devils of Loudon* that is Ken Russell's *The Devils*. Graphic violence and sexual perversion caused critic Alexander Walker to describe it as "monstrously indecent" and little more than "the masturbation fantasies of a Roman Catholic childhood." Russell responded by hitting Walker over the head on live TV with a copy of the rolled-up newspaper in which the review had appeared.[12] The catchpenny dreadfulness of Ted Hooker's *Crucible of Terror* starred Mike Raven as a crazed sculptor who saves himself the trouble of sculpting in clay by casting dead bodies, while Hammer returned with a gender-swapped variation of Robert Louis Stevenson's celebrated tale of duality with Roy Ward Baker's *Dr. Jekyll and Sister Hyde*. Peter Collinson's *Fright* had Susan George terrorized by the crazed father of a child she finds herself babysitting. Dropping the RP accent he had used in *Scars of Dracula*, Dennis Waterman, who plays her boyfriend, is eventually murdered—a fate he managed to avoid in the Dracula film. The father of the child was played by Ian Bannen, who at this time specialized in unhinged roles, appearing two years later as a suspected child murderer opposite Sean Connery in *The Offence*. In 1974 he portrayed a tyrannical father who is killed by voodoo in *From Beyond the Grave* (dir. Kevin Connor).

In many ways *Fright* was Hammer Film manqué. It was produced by Harry Fine and Michael Style, who had presided over *The Vampire Lovers*, in which George Cole played the part of Henry Morton. Cole also appears in *Fright*. Fine and Style would go on to produce the two sequels of the Karnstein trilogy, the screenplays of which were written by Tudor Gates, who also scripted *Fright*; Harry Robinson, who composed the music for the Karnstein films, also scored Collinson's film. Its premise of a young woman in danger from a psychopath in a domestic context would be repeated the same year in Sam Peckinpah's *Straw Dogs*, which again starred Susan George, whose character is anally penetrated. The year of 1971 enjoyed three British film premières for Susan George. In Pete Walker's sexploitational thriller, *Die Screaming, Marianne*, she enlivens the opening title sequence by dancing to Cyril Ornadel's poster-paint brass music. Though scantily clad with chains around her loins, her dance moves are comparable to gyrations of the gatecrashers at the beginning of *Dracula A.D. 1972*. For those who criticize the clothes and slang of the teenagers of that film, it is instructive to see sequences like this to demonstrate that *A.D. 1972* was not so very far behind the times.

John Hough's *Twins of Evil* (1971) invigorated what had been the rather limp pulse of Jimmy Sangster's *Lust for a Vampire* (1971). *Playboy* Playmates Madeleine and Mary Collinson, who played the title roles of Hough's superior vampire tale, revealed their cleavages accordingly, but with nowhere near as much full-frontal nudity as we find in Ray Austin's *Virgin Witch* the following year. However, Austin sensibly handled the story to produce something rather more interesting than soft porn, and the sinister mood of the film is considerably aided by Ted Dicks's cimbalom-colored score. A respectable doctor (Neil Hallett) turns out to be a white witch. In the best Dennis Wheatley manner, he wears a dinner jacket and bow tie at dinner, and his home is comfortably appointed. His assistant (Patricia Haynes) is, however, more interested in following the left-hand path, and she also has lesbian tendencies. When two enthusiastic virginal sisters spend the weekend at the doctor's country retreat, thinking they are only there for a topless fashion shoot, they are initiated into the doctor's coven. The extended orgy that follows is more sexually explicit and, perhaps because of that, far less disturbing than the Black Mass in *Dracula A.D. 1972*. The elder of the two girls ultimately kills the doctor's assistant and then takes her place. The insistence on nubile female nudity and male assault upon it very much helps to explain the zeitgeist that enabled the sexual predation of figures like the British D.J. Jimmy Savile, the TV presenter Stuart Hall, and the entertainer Rolf Harris. The presentation of young women as objects of titillation and exploitation was so ingrained in the dominant ideology of the time that sexual exploitation, if not outright rape, was expected if not positively incited. Hammer's approach to nudity never went as far as it did in *Virgin Witch*, *Die Screaming, Marianne*, or *Straw Dogs*. Though set in the present day, the aura of Gothic horror in *Dracula A.D. 1972* distances it from reality, as does the rather more formal dialogue of Van Helsing, not to mention the mildly caricatured slang of the teenagers. The film is nonetheless representative of the mood of the time in which it was filmed. Another aspect that unites all these films is the predominantly middle-class milieu in which they operate. Received pronunciation was still very much the norm (there is very little common parlance and very few regional accents), and middle-class environments predominate: country houses, well-furnished living rooms, elegant restaurants, suits and ties for the men, elegant day and evening wear for the women. Hammer, always a very middle-class organization, by 1972 was distinctly middle-aged.

Things were a little different in *Get Carter* (dir. Mike Hodges, 1971), in which a shotgun-wielding Michael Caine returns to northeast England to exact vengeance on those responsible for the murder of his brother. The regional accents and working-class environments of this modern-dress vendetta were in stark contrast to Peter Sasdy's *Hands of the Ripper* for Hammer, in which Eric Porter's Freudian psychiatrist attempts to diagnose and cure the daughter of Jack the Ripper. Statistically, it is just as violent as *Get Carter* (Porter has a sword thrust into his midriff, a maid has her throat slashed, a medium is stabbed, and Dora Bryan is skewered with a coal poker), but the period setting and middle-class context somewhat softens these various blows by comparison. Christopher Lee and Peter Cushing were reunited in Amicus's faithful adaptation of *Dr. Jekyll and Mr. Hyde*, unfaithfully entitled *I, Monster* and directed by Stephen Weeks, while academic arrogance was clumsily exposed in Robert Hartford-Davis's *Incense for the Damned*, in which Cushing played a rather nastier professor than he would play in *Dracula A.D. 1972*.

Stephanie Beacham warmed up for the horrors of *A.D. 1972* in Michael Winner's *The Nightcomers*, in which she played Miss Jessel, the governess of Henry James's novella, *The Turn of the Screw*. Winner's film, however, is a prequel to the story that formed the basis of Jack Clayton's 1967 adaptation, *The Innocents*. Michael Hastings's screenplay attempts to explain what happened before the new governess arrives at Blye, and how the children, Miles and Flora, were corrupted by her and her lover Peter Quint (Marlon Brando). Quint engages in sadomasochistic bondage sessions with Jessel, hog-tying her with rope. The children observe these goings-on, imitate them, and eventually murder Quint and Jessel. The sex scenes are salacious rather than scary, while the much more stylized seductions of Christopher Lee's Dracula in *A.D. 1972* are far more frightening than Brando's. *The Nightcomers* also features a curious foreshadowing of the opening prayer for the Burial of the Dead, which, as we know, immediately precedes the main title of *A.D. 1972*. In Winner's film, this occurs when the parents of Miles and Flora are interred. Hindsight makes connections that certainly weren't intended, but Stephanie Beacham being in both films makes them seem significant.

By the time the Dracula film was finally unleashed on September 28, 1972, a raft of competing horror films had also been released. In March, Peter Sasdy's *Doomwatch* appeared. Amicus also released Freddie Francis's compendium horror film, *Tales from the Crypt*, that month. Robert Young's *Vampire Circus*, for Hammer, followed in April, while in June audiences were given the answer to *What Became of Jack and Jill?* (dir. Bill Bain). Hammer returned in July with Jimmy Sangster's psychological thriller *Fear in the Night*, alongside Alastair Reid's *Something to Hide*, with Peter Finch, while Pete Walker's *The Flesh and Blood Show* was unleashed five days before *Dracula A.D. 1972*. With the exception of *Vampire Circus*, which was set in 1825, all these films provide fascinating snap-shots of the early 1970s in Britain. There was a distinct chill in the air.

Peter Sasdy's *Doomwatch*, a spin-off of the popular BBC television series of the same name, was a fairly thin story about chemical dumping by the Ministry of Defence and the inevitable governmental cover-up. It formed part of the fashion for horror films in that the consequence of this pollution was a form of agronomy, which results in horrific disfigurement. The main titles feature shots of dead birds on a beach, covered in oil, reflecting the oil slicks from leaking tankers that were making headlines at the time. It begins rather as would Robin Hardy's *The Wicker Man* the following year, as Ian Bannen arrives on a remote Cornish island to find out what's been going on among the suspicious and secretive inhabitants. What he eventually discovers is that a chemical firm has been experimenting with pituitary growth hormone, originally developed as a livestock feed additive. When this didn't work out, the hormones were dumped in the sea. Consumed by fish, which were then eaten by the islanders, horrific results ensued. All that remained of hippie optimism in this film were the flamboyant cravats worn by the trendier of the scientists.

Tales from the Crypt features five stories, which also reflect the time in which it was made. The first stars Joan Collins, who murders her husband on Christmas Eve, and it is valuable as a record of '70s interior design, showcasing acid green cushions on white leather sofas, the inevitable burlap lampshades of the decade, louvered doors, and rubber plants. The following story about a car crash, starring Ian Hendry, features equally inevitable orange lampshades and characteristic floral wallpaper. (Apparently, producer Milton Subotsky hated these sets.) The third story won Peter Cushing an award (the Lincoln d'Or Award in France for Best Actor) as a cruelly tormented pensioner, Grimsdyke, who exacts supernatural revenge on his heartless neighbors, reflecting the ruthless redevelopment and gentrification that was beginning to affect the country. Grimsdyke lives in a shabby little house, which his neighbors want demolished. (In fact, the house is still standing 40 years later.) The middle classes are punished in this story, as they are in the following one, which reworks W.W. Jacobs's famous story, "The Monkey's Paw." Here, Richard Greene plays a wealthy businessman who falls on hard times. Pursued by Death on a motorcycle (a motif that would appear in Don Sharp's *Psychomania* the following year), he has an accident and dies, only to be brought back in agony by his wife, who is granted three wishes by a jade antiquity. These, predictably, only make matters worse. Finally, in the last story, Nigel Patrick plays the tyrannical superintendent of a community of blind men, who is eventually punished by them for his cruelty. Social unrest, distrust of authority, and a sense of social collapse are all reflected in all of these stories.

Filmed in 1970 but delayed in its release until June 1972, *What Became of Jack and Jill?* has Vanessa Howard and Paul Nicholas as frustrated young things who gaslight Mona Washbourne's Alice Tallent, the doting grandmother of Nicholas's Johnnie Talent. He and his girlfriend want Alice's money, so they attempt to induce a heart attack. The major theme here is the generation gap and the fear of delinquency, but it also records the dank, shabby reality of suburban London at the time, in which not everything and everyone was "swinging."

Fear in the Night is one of Jimmy Sangster's many reworkings of Henri-Georges Clouzot's *Les diaboliques* (1955). Set in a boy's boarding school during the holidays, Ralph Bates and Joan Collins play lovers who attempt to drive Judy Geeson's psychologically disturbed character mad and kill Peter Cushing, who plays Collins's husband. One of the most evocative scenes takes place in a service station in the fog. The brutalist concrete of this place in the middle of nowhere (actually Toddington Service Station on the M1) powerfully evokes the sense of anomie that was and would increasingly be felt during the 1970s—complete with more orange curtains. Bates broods over his tortuous plans beside a rack of Marble Arch LPs, wearing an expression that indicates the generally bleak mood of the decade. As we shall see, concrete underpasses and cars feature in the main title sequence of *Dracula A.D. 1972*. The prologue of the latter also features Tykes Water Bridge, also seen in *Fear in the Night*.

Something to Hide, a follow-up to Alastair Reid's *The Night Digger*, is a marvelous study of how shabby Britain had become by this time. Admittedly, the action takes place on the Isle of Wight, but the grunginess of the beach outside Peter Finch's cottage, littered with garbage, is indicative of the wider picture. His house is also a mess, as indeed is his personal life, having buried his wife (Shelley Winters) in the sand after a domestic accident, and burned the dead baby of a hitchhiker (Linda Hayden), whom he foolishly puts up for a while. His boss at the council offices (Colin Blakely) is desperate to improve the tourist trade by thinking up slogans. By this time, Brits were jetting off to Greece and Spain for their holidays, leaving the Isle of Wight to the elderly and underprivileged.

Pete Walker's exploitative *The Flesh and Blood Show* is distinctly self-referential, featuring actors who had already been associated with horror films, such as Jenny Hanley (*Scars of Dracula*), Robin Askwith and Candace Glendenning (*Tower of Evil* [dir. Jim O'Connally]), and Judy Matheson and Luan Peters (both of whom appeared in *Lust for a Vampire* and *Twins of Evil*, with Matheson also featuring in *Crucible of Terror*). Here, they play actors rehearsing for a horror play called *The Flesh and Blood Show* in a derelict theater on a deserted, fog-shrouded seaside pier. The murders that propel the plot are committed by a crazed actor who haunts the theater, played by Patrick Barr, who would appear as Lord Carradine in the following year's *The Satanic Rites of Dracula*. The gloomy "end of the pier" mood complements the seaside shabbiness of *Something to Hide*.

In November, soon after the release of *Dracula A.D. 1972*, Gary Sherman's *Death Line* opened with a particularly seedy scene that begins with a man in a bowler hat contemplating the adverts outside a Soho strip-show theater. This is James Manfred, O.B.E., played by James Cossins, who was well known to Hammer fans for his roles in *Blood from the Mummy's Tomb* (1971) and Roy Ward Baker's *The Anniversary* (1968). In the latter, he played a gentle cross-dresser, but in *Death Line* he is a rather nastier character who has more in common with the sadistic lunatic asylum orderly he played in the former. Manfred is obviously upper class, dressed in a regulation pinstripe suit and old Etonian tie and carrying a furled umbrella, and this sets up the film's underlying theme of class conflict. During the titles, which artily move in and out of focus, accompanied by some very sleazy music, Manfred is shown entering and exiting this seedy theater, circumspectly maintaining his dignity as he makes his way to the Russell Square tube station.

On the otherwise deserted late-night platform, he propositions a woman in a red plastic raincoat, assuming she is a prostitute, a taste for which his visit to the strip show has obviously stimulated. Manfred treats her like cheap meat for sale, little realizing that he will soon be meat for consuming shortly afterwards. "Little flirt," he sneers. "Look darling, God knows if you're worth it but fortunately I can afford to find out." Teasing her by snatching the money away from her as she reaches out for it, he says, "Payment on delivery, my darling." Infuriated, the woman knees him in the groin and runs off, just before "something" advances towards him. The film is ostensibly about cannibalism, but is much more about the state of Britain at the time. It is *Death Line*'s background of class conflict, along with a discussion of capitalism's callous treatment of the workers, that makes what would otherwise be just a grisly cannibal film rather more interesting. Christopher Lee's MI5 agent, Stratton-Villiers, refers to "missing dentists and missing greengrocers" as though dentists and tradesmen don't really matter. Manfred's disappearance does, however. He suggests to Donald Pleasence's lower-class copper, Calhoun, that he should go back to "planting pot on people" and stop meddling in things he is too lowly to be entrusted with. The elitist arrogance of Stratton-Villiers of course chimes with capitalism's callous treatment of the buried, expendable, and somehow subhuman workers. It is debatable if callousness is in fact worse than cannibalism.

Again, this film is a valuable time capsule of '70s fashion. Sharon Gurney's Patricia wears yellow "kinky" boots, for example, along with a Suzi Quatro hairstyle, and there are also the furnishings and props that evoke the period just as effectively. After Patricia temporarily leaves Alex after an argument, we watch him contemplating a Newton's cradle, which became a popular "executive toy" on the desk of many a policeman and office manager in the 1970s. Indeed, Inspector Murray plays with one in *Dracula A.D. 1972*. It's also salutary to return to a world of typewriters and rotary style telephones, filing cabinets and policemen wearing tunics with whistles, long before the internet age. Perhaps reassuringly, the Underground is in many ways largely the same as it was—minus, one hopes, the cannibal element.

1972 also saw the release of Bob Clark's "comedy-horror" film called *Children Shouldn't Play with Dead Things*, which shares many of its themes and motifs with those of *Dracula A.D. 1972*. Filmed on a tight budget ($50,000), it lacks the professional gloss of Alan Gibson's direction but nonetheless features a group of T-shirted and be-jeaned young people, slightly older than teenagers, who visit an Isle of the Dead off the coast of Miami, and there encounter zombies. Like the cast of *The Flesh and Blood Show*, they are all actors, under the leadership of a sadistic theater director played by Alan Ormsby, who presents a kind of Johnny Alucard figure, complete with satanic goatee and striped trousers. Threatening his troupe with dismissal if they chicken out, he stages an elaborate hoax in which other actors, pretending to be corpses, attack the troupe; but later, he and his friends have to deal with the genuine undead. The cynical attitude of the group in general, who continually indulges in graveyard humor, not to mention their willingness to disinter dead bodies at the command of their director, all suggest the painful post–Manson hangover of the hippie trip. The graveyard is actually more genuinely disturbing than St. Bartolph's, and truly worthy of Jessica's comment in that film: "The operative word is 'yuk.'" There are other parallels with *A.D. 1972*. Raising the dead obviously unites both films, as does the use of masks by the actors to frighten each other. Two of the actors in *Children Shouldn't Play with Dead Things* pretend to be corpses, with suitably decaying features. In *A.D. 1972*, William Ellis's Joe Mitcham wears a skull mask to scare Jessica after she sees Lawrence Van Helsing's grave. Another important parallel is Carl Zittrer's electronic score, which can usefully be compared to the radiophonic "Electric Storm in Hell" from Delia Derbyshire's collaboration with the White Noise, which is used in the Black Mass scene of the Hammer film. Alan (Ormsby) also stages his own Black Mass. He dons a blue robe, draws a pentagram in chalk, lights black candles, and sprinkles the dried blood of an unborn infant into the graves, much as Alucard Senior buries Dracula's dried blood into ground near Van Helsing's grave. Anya (Anya Ormsby) is similar to Caroline Munro's Laura Bellows in *A.D. 1972*, being rather more in tune with the diabolical goings-on than the others. Just as Laura enthusiastically agrees to lie on Alucard's altar (until she's covered with blood, of course), so does Anya gaze into the eyes of a disinterred corpse. Alan then delivers his invocation, which again has quite a lot in common with Johnny's invocation, mentioning, as it does, several demons:

> O, Great Diviner, Master of the Three Worlds, Disciple who became Master, Lord of the Netherworld, Lord of Night, Prince of Darkness, Despoiler of Light, Diviner of Powers, Redeemer of Passion, Crucible of Flesh; by the blood incarnate, by the flesh made proud, by the soul devoured of itself, by these words we do implore, by these deeds we do supplicate and call upon the grace of thee, Lord Almighty of the Underworld, to release the souls of all thy servants who lie here unredeemed, to release them to serve thy servant, bending their wills always to His, to thine own. By the blood of babes unborn, by the inversion of the Savior, by the bond of thine own hand, we do entreat thee: deliver them up to us, to command in thy name to serve our will and thine own, by Lucifer, Beelzebub, Mephistopheles, Arkanes and all the underlords, we do entreat, let them rise, let them rise up, *Spiritus aquitani*, *salvate*, let them let them rise up, Satan: god of all.

When nothing happens after all that, Jeffrey (Jeff Gillen) remarks, "They must be out to lunch," which isn't the tone Alan wants, and which *A.D. 1972* dispenses with altogether by the time things have begun to get out of hand.

Sadly, 1972 witnessed increasing violence from the IRA, with Bloody Sunday (January 30), the bombing of Aldershot barracks (February 22), and Bloody Friday (July 21). A few days before *A.D. 1972* was released, a parcel bomb killed a diplomat at the Israeli embassy in London. Such attacks are unfortunately more commonplace now than they were then, when they very much signaled the ugly face of modern Britain. Society was predicted to become a much more violent place, propelled by technology, which would, of course, facilitate our subsequent fantasies. In this respect, *Dracula A.D. 1972* was Janus-faced. The Gothic aspects obviously looked to the past, and in the appearances of Lee and Cushing, very much to Hammer's own past. The hippie idiom, which was a few years out of date by that time, was also retrogressive, but Laura Bellows's severed head being discovered by boys playing on a building site, and investigated by detectives from Scotland Yard, pointed very much in the direction British television was soon to head with Ian and Troy Kennedy Martin's hard-headed police series, *The Sweeney*, which plunged audiences into cockney slang, London's criminal underworld, Flying Squad coppers with guns (British police shows before had always lacked that potent sexual excitement), and a liberal dose of prostitutes, nudity, and general misogyny. In *Dracula A.D. 1972*, Michael Coles as Inspector Murray and David Andrews as his detective sergeant are indeed somewhat politer and better dressed templates for John Thaw's Detective Inspector Jack Regan and Dennis Waterman's Detective Sergeant George Carter in *The Sweeney*. Politer though Murray is, he does anticipate the rougher language, which would be regularly employed by the Regan and Carter, in one line delivered to his sergeant: "I bet you a pound to a pinch of shit that there's a little bit of hash somewhere at that party." It's easy to regard this from our own perspective as being rather tame, but from within Hammer's own boundaries of what was and was not acceptable at the time, such language was powerfully transgressive, as was Johnny Alucard later calling Cushing's Van Helsing a "bastard." Though that word does indeed appear in a friendlier context in the second volume of Cushing's memoirs, it is well known that he was very much opposed to "bad" language in films, the lack of which in Hammer films he later identified as one of their many attractions:

> According to those who write to me, they feel that the producers of today's epics in this genre rely too much upon brutal savagery, explicit sex scenes, nudity, obscene language, special effects, and little or no characterization. They find all this repellent and are sickened by the general decadence offered to them in the name of entertainment, so different from that of yesteryear.[13]
>
> Today's generation say they prefer the Hammer pictures because they left a great deal to the imagination. There was no foul language, no gratuitous violence and, in the end, good always triumphed over evil.[14]

One should not forget that Hammer's early successes were reviled by the critics, one of whom described them as being "for sadists only."[15] With regard to expletives, no Hammer film before *Dracula A.D 1972* (or indeed after it) included vocabulary such as "shit" and "fuck," which are now so ubiquitous as to have lost most of their power. Such language was rarely heard in any British movie of the time. It didn't feature in *The Sweeney* either. No one could say those words on British TV with impunity. Kenneth Tynan was the first to say "fuck" on a live broadcast in 1965, followed by the Sex Pistols in December 1976 on the Bill Grundy Show on ITV. (Susan George does say it, *sotto voce*, in *Fright*, and Donald Pleasence does say "shit," and mouths "fuck," in Gary Sherman's *Death Line* [also 1972], but these were very much exceptions that broke the rule at that time.) Given this context, Don Houghton's adoption of "shit" and "bastard" are worth noting. Indeed, it is still disconcerting to hear Peter Cushing, so revered as the saint of British cinema, being called a "bastard."

Interlude One: Chelsea

> "Chelsea"
> —Old English term for "landing place
> [on the river] for chalk or limestone."
> —Wikipedia

A CURIOUS COINCIDENCE WITH *Dracula A.D. 1972* lies in the name of a prolific writer of vampire stories. This is the American author of vampire novels, Chelsea Quinn Yarbro, but the choice of the London district as a location for fashionable vampires was not as arbitrary as one might think. Though Chelsea became a hub of 1960s fashion after Mary Quant opened her boutique, Bazaar, on King's Road in 1955, it had long been the home of artists and intellectuals, who had moved there in the 19th century. One reason why so many artists, particularly of the Pre-Raphaelite Brotherhood such as Dante Gabriel Rossetti and William Holman Hunt, as well as the high priests of the aesthetic movement, such as Oscar Wilde and James McNeill Whistler, were attracted to it (and in particular to Cheyne Walk) was that it was then much cheaper than anywhere else, while being close enough to the West End to keep in contact with their prospective clients. Now, of course, it is one of the most affluent and costly of London locations.

Chelsea also has an association with the macabre and occult. Its most famous Victorian resident between 1834 and 1845 was Thomas Carlyle, the so-called "Sage of Chelsea," who resided at what was then No. 5 Cheyne Row (now No. 24), which became a hub of the Victorian intelligentsia. Intriguingly, Carlyle peppered his study of *The French Revolution* (1837) with the kind of imagery one finds in the Gothic novels that were so popular in his infancy:

> the Palais-Royal shall again, and more than ever, be the *Sorcerer's Sabbath* and *Satan-at-Home* of our Planet.[1]
>
> There, in these Dens of Satan, which one knows, and perseveringly denounces, do Sieur Motier's mouchards consort and colleague; battening vampyre-like on a People next-door to starvation.[2]

However, he wasn't the only Chelsea resident to be associated with "vampyres." Rossetti, who lived at 16 Cheyne Walk, had famously buried a volume of early poems in the Highgate Cemetery grave of his wife, Elizabeth Siddal, whose body he later exhumed to retrieve the poems. He found it "quite perfect on coming to the light of the fire on the surface, and that when the book was lifted, there came away some of

Rossetti's Residence—**Queen Anne's House, 16 Cheyne Walk, Chelsea (photograph by David Huckvale).**

the beautiful golden hair in which Rossetti had entwined it."[3] This distinctly Gothic, pseudo-vampiric experience very probably influenced that other Chelsea inhabitant, Bram Stoker, when he was writing *Dracula* some years later. (For a while Stoker lived at 27 Cheyne Walk, until he moved to 17 St. Leonard's Terrace in 1891.)

Rossetti's house, also known as the Queen's House, is a Queen Anne–style building, described by Hall Caine, the dedicatee of Stoker's novel and Rossetti's close associate, as being "much mutilated by the introduction of unsightly bow windows, the brick work falling into decay, the paint in need of renewal, the windows dull with the dust of months, the sills bearing more than the suspicion of cobwebs, the angles of the steps to the porch and the untrodden flags of the little court leading up to them overgrown with moss and weed while round the walls and up the reveals of door and windows were creeping and tangled branches of the wildest ivy that ever grew untouched by shears." Caine continues:

> Such was the exterior of the house of the poet-painter when I walked up to it on the autumn evening of my earliest visit. The interior of the house, when with a trembling heart I first stepped over the threshold, seemed to be at once like and unlike the outside. The hall had a puzzling look of equal nobility and shabbiness, for the floor was paved with white marble, which was partly covered by a strip of worn-out coconut matting.....
>
> The studio was a large, irregular room, measuring perhaps, thirty feet by twenty, and structurally puzzling to one who saw it for the first time. The fireplace was at one end of the room, and on either side of it hung a number of drawings in chalk, chiefly studies of female heads, all very beautiful, and all by Rossetti himself. Easels of various size, some very large, bearing partly-painted pictures in different stages of progress, stood at irregular angles nearly all over the floor, leaving room only for a few pieces of furniture. There was a large sofa, under a Holland cover, somewhat baggy and soiled, two low easy chairs similarly appareled ... a large bookcase with a glass front surmounted by a yellow copy of the Stratford bust of Shakespeare.... Two carved cabinets, and a little writing desk and cane-bottomed chair were in the corner, near a small window, which was heavily darkened by the thick foliage of the trees that grew in the garden beyond.[4]

This general sense of clutter is somewhat reminiscent of the admittedly more bourgeois and elegant interior of Lorrimer Van Helsing's so-called "mausoleum" of a study in *Dracula A.D. 1972*.

Stoker's Home—27 Cheyne Walk, Chelsea (photograph by David Huckvale).

Another curious Chelsea interior was described in Arthur Ransome's book *Bohemia in London*. In the chapter entitled "A Chelsea Evening," he describes the studio of the artist Pamela Colman Smith, whom he refers to as "Gypsy." She is best known today for having illustrated Bram Stoker's novel, *The Lair of the White Worm*, as well as designing the Rider-Waite Tarot card deck for the occultist and member of the Order of the Golden Dawn, A.E. Waite:

> A woolly monkey perched ridiculously on a pile of portfolios, and grinned at the cast of a woman's head, that stood smiling austerely on top of a black cupboard, in a medley of Eastern pottery and Indian gods. The mantel-shelves, three stories high, were laden with gimcracks. A low bookcase, crammed and piled with books, was half hidden under a drift of loose pieces of music. An old grand piano, on which two brass bedroom candlesticks were burning, ran back into the inner room, where in the darkness was a tall mirror, a heap of crimson silks, and a low table with another candle flickering among the bottles and glasses on a tray. Chairs and stools were crowded everywhere, and on a big blue sofa, against a wall, a broadly whiskered picture-dealer was sitting, looking at a book of Japanese prints.[5]

William Hope Hodgson's fictional occult detective, Thomas Carnacki, was said to have lived at 472 Cheyne Walk, whither his guests visited to hear his occult adventures, after which they "went out on to the Embankment and presently through the darkness to our various houses."[6] Further along Cheyne Walk, Carlyle Mansions had also been home to T.S. Eliot, Henry James, and Ian Fleming, whose James Bond has been supposed to have lived at nearby 30 Wellington Square. W. Somerset Maugham, who also lived there, had met the infamous magician Aleister Crowley in Paris and based the character of Oliver Haddo in his novel, *The Magician*, on him. Crowley, who like 007 resided in Wellington Square, described how he came to settle there in his "autohagiography":

> I had alighted at a horrible hotel in Russell Square thronged with hustling hooligans of the middle classes. My heart sank at the thought of going back there. I wanted to save the fivepenny bus fare. I came to the corner of Wellington Square and was suddenly seized with a direct inspiration to try my luck. "Try the sacred numbers, especially the Secret Key of *The Book of the Law*—31!" Fagged as I was, I obeyed. The first number connected with my work was this very "31" and in the window was a card "Apartments to Let." A van stood at the door, which was open, I went in. The landlady showed me a large front room on the first floor, with French windows opening upon a balcony which overlooked the spirit-soothing oasis of the square; the small green oblong with its ancient trees. It was lean and comfortable, the rent reasonable, and the people of the house sympathetic and intelligent. The bow drawn at the venture had hit the ideal at the first twang of the string. The miracle was the more striking that the card had not been in the window till a few hours before; they had in fact not finished moving in.[7]

Colin Wilson, whose book on *The Occult* graces Van Helsing's shelves in *A.D. 1972*, also lived in Chelsea for a while, and another Chelsea square—Cadogan—attracted several more luminaries of the macabre. The occult novelist Dennis Wheatley occupied a ground floor flat at No. 60, and could claim neighbors in the fantasy animator Ray Harryhausen and horror film stars Boris Karloff and Christopher Lee. Lee described his flat in Wellington Square as being "on a level of the tops of the plane trees. Not for the first time, the nearby King's Road was becoming notorious, but we hardly felt the vibrations of that. It was very peaceful. We made the walls apple green and came through gold curtains to face the sun. Our immediate neighbour was the delightful, soothing Boris Karloff. In the mews behind lived an owl."[8] He also recalled of Karloff: "When we came out of our houses simultaneously, people expected to see body-bags dumped on the pavement."[9]

Among Chelsea musicians were three with pronounced interests in the occult and the weird. Cyril Scott had already led a fascinating life on the Continent and at home when he moved to Chelsea in the early years of the 20th century. Not only a composer, but also a poet (of rather purple passages), homeopathist, and occultist, Scott continued to pursue his manifold interests in this part of London, which he describes in his first volume of autobiography:

> Thus on a sunny autumn morning a cart containing some very peculiar-looking furniture drove up in front of a terrace facing the top of Oakley Street and was unloaded, much to the amusement of a few onlookers, by the driver and an elderly loafer, and carried up the narrow stairs to my room. Among this furniture was a very old stained-glass window which I had bought in Paris, a wooden contraption which looked like a cross between a confessional box and choir stalls. Indeed, my mother had often stood in front of this piece of furniture and laughed in that manner expressive of pity for one who, in her estimation, obviously has a screw loose *somewhere* ...
> The selection of King's Road, Chelsea, as a place of habitation was, I grant, a rather peculiar one, but then I hoped that the continuous rumble of traffic would drown my bugbear, the noise of barrel-organs.[10]

An Indian named R.C. Hiralal wrote an astonishing article about his visit to Scott's Chelsea residence:

> At five hours after noon, I presented myself at the residence of the renowned musician, a house of many chambers, and was ushered by a servant in lamp-black garments into a closet resembling the antechamber of a prince; for it was adorned by a canopy and rich in upholstery, as the throne of a Maharakah is covered with a dome and rich in cushions. Furthermore it was lighted by windows with variegated panes and abounding in purple and red and saffron or blue, as the window of occidental temples abound in pigmented glass, portraying the picture of the avatar of the West and His disciples; furthermore it was decorated by walls of gold and a lapis lazuli ceiling prinked with stars, as the welkin is in all seeming dyed by the colour blue and at night-time prinked with the Milky Way.[11]

Scott soon discovered that actress Ellen Terry lived almost opposite. She, of course, had been the leading lady at Sir Henry Irving's Lyceum Theater, whose business dealings were managed by none other than Bram Stoker. During his stay in Chelsea, Scott also attempted to form a Vedanta Society, having been inspired to do so after hearing Swami Abhedananda speak. The Society existed for about a year and came to "an abrupt end" as "we could not collect enough members to maintain the Swami over here, in spite of all our efforts. ... I think, nevertheless, that the forming of societies is not one of my talents, so do not anticipate further efforts along that line of endeavor."[12] His fascination with the Swami did, however, anticipate the similar influence of the Maharishi Mahesh Yogi on the Beatles in the 1960s.

Scott's contemporary, the composer John Ireland, who lived at 43 Markham Square, was fascinated by the weird mystical writings of Arthur Machen, who influenced some of his compositions, most notably "The Scarlet Ceremonies," which forms the finale to his set of three piano pieces called *Decorations*. His *London Pieces*, also for piano, begin with an elegiac barcarole called "Chelsea Reach," inspired by the flickering of gas lamps in the waters of the Thames, which he saw while driving over Battersea Bridge in his Morgan motor car in 1917. The visual poetry of the scene had already been described by Whistler in his "Ten O'Clock Lecture":

> And when the evening mist clothes the riverside with poetry, as with a veil, and the poor buildings lose themselves in the dim sky, and the tall chimneys become campanili, and the warehouses are palaces in the night, and the whole city hangs in the heavens, and fairy-land is before us....[13]

It is very much this quality that Alan Gibson so expertly captures in his shots of the river (including Battersea Bridge) in *Dracula A.D. 1972*—particularly the shot of the setting sun over Chelsea Embankment, which intercuts Van Helsing's preparations for his encounter with Dracula in the graveyard of St. Bartolph's.

Another Chelsea composer with a consuming interest in the occult was Philip Heseltine, who also went by the nom de plume of Peter Warlock. He had discovered the writings of Aleister Crowley in 1917, and he eventually felt sufficiently in tune with supernatural forces to claim:

> I have travelled in the dark, often ignorant of the fact I was travelling at all. I have received very definite and detailed communications concerning music from sources which the ignorant and unheeding world call supernatural: and that there is unlimited power behind these sources.[14]

Like Jekyll and Hyde, Warlock released a personality that Heseltine had been unable previously to negotiate. Influenced by Crowley's philosophy, "Do what thou wilt shall be the whole of the law," Warlock experimented with drugs, alcohol, and sex, preoccupations that led to an increasingly hedonistic lifestyle. Why he killed himself remains an open question. Some believe he was murdered by composer Bernard van Dieren, others that he committed suicide due to depression and mental illness. Art critic Brian Sewell, who eventually learned that he was Hesseltine's illegitimate child, believed that it was his birth that proved to be the final straw, but whatever the cause, Peter Warlock was found dead on the morning of December 17, 1930, overcome by carbon monoxide from a gas fire in his Chelsea home in Tite Street.

The residence of Oscar Wilde was 34 Tite Street at the time of his disgrace and imprisonment, and a nearby residence in Tite Street had briefly been home to Hammer films' most celebrated "house" composer, James Bernard, who so sonorously accompanied all but two of the company's Dracula films. Formerly, he and his partner, Paul Dehn, had lived together at 19 Brammerton Street, another Chelsea location, which was where he conceived the famous "Dra-Cu-La" theme for Hammer's first Dracula film in 1958:

> I was working on one floor of our house. Paul had been working on another upper floor, tapping away on his typewriter at whatever he was doing, and I shouted up, "Paul, do you think this is too obvious to just try and say 'Dracula' in the music?" He was very musical. He could play the piano and had a nice light tenor voice, so I valued his opinion. He said, "No! No! That's it! Use it! Don't be shy! You've got it!" He was very encouraging. So that was it. "Dra-Cu-La!"—and then the next bit was, "Beware of Dra-Cu-La! Dra-Cu-La! DRA-CU-LA! Watch out for DRA-CU-LA!—terribly childish."[15]

It is, therefore, more than appropriate that this theme opens Dracula's arrival in Chelsea at the very beginning of *A.D. 1972*. With growing success, Dehn and Bernard decided to move to the somewhat grander location in Tite Street. However, Dehn died soon after they moved in, and Bernard decided to sell up and move to Jamaica, following in the footsteps of that other Chelsea luminary, Ian Fleming. He eventually returned to Chelsea, living for several years in a compact but comfortable flat in Oakley Gardens before his death in 2001. One of Bernard's greatest scores for Hammer was *The Devil Rides Out* (dir. Terence Fisher, 1968), which starred that other Chelsea resident, Charles Gray, who lived in Ennismore Gardens.

Thus does the psycho-geography of the area feed into background and aura of Gibson's film. Previous films had exploited this mood to similar effect. As early as 1928, Anthony Asquith had captured its bohemian quality in *Underground*, in which an electrician and a railway porter both fall in love with the same woman on the London Underground. The otherwise humorous nature of the film becomes much darker in the climax, set against the backdrop of Lots Road Power Station, which would later appear in Michael Winner's *I'll Never Forget Whatshisname* in 1967, as well as in Alan Gibson's *Goodbye Gemini*, where it is beautifully photographed against the setting sun. Though filmed entirely in Hollywood in 1936, *Dracula's Daughter*, starring Gloria Holden, had been partly set in Chelsea, where Holden's Countess Marya Zaleska has her studio. It is there that she famously seduces a young woman in what is often regarded as the first "lesbian" scene in a vampire movie. The studio is situated over a bookshop, the proprietor of which confesses, "there's some strange goings on up there." As in *A.D. 1972*, one of Zaleska's victims is found lying on the Thames Embankment. The Chelsea Embankment also features in Winner's

Wilde's House Beautiful—34 Tite Street, Chelsea (photograph by David Huckvale).

film, along with Douglas Hickox's *Theatre of Blood* in 1973, and earlier in *The Party's Over*, directed by Guy Hamilton in 1965.

A valuable record of Chelsea at the height of its '60s power, *The Party's Over* starred Oliver Reed as the leader of a group of beatniks, who live the bohemian

Where "Dra-cu-la" Was Born—James Bernard's home at 19 Brammerton Street, Chelsea (photograph by David Huckvale).

lifestyle that had begun to fade away by 1972. With its free love, drugs, and implied necrophilia, the film was considered shocking at the time, and though not a horror film it does contain some genuinely horrible things (a man commits suicide by falling off a roof), as well as imagery that isn't far removed from science fiction and even zombie films. The opening credits play out over shots of the assembled beatniks making their way over the Albert Suspension Bridge in Chelsea (that immediately recognizable structure, some impressive shots of which were also to appear in Jack Cardiff's horror film, *The Mutations*, in 1974). The beatniks (called "Chelsea aborigines" in a later scene) then wander impassively in their post-party fatigue through Glebe Place—not far from James Bernard's residence in Bramerton Street. Other important Chelsea sites can be seen throughout the film: Cadogan Street, Redcliffe Gardens, and the Chelsea Police Station in King's Road. (This latter also appears in Basil Dearden's two social commentary thrillers, *Sapphire* [1959] and *Victim* [1961], the latter starring Dirk Bogarde as a homosexual barrister.)

Bogarde returned to Chelsea in 1963 for Joseph Losey's *The Servant*, in which he plays a manipulative and psychologically vampiric "gentleman's gentleman" named Barrett, who dominates his weak-willed, effete employer, Tony, played by James Fox. The implication is that both are homosexual, but Barrett is definitely the dominant partner. Indeed, Tony says of Barrett, "He's a vampire too on his days off." There are ways of looking at this film as a kind of horror story akin to Polanski's study of sexual repression in *Repulsion* (1965). Like *The Servant*, *Repulsion* largely takes place within claustrophobically domestic confines. Barrett gradually corrupts Tony, draining his self-respect and ultimately usurping his position. Intriguingly, as soon as Tony makes his comment about Barrett being a vampire, we see Barrett's reflection in a mirror, an inverted reference to the belief that vampires cast no reflection. That Losey chose to locate all this in Chelsea is significant, given the associations of the place, as well as it being an appropriately wealthy area for the upper-class Tony to live in. No. 30 Royal Avenue, the house chosen for Tony's residence, is similar to Van Helsing's home in *A.D. 1972*, with similarly arched windows, transom window over the front door, stucco ground floor façade, railings, and area. Losey obviously felt in tune with the place as he later moved into 31 Royal Avenue, directly opposite "Tony's" house, and remained there between 1966 and 1984, as is commemorated by one of the many blue plaques in the area.

Two years after *Repulsion*, Cadogan Gardens and Langton Street appeared in *The Sorcerers*, Michael Reeves's 1967 allegory of '60s psychedelia and cult of youth. A less well-known film traded even more on Chelsea's trendy reputation. This was David Miller's Euro-spy thriller, *Hammerhead* (1968). It isn't quite so stylized as *Modesty Blaise*, Losey's satire on the James Bond films, and Miller plays it straight, but due to the film's stylistic excesses, he ends up unintentionally satirizing himself. It starts with its most striking sequence, over which the main titles are superimposed. This is a "happening" in which an avant-garde artist (played by Douglas Wilmer) shoots a shop dummy, which is then substituted by Judy Geeson wearing the same outfit. After several more dummies are destroyed, a human "victim" is placed in a giant hamburger roll, which, to the crowd's delight, the artist's assistants then cover in paint masquerading as ketchup, which they pour from a giant bottle.

The whole is accompanied by semi-clad and topless women playing a variety of musical instruments (tuba, cello, accordion). The music for this sequence was scored by another of Hammer's later composers, David Whitaker, and the musical cue is titled "Chelsea Happening." In fact, it was all filmed further north in the converted railway engine shed in Chalk Farm called the Roundhouse. Chalk Farm, however, had none of the trendy associations of Chelsea, so the audience is persuaded to believe this all takes place in SW10. To cement the connection, we see one of the assembled hippies who are assembled to watch this drug-fueled, soap-bubble filled extravaganza wearing a T-shirt emblazoned on the front with "Meet Me" and on the back "In Chelsea." A poster on stage similarly announces, "See You in Chelsea."

In terms of the kind of thing that was happening in the alternative culture of the 1960s, this opening sequence now looks almost like documentary footage. It is no more "way out" than what goes on in *A.D. 1972*; only its earlier date lends it perhaps a little more authenticity. As in *A.D. 1972*, the police eventually arrive to break up this outrage against "public decency," and, like the party gatecrashers in Gibson's film, the hippie crowd runs off to avoid being "busted." Vince Edwards, who plays the sub–Bond (and, by comparison, rather "square") hero, Charles Hood, lives in a bachelor pad situated in a back street not unlike the one where Johnny Alucard hangs out. His arrival there is observed by a secret agent, played by Patrick Cargill, before he went on to complain about the party in *Father, Dear Father*.

Pete Walker's sexploitational thriller, *Die Screaming, Marianne*, came out in 1971 and brought more conventional if relatively mild horror to Chelsea, featuring shots of Chelsea Town Hall in King's Road; however, most of the action is set in Portugal. After *Dracula A.D. 1972* cemented the connection between the somewhat seedy elegance of Chelsea and the horror genre, later horror films took their cue from Gibson's example. Douglas Hickox's *Theatre of Blood* (1973) chose Cheyne Walk as

Chelsea Embankment, A.D. 2024 (photograph by David Huckvale).

the location for the scene in which Jack Hawkins's theater critic, Solomon Psaltery, strangles his wife (Diana Dors), while Robert Coote's Oliver Larding is drowned in a vat of malmsey in a wine cellar in Chelsea's Justice Walk. Peter Sasdy's *I Don't Want to Be Born* followed in 1975, featuring scenes shot in King's Road, Markham Square (along with the pub, the Markham Arms), and 32 Wellington Square, which was chosen as the home of a married couple played by Ralph Bates and Joan Collins, who have produced a demonic baby. Caroline Munro, her head convincingly reattached to her body by this time, also features as a concerned family friend.

A very useful document of the times appeared the following year in Massimo Dallamano's adaptation of Oscar Wilde's *The Picture of Dorian Gray*. *The Secret of Dorian Gray* followed the outlines of the story faithfully enough but set everything in 1976, with Helmut Berger, at the height of his beauty, in the title role. Not only do we see the Albert Bridge, Battersea Park, and power station but also, toward the end, astonishing shots of Berger walking down King's Road, past Markham Square, and entering the Chelsea Potter pub, wearing an outlandish brown and cream, pseudo zebra-striped coat with a brown fedora hat, attracting attention from passersby whose outfits are no less "trendy" than those in *A.D. 1972*. For those who might think the outfits in Gibson's film were "past it" by that time, Dallamano's film demonstrates that they weren't—even four years later.

Five

The Occult

> "To us it has been a serious, lifelong study"
> —Van Helsing in *Dracula A.D. 1972*

THE OCCULT REVIVAL OF THE 1960s had its roots in the 19th century. With the decline of established religion in the wake of Charles Darwin's *Origin of Species* and the advance of science, alternative movements began to emerge to satisfy the need for meaning and purpose. In the 1850s, Spiritualism in America grew from humble origins to attract adherents across the globe. When interest in Spiritualism began to wane, Madame Blavatsky introduced Theosophy to the spiritually hungry, which attempted to synthesize all the world's religions into a "Secret Doctrine," which was also the title of the Bible she wrote to promote her movement. Prominent advocates of Theosophy, which charted humanity's spiritual evolution through seven "root races," included the composers Alexander Scriabin and Cyril Scott and the artists, Piet Mondrian, Paul Klee, and František Kupka, all of whom initiated European modernism. Poet W.B. Yeats was also a theosophist before his attention was drawn to the Order of the Golden Dawn, which promised a more practical experience of magical phenomena. Writers Algernon Blackwood, Arthur Machen, and J. Brodie-Innes were all later members of the Golden Dawn, as was Aleister Crowley, who eventually broke free to form his own religion of Thelema, for which he wrote his own Bible, "The Book of the Law," in 1904.

On the continent of Europe, writers such as J.-K. Huysmans, Jean Lorrain, and Joséphin Péladan wrote novels about the occult underworld of Paris, as did Gustav Meyrink and Hanns Heinz Ewers in Austria and Germany. In England, the Society for Psychical Research investigated the often spurious claims of the new gurus who sprang up along with the resurgence of interest in Spiritualism after the First World War, when so many people sought communion with those they had lost in the slaughter. Occult novels became even more popular. Dion Fortune, a former member of the Golden Dawn before founding her own order (the Order of the Inner Light), published five occult novels between 1927 and 1957, but the most famous purveyor of occult fiction was surely Dennis Wheatley, who wrote nine novels with occult themes, the most famous of which, *The Devil Rides Out*, began his association with the genre in 1934.

By the time Crowley died in 1947, the Second World War had somewhat drained enthusiasm for the occult, especially in light of Hitler and Nazism's dangerous fascination with the subject, but baby boomers, caught up in the hippie movement of the late 1950s and '60s, rediscovered the writings of Crowley, who was eventually enshrined as one of "the people we like and admire" on the cover of the Beatles' *Sgt. Pepper* album in 1967. By the time Crowley's books were reprinted in the early 1970s, the Beast was back in business.

In Robert Irwin's novel, *Satan Wants Me*, an apprentice hippie magician, Peter, buys a copy of this influential LP and plays it repeatedly:

> I need to hear music again and again in order to internalize it. "Sgt. Pepper" is this summer's record, yet by autumn I know that all its tunes will be dead and lifeless in my ears. Only perhaps in returning to the record years later will I be able to capture some of that initial summery enthusiasm. For now, on a June morning, the record is amazing—that wall of sound, the tracks sliding into one another, and the kaleidoscopic tumble of lyrical images and sound effects. The music is brassy and percussive as the sleeve is gaudy. ... This is the music of the summer of 67 and by putting it on the turntable I shall always be able to return to that momentous summer. But then who will I be when I play this record in twenty years time?[1]

Conspiracy theorists liked to suggest that the opening line of the album, about it having been 20 years to the day since Sergeant Pepper first taught the band to play, was a coded message, implying that Sgt. Pepper was a cipher for Crowley himself. Alas, Crowley died on December 1, 1947, rather than on June 1, the day the album was released: 20 years, certainly, but not to the day. The Beatles themselves have often been considered occultists, posing as they occasionally did with "satanic" hand gestures, which it is fairly safe to assume were merely part of the fashionable bric-a-brac of the time. The appeal of Crowley was his anti-establishment, "do what thou wilt" philosophy, alongside his anti–Christian polemics, but agreeing with these ideas alone do not make one a Satanist. The occult trappings of Anton LaVey, who founded the Church of Satan one year before the Summer of Love, were also largely gestural. LaVey believed in neither God nor Satan as supernatural forces but rather as personifications of strictly human impulses. Satan, for LaVey and his followers, thus became a symbol of personal freedom and self-determination. Indebted to the atheism of Percy Bysshe Shelley and the humanist anti–Christian philosophy of Friedrich Nietzsche, whose theory of the Will to Power has much in common with Crowley's statement, "Do what thou wilt," LaVey's creed is in fact politically radical—and, despite appearances, highly secular. It is a philosophical system masquerading as a religion, psychology disguised as Satanism. His use of "satanic" imagery is much the same as Nietzsche's use of contentious imagery in his books, one of which is called *The Anti-Christ*, another *Twilight of the Idols*. This aspect of Satanism was completely overlooked by Hammer in *Dracula A.D. 1972*, which took a more Wheatley-esque, strictly Christian, and conventional approach to the subject, overlooking this significant aspect of the occult revival of the time.

Another of the luminaries on the cover of *Sgt. Pepper* was the Swiss psychoanalyst C.G. Jung, who was also engaged in occult research. His complete works feature eight essays on the subject, including "On the Psychology and Pathology of So-Called Occult Phenomena," "On Spiritualistic Phenomena," "The Psychological Foundations of Belief in Spirits," "The Soul and Death," and "On Spooks: Heresy or Truth?" Indeed, Jung based much of his theory on neo-paganism and 19th-century occultism, eventually coming to believe himself to be the Aryan Christ. The avant-garde composer Karlheinz Stockhausen, who also features on the *Sgt. Pepper* cover, also had deep interest in esoteric wisdom, which went so far as leading him to believe he was from another planet. Another famous *Sgt. Pepper* face was that of Aldous Huxley, whose study of the effects of mescalin in *The Doors of Perception*, published in 1954, inspired Jim Morrison to name his rock group the Doors in 1965. The album's back cover features a photograph of the band posing with a small bust of Beethoven, which sufficiently resembles Crowley for fans to have mistaken it for the Beast 666 himself. Drug use was, of course, a major reason for the occult revival of the period: transcendental experiences re-defined not only what the body was for those who indulged, but also rearranged reality, leading to the idea that it could be radically transformed. Such bewildering experiences required a "new" framework and imagery, which established religion and conventional social mores could no longer offer. Occultism was the solution for many. With the collapse of the hippie dream in the 1970s, occultism became even more significant, as it provided a balm for the pain of disillusionment.

Jimmy Page, lead guitarist of Led Zeppelin, was also fascinated by Crowley's ideas, and in 1971 he purchased Crowley's home, Boleskine House, on the shores of Loch Ness, in which to house his considerable library of occult volumes. He even had "Do what thou wilt" inscribed on the vinyl of Led Zeppelin's third album, *Led Zeppelin III* (1970). Though Page spent little time at Boleskine, his friend Malcolm Dent did. Dent apparently experienced some terrifying paranormal experiences there, which adherents of the occult have suggested were demonic entities left behind by Crowley after he aborted his invocation of *The Sacred Magic of Abra-Melin the Mage*, for which he had specifically purchased Boleskine House, as it offered the kind of space and architectural layout required by the ritual.

The release of *Sgt. Pepper* crowned the Summer of Love at the Monterey International Pop Music Festival in California that year. Monterey was the zenith of the hippie movement, with its aim to transform society via drugs, sex, and music. One hundred thousand people gathered at the Monterey County Fairgrounds near San Francisco, for which John Phillips's song, "San Francisco," became an anthem. Phillips, who was one of the Mamas and the Papas, was also an associate of Charles Manson, and Roman Polanski for a while wondered if he had organized the murder of Sharon Tate as a revenge for Polanski's affair with Phillips's wife, Michelle.

> I'd had a one-night stand with Michelle while Sharon was filming in Rome. Now it was essential for me to know if she'd ever told him. I went to see her, duly wired up; we talked a lot about John's violence and the intensity of his rages. Yes, Michelle said, she'd told him. Could the knowledge really have provoked such a bout of murderous fury?[2]

The murder, along with the shock impact of Polanski's occult film *Rosemary's Baby* the following year (which also saw Hammer release *The Devil Rides Out*), helped cement the idea that Monterey had been some kind of satanic convention. Whether satanic or not, occultism was definitely in the air. Kenneth Anger's occult film, *Lucifer Rising—A Love Vision*, was released in the same year as *Dracula A.D. 1972*. It was originally to have featured music by Jimmy Page, but this was replaced with a score by the convicted murderer and cohort of Charles Manson, Bobby

Beausoleil—forming the only film soundtrack "recorded entirely in prison." Page does however appear in the film itself, gazing up at a photograph of Crowley. Marianne Faithfull also appears (as Lilith), along with Mick Jagger's younger brother, Chris.

Rock and pop also peppers Robert Irwin's *Satan Wants Me*. The "soundtrack" of the novel features references to Alan Price's "Simon Smith and His Amazing Dancing Bear," Jeff Beck's "Silver Lining," the Rolling Stones' "Have You Seen Your Mother, Baby?" Jefferson Airplane's "White Rabbit," the Beatles' "Strawberry Fields Forever," Pink Floyd's "Piper at the Gates of Dawn," and Procol Harum's "Whiter Shade of Pale." Irwin's novel is a rather more realistic account of the lifestyle Hammer bravely attempted to convey (three or four years too late) in *A.D. 1972*. The hero, Peter, is similar to Alan Gibson's swinging middle-class hippies who hang out at the Cavern Club. Peter's equivalent of the Cavern Coffee Bar is a place called Middle Earth. Like Johnny Alucard and Marsha Hunt's Gloria in *A.D. 1972*, he listens to drug-drenched prog rock. ("They were all zonked when they recorded this," Johnny explains when he puts a record on in *A.D. 1972*. "Aren't they always," Gaynor replies wearily. Peter similarly confesses to "scoring four ampoules of methedrine, a couple of ampoules of amyl nitrate, half a dozen cubes of LSD, a tiny sachet of heroin and a couple of grams of dope.") Also, like the teenagers of *Dracula A.D. 1972*, Peter gets involved with the occult, joining an organization called the Black Book Lodge, as part of his Ph.D. research at the London School of Economics for a thesis on "Intergroup dynamics and peer-group reinforcement on a North-London coven of sorcerers." The lodge members, however, are convinced he is a reincarnation of Crowley.

1971 also witnessed the release of David Bowie's *Hunky Dory* album, which also reflected Bowie's interest in Crowley. The song "Quicksilver" includes a reference to the Golden Dawn, along with Crowley's habit of biting his "scarlet women" on the lips—Bowie refers to this as "kissing the fang of a viper."

Even more significant, perhaps, was the absorption of the occult into children's and mainstream television in Britain at the time. *Escape into Night* was an adaptation of Catherine Storr's 1958 novel, *Marianne Dreams*, directed by Richard Bramall and screened between April and May of that year. Though it would be regarded as profoundly disturbing for young people today, *Escape into Night* plunged into a world of psychological fantasy in which Marianne (Vikki Chambers), who is convalescing at home from a riding accident, finds that she can enter a world of her own creation, which she draws in a sketchbook. She finds herself in a frighteningly empty house, where she encounters an invalid boy (Steven Jones) who is threatened by malevolent beings in the form of stones with a single eye, who chant, much in the manner of the Daleks that were terrifying children in *Doctor Who* at the time, "We're coming!"

Ace of Wands was a product of hippie occultism brought into living rooms at teatime after school. Each episode began with a magic circle enclosing a pentagram. A pair of eyes was then superimposed on this, adorned with mystical symbols which would have been happily worn by the hippies at Woodstock. A hand then makes magical passes, all accompanied by Andy Bown's psychedelic theme song, which is in essence a kind of occult incantation. The hero of the series, played by

Michael MacKenzie, is a magician called Tarot who possesses genuine psychic powers, which he uses to solve occult mysteries with the assistance of his young friends. *Ace of Wands* was preceded a few years before by Alan Garner's adaptation of his own novel, *The Owl Service* (dir. Peter Plummer, 1969–70), in which three teenagers (played by actors who were actually all in their twenties, as were the "teenagers" of *A.D. 1972*) reenact an ancient love triangle. Garner based his deeply disturbing story on the Welsh folk classic, *The Mabinogion*, and while not occult in the classical sense, it certainly channels the supernatural, verging as it does on folk horror. Folk horror itself had begun to establish itself in films such J. Lee Thompson's *The Eye of the Devil* in 1966, which starred David Niven as an aristocrat who must sacrifice himself to save the ailing grape harvest in his French chateau. It also characterized James MacTaggart's "Robin Redbreast" in 1970, which formed part of the BBC's celebrated and influential *Play for Today* series. Other television series had explored the occult in the 1960s, such as *Mystery and Imagination*, adapting, among other stories, J. Meade Faulkner's "The Lost Stradivarius," Robert Swindells's "Room 13," and "Casting the Runes," "Lost Hearts," and "The Tractate Middoch," by M.R. James, along with Bram Stoker's *The Jewel of Seven Stars*, which was the last of the three episodes to be broadcast in 1970. The BBC also began to screen its acclaimed *Ghost Stories for Christmas*, with an adaptation of M.R. James's "The Stalls of Barchester Cathedral" in 1971, followed by "A Warning to the Curious" in 1972. Nigel Kneale's *The Stone Tape*, with its thesis that ghosts are "recordings" of the past preserved in the very fabric of a building, along with a six-part anthology of occult stories in another series called *Dead of Night*, were also screened on British TV in 1972.

It was into this occult subculture that *Dracula A.D. 1972* made its debut. Hammer had first flirted with the occult in *The Kiss of the Vampire* in 1963, in which an occult ceremony called "Corpus diabolo levitum" is performed within a magic circle, complete with pentagram, grimoire, and incantations. After Don Sharp followed this up by directing *Witchcraft* for Robert Lippert in 1964, in a contemporary story concerning a witch who comes back from the dead to avenge the desecration of her grave, Hammer (which was closely connected to Lippert) went on to explore witchcraft in Cyril Frankel's *The Witches* (1966), with Joan Fontaine encountering Kay Walsh's Stephanie Bax, who plans to transfer her soul into the body of a teenager—all set, once again, in what was then the present day. Elaborate occult ceremonies formed some of the more interesting aspects of Hammer's *The Vengeance of She* in 1968, but these were not representation of a Black Mass in the conventional sense, and anyway, they took place in the faraway land of Kuma, where Kallikrates (John Richardson) awaits the return of his lost Ayesha, whom he thinks he has found in the shape of Olinka Berova. Putting a real Black Mass on screen was more of a challenge, as Christopher Lee explained:

> Conservative, Hammer had always worried about the Church's reaction to the screening of the Black Mass. But we thought the charge of blasphemy would not stick if we did the thing with due attention to scholarship. I appointed myself black technical advisor, as well as playing a goody, and spent many hours in the British Museum guddling for Satanic trout, and came up with a useful catch, notably a genuine prayer of exorcism we used at the end. [In fact, a spell to trap the Devil in a bottle by one Armadel, from his seventeenth-century *Grimoire ou*

la Cabale.] And I had the friendship of Dennis Wheatley, the author of the story, who lived on the other side of the square from me in Chelsea.[3]

The film in question was, of course, *The Devil Rides Out*, which had emerged from the Summer of Love the previous year. Set in the 1930s milieu of Wheatley's novel, it was an advance from the early 20th-century period of *The Kiss of the Vampire*, nudging Hammer ever closer to what would happen in *Dracula A.D. 1972*. In fact, Robert Irwin distorts history a little in *Satan Wants Me*, having *The Devil Rides Out* released in 1967, rather than the following year, to make it coincide with the momentous events of the Summer of Love:

> I wanted to see *The Devil Rides Out*, which was playing at the Electric in Portobello Road.... I grooved on the film, especially Charles Gray being sleek and unctuous as the Satanist Mocata and the scene where Christopher Lee (playing the Duc de Richelieu) faces out the forces of Evil from within the pentacle.[4]

By this time, Polanski was ready with *Rosemary's Baby* (also in 1968), followed three years later by Paul Wendkos's *The Mephisto Waltz*, in which Curt Jurgens played a concert pianist who, when he knows he is about to die from an incurable illness, transfers his soul into the body of a music critic played by Alan Alda. Occult ceremonies with pentagrams and black candles in the traditional manner appeared in the same year's *Twins of Evil*, this time set in 17th-century Styria, after which the satanic floodgates then opened wide with *The Exorcist* in 1973 and *The Omen* in 1976. *Dracula A.D. 1972* was thus part of a much larger fashion for placing occult subject matter in contemporary settings, and in this respect it is more useful to regard Gibson's film as an occult film in which Lee's Dracula has more of Satan about him than of Stoker.

The black magic shown in the film is more explicit than the satanic ceremony

"Dig the music, kids!"—Christopher Neame as Johnny Alucard in *Dracula A.D. 1972.*

in *Taste the Blood of Dracula* on which it is based, but they have much in common. Both take place in a deconsecrated church, both desecrate a Christian altar with satanic imagery (*Taste the Blood* decorates it with astrological sigils, whereas *A.D. 1972* opts for the Liberace-esque monogram "D" for Dracula). The glass vial in which Dracula's dried blood is kept in *Taste* is much the same as the one we see in *A.D. 1972*, and Courtley cuts the palm of his hand to drain the blood from it onto the blood powder much as Johnny will slash his wrist. Courtley's invocation appeals to "ye timeless ones—ye elemental of the earth and of the air, and of fire and of water."

> In the most august dread of the supreme Prince of Darkness, and of his arch angels, and angels of darkness and his legions—and draw near and do my bidding. I command! I command! I command!

Johnny is more specific. He calls upon a host of demons. The first of these is Andras, "grand marquis of Hell," who commands 30 legions of demons. His angelic body has the head of an owl or a raven and he rides on the back of a black wolf, stirring up discord and rebellion.

Next is Behemoth, whom Johnny calls "arch-devil of the black delights." Associated with the Angel of Death, Behemoth is also described as eating grass like an ox. In the Bible's Book of Job, he is associated with gluttony. Milton described him in *Paradise Lost* as being of immense size:

> Behemoth, biggest born of earth, upheav'd
> His vastness: fleeced the flocks and bleating rose,
> As plants: ambiguous between sea and land
> The river horse and scaly crocodile.[5]

"Asmodeus, the destroyer" is Johnny's third demon. Originally a Persian entity, he was placed in the highest order of the seraphim in Hebraic religion. He helped build Solomon's Temple, summoning various other demons to help in the work by means of a magic ring, which might suggest that Johnny's appellation is inaccurate, but Asmodeus has three heads (a bull, a man, and a ram) and also breathed fire, so had plenty of destructive potential. He was also claimed as one of the seven princes of Hell, each prince equating to one of the seven deadly sins. Asmodeus was in charge of Lust, and "burns with desire to tempt men with his swine in luxuriousness and is the prince of wantons"[6]

Astaroth is the next to be summoned: a foul-smelling demon who sits on the back of an infernal dragon, holding a viper in his right hand.

Beelzebub follows, who, according to Milton, is:

> Majestick though in ruin: sage he stood
> With *Atlantean* shoulders fit to bear
> The weight of mightiest Monarchies; his look
> Drew audience and attention still as Night
> Or Summers Noon-tide air, while thus he spake.

Known as "Lord of the Flies," he was regarded by the Jews as the greatest of demons. Milton referred to him as next in power to Satan "and next in crime."[7] Johnny says "Beelzebub" is one of the "many names of Satan."

Lucifer is now invoked—the most beautiful of the angels in heaven, the morning star, the symbol of wisdom and insight, whom Gnostic belief claims as a force for good, as he overthrows the tyranny of God and endows humanity with freedom, but Johnny regards him in a more traditional light—or darkness. Johnny also calls upon Belberith, Hell's secretary and archivist, along with Leviathan, the immense female sea dragon that is impervious to weapons, whom Milton called "the Arch-Fiend." He was worshipped in the form of a phallus, and medieval legend had it that after visiting earth to witness human marriage, he fled back to Hell, grateful that no such thing existed there. It is appropriate that such a misogynist demon is the one Johnny invokes before spilling his blood over Laura, who becomes Dracula's first victim.

Several of these demons had appeared (in sculptural form) in Freddie Francis's *The Skull*, made for Amicus in 1965. During an auction at which they are to be sold, Lee and Cushing play competing collectors of occult antiquities. The statues are meant to have been fashioned after descriptions in a genuine antiquarian book, namely, *The admirable historie of the possession and conuersion of a penitent woman. Seduced by a magician that made her to become a witch, and the princes of sorcerers in the country of Prouince, who was brought to S. Baume to be exorcised, in the yeere 1610. in the moneth of Nouember, by the authority of the reuerend father, and frier, Sebastian Michaëlis, priour of the Couent Royall of S. Magdalene at Saint Maximin.*

Michael Gough, who plays the auctioneer in that film, describes Lucifer as he "who commands all." Beelzebub is "the prince of the seraphim who tempts men with Pride." Leviathan "tempts men with heresies and sins repugnant unto faith," and finally, Belberith, "prince of the fallen cherubim who tempts men to be quarrelsome and contentious and to commit murder." Thus, *The Skull* foreshadows Johnny's Black Mass by seven years. Cushing's Dr. Christopher Maitland starts out as a disbeliever in the occult, despite his extensive collection of occult objects, which Patrick Wymark's Marco, the dealer who works for him, describes while wandering around his carefully curated hoard: "the crux ansata fashioned from a thigh bone, that shriveled hand of glory, stolen from a grave in Mainz, this knife: Giles de Retz's, the notorious wife-murderer—Bluebeard." Cushing explains, "It's because people all through the ages have been influenced and terrorized by these things that I carry out research to try and find the reasons why. It's all part of the unknown, and the unknown is always intriguing." Cushing keeps his collection in a book-lined study, and thus foreshadows the equally bookish Lorrimer Van Helsing, who, by contrast, never has any doubt as to the real dangers of the occult. Marco's next offerings are first a biography of the Marquis de Sade bound in human skin, and then the possessed skull of the Marquis himself—whose name is now associated with "the cruelty and savagery that is in all of us." (The true picture of de Sade as profound philosopher of the human condition, albeit a pornographic one, is glossed over for the purposes of the film.)

We don't get to see what books actually line Maitland's study, but we do get a chance to see the Van Helsing's library in more detail in *Dracula A.D. 1972,* and it is a mark of the loving attention to detail in this film that an entire shelf of his library is filled with genuine occult titles, some only recently published at the time the film was made. These include Arthur Edward Waite's *The Secret Tradition of Alchemy—Its Development and Records* from 1937, along with his somewhat turgid account of

"These are scientific works..."—Professor Van Helsing's library in *Dracula A.D. 1972*.

Rosicrucianism in *The Brotherhood of the Rosy Cross* (1928), in which he writes, à propos of the Count St. Germain, "that although there are no occult sciences there are secret arts, and there is very full evidence that he was versed in these."[8] Van Helsing, however, is very much of the opinion that the occult is indeed a science. "This is not a subject to fool around with," he admonishes Jessica, who is casually flipping through a *Treatise on the Black Mass*. "These are scientific works." The *Treatise* itself is presumably a studio mock-up (I have been unable to trace the existence of it or its author, one Dr. J. Torshauser): not so the other books, among which is Bernard Bromage's *The Occult Arts of Ancient Egypt* (1960), which is again written from the point of view of a believer:

> There is no truth in occultism more true than this. To play with fire is to invite the risk of fire; and the demons who serve the interests of would-be destroyers, are not loyal demons! ... They do the will of their temporary masters only so long as they cannot wriggle away into some more independent sphere.[9]

Such sentiments are reminiscent of Dennis Wheatley's famous warning at the beginning of *The Devil Rides Out*, which Peter, the narrator of Irwin's *Satan Wants Me*, quotes:

> Should any of my readers incline to a serious study of the subject, and thus come into contact with a man or woman of Power, I feel that it is only right to urge them, most strongly, to refrain from being drawn into the practice of the Secret Art in any way. My own observations have led me to an absolute conviction that to do so would bring them into dangers of a very real concrete nature.

"What a wonderful come-on," Peter adds.[10]

Another of Van Helsing's books is Rollo Ahmed's *The Black Art*, published, with an introduction by Dennis Wheatley, by Jarrolds in 1967. Wheatley had met Ahmed when engaged in the research for *The Devil Rides Out*, and was rather taken with him. Indeed, he may have been the inspiration for both the Egyptian servant in that novel and, according to Wheatley expert Ken Gallagher,[11] Dr. Saturday, the voodoo high priest in *Strange Conflict*. Wheatley was in fact instrumental in Ahmed writing *The Black Art*, as he recommended him to his own publisher, Hutchinson, when Hutchinson had asked Wheatley to write a serious study of the occult. Feeling unable to do this at the time, he suggested they approach Ahmed.

Van Helsing also owns a copy of Indries Shah's 1956 *Oriental Magic*, and the Richard Wilhelm–C.G. Jung edition of the *I Ching*, first published in 1968. As Lorrimer explains, "our family, Jessica, has a tradition of research into the occult. To us it has been a serious, life-long study." It would be amusing to think that the Wilhelm edition of the Chinese fortune-telling system had been handed down to Lorrimer from the Lawrence Van Helsing who visited China in Roy Ward Baker's *The Legend of the 7 Golden Vampires*, but alas, that film was yet to be made (it didn't appear till 1974), and anyway, according to *Dracula A.D. 1972*, Lawrence Van Helsing died in 1872, while the action of *The Legend of the 7 Golden Vampires* takes place in 1904.

The library continues with Francis A. Yates's *Giordano Bruno and the Hermetic Tradition*, published by the University of Chicago Press in 1964, a book that later inspired Philip Pullman's trilogy, *His Dark Materials*. Yates argues that the Renaissance Roman Catholic priest, Bruno, was burned at the stake for advocating the Hermetic tradition. More recently published, from the perspective of 1971, is W.B. Crow's *A Fascinating History of Magic, Witchcraft and Occultism*, published by Wilshire Book Co. in 1968. Colin Wilson's even more recently published *The Occult* (1971) also graces the shelves. Wilson was a mixture of skeptic and adherent. Even so, he was not pleased with the publisher's blurb, which claimed it was "The ultimate book for those who would walk with the Gods"—another rather effective "come-on." Philip Toynbee described it as "a cheerful perambulation through the marshes, forests and badlands of magic and superstition ... which should encourage those who share Wilson's conviction that man must evolve in order to survive, and that his only path of evolution lies in the development of his neglected paranormal faculties." In it, Wilson does indeed discuss vampirism, which he regards as "frustrated sexuality turned to aggression":

> But this is not to assert that vampirism is merely a superstition or a delusion. Examples of it are so well authenticated that it would be absurd to try to maintain a strictly rational position. We are again in the realm of the borderland of the mind where strange forces can erupt from the subconscious and take on apparently material shape.[12]

He refers to Dion Fortune, who interpreted vampirism as a draining of psychic energy in her book *Psychic Self-Defense:*

> Now, vampirism is contagious; the person who is vampirised, being depleted of vitality, is a psychic vacuum, himself absorbing from anyone he comes across in order to refill his depleted sources of vitality without realizing their significance, and before he knows where he is, he is a full-blown vampire.[13]

While Van Helsing would have agreed with Wilson's comment about the well-authenticated examples of vampirism, he would not have agreed with Fortune's psychic explanation, as his own grandfather had collected "conclusive proof" that vampires exist in the classical sense of the term. We never find out if Lorrimer has actually practiced magic himself, but he does own a copy of Marius Malchus's translation of *The Secret Grimoire of Turiel*, which was also hot off the press when the film was made, this particular edition having been published in in 1971. Dennis Wheatley would later provide a cheaper paperback alternative of the same ritual in Volume 21 of his *Library of the Occult*, which he introduced with the words: "Finally we give 'The Secret Grimoire' of Turiel which portends to tell one how to raise a demon. But if you try and fail, please don't ask me for your money back."[14] This rather more jovial "come-on" has much in common with the way in which the publishers advertised Wilson's book, which was very much symptomatic of the time: "OVER 500 SECRETS EXPLORED...THE COSMIC SYMPHONY: OURS TO KNOW, WORSHIP & ENJOY. HEAR IT HERE." In *Dracula A.D. 1972*, Bob dismisses this modish fashion for the occult as "Sunday supplement stuff: Ouija boards, crystals balls," to which Joe Mitcham responds by miming a celestial telephone call: "Is there anyone down there wishing to talk to anyone up here? Ooo, it's for you, Sapphire." (It is interesting that he refers to Marsha Hunt's Gloria as Sapphire, as this was the name of the first British film to address racial prejudice, which, of course, still had a long way to go in the early 1970s.)

Turiel is one of 200 fallen angels listed in *The Book of Enoch*: "Messenger of the Spirits of Jupiter, appointed thereunto by the Creator of all things visible and invisible." The whole grimoire devoted to him is in fact an incredibly devout text, with many appeals to God for divine protection. The magician asks Turiel to appear "in the form of a beautiful angel clothed in white vestures, gently, courteously, kindly, and affably entering into communication with me, and that he neither bring terror nor fear unto me." When Turiel finally appears, the invoker must ask, "Comest thou in peace, in the Name of the Father, and of the Son, and of the Holy Ghost?"

> Wilt thou confirm thyself unto me at this time, and from henceforward reveal all things unto me that I shall desire to know and teach me how to increase my wisdom and knowledge, and show unto me the secrets of the Magick Art, and of the liberal sciences, that I may set forth the praise and glory of Almighty God?[15]

Another volume on Van Helsing's shelves is Moses Gaster's 1896 classic of Hebraic magic, *The Sword of Moses—An Ancient Book of Magic*, reissued by Weiser in 1970. Gaster, who was born in Bucharest, was a scholar, manuscript collector and Zionist who eventually moved to England, having been expelled from Romania, but there the parallel with Count Dracula ends.

The ceremonial magician and Hermetic Kabbalist William Gray (who knew Victor Neuberg, Crowley, and Dion Fortune) obviously interested Van Helsing as well, as he owns a copy of his 1970 introduction to ritual magic, *Inner Traditions of Magic*. This book complements Gaster's work, for, as Gray's biographers explain, "real esotericism was not just dressing up in handsome robes and manipulating symbols for the sake of so doing. It was knowing how to apply the meaning of such symbols to Life itself, for the purpose of altering or directing its energy in accordance with intention. For example, a Magical Sword was not the physical symbol one handles in Temple practice, but its qualities as applied to the human being. Flexibility, sharpness, keenness, brightness, pointedness of action, and everything else to be thought of in connection with a well-balanced blade."[16]

The prolific communist novelist and historian Jack Lindsay published his *Origins of Alchemy in Graeco-Roman Egypt* in 1970, a copy of which also forms part of Van Helsing's collection, as does Alice A. Bailey's *A Treatise on Cosmic Fire* from 1925, and Paul Carus's 1900 *History of the Devil and the Idea of Evil*, which would have been of particular interest to Van Helsing, who believes that evil is more than just an idea. "There is a Satan," he tells Inspector Murray.

He has also read *The Meaning of Witchcraft* (1959) by the father of modern witchcraft, Gerald Gardner, along with A.E. Wallis Budge's translation of *The Egyptian Book of the Dead*, *The Book of Thoth*, Cecil L'Estrange Ewen's *Witchcraft and Demonianism* (1933), Paul Huson's *Mastering Witchcraft* (1970), a study of the Kabbalah, and, of course, the entirely fictional *The Legend of Dracula the Vampire* by Lawrence Van Helsing. However, by the time he replaces the *Treatise on the Black Mass*, which Jessica has selected for "a quiet bit of mind-blowing," and pulls out his grandfather's work, we can see that all the books have been rearranged since Jessica's entrance. Presumably the set had been dismantled and re-erected between filming these two sections of the scene.

For the occult ceremony in St. Bartolph's, a pentagram within a magic circle, with astrological sigils, has been inscribed on the floor. An inverted crucifix stands on the altar. Black candles flicker in the dark. Johnny wears black robes, and despite Laura's suggestion that Jessica wear one of "the silken shrouds of death" he has thoughtfully provided, no one else puts on anything ceremonial. Johnny baptizes Laura "by the six thousand terrors of hell" along with liberal quantities of his own blood. This overflows the chalice on contact with Dracula's sanguinary remains, just as it had done in *Taste the Blood of Dracula*, and Dracula's grave begins to rise and fall as the magic makes its effect. According to the film's producer, Josephine Douglas, Lee, who had just returned from playing Vlad Tepes in Romania, added his own touch to the proceedings:

> He had a box, and he brought it back all the way from Dracula's castle Transylvania—a box full of earth he ceremoniously sprinkled into this tomb on the set before he got into it, because he said it would give the scene an authenticity that it might otherwise be lacking. I never could make out whether he was sending us all up or whether he really believed it. I know he did it with the utmost seriousness.[17]

Douglas refers here to the closing scenes of Dracula's immolation. For the vampire's reappearance in the 20th century, Lee was not required to lie down in the earth, but simply to stand, extending his hand in a papal gesture, showing that the ring, previously on Johnny's finger, has been magically transferred to his own. Over the years, Lee repeatedly warned against the dangers of dabbling in the occult. If you do, "you'll not only lose your mind, but you'll lose your soul," he said in 2011.[18] In this, he was no doubt influenced by his friend Dennis Wheatley, so there is the possibility that he did indeed take this odd ceremony seriously, but if so, wasn't he guilty of dabbling himself?

The exorcist and self-styled vampire hunter, Bishop Sean Manchester, has no hesitation about the reality of the occult—and in particular about the reality of vampires.

> In Satanism, which frequently embraces vampirism, the use of blood as a base for elementals to manifest and materialize is also used. There is a correlation between the almost

> anti–Christ figure the vampire represents by its complete turning upside down of the resurrection to come and the gift of life ever after which is turned into this filthy parody called the undead. ... Staking is the second most potent method of exorcism next to cremation. Ideally the wood should be of aspen or whitethorn, possibly blackthorn ... the preferred wood is due to the tree being believed to have have provided the wood for the crucifixion and the species used for the crown of thorns.[19]

He believes that vampires are dead bodies animated by demonic forces, and has explained the disbelief that followed his claims that vampires are genuine phenomena as evidence of T.S. Eliot's remark that human kind cannot bear very much reality. Vampires are apparently too much reality. But "it's very difficult to dismiss something that real by ignoring it."

Manchester came to fame—some would say infamy—during his involvement with the so-called Highgate Vampire phenomenon in 1968, which reached its peak in 1970 when he appeared on television, announcing that he would perform an exorcism on Friday, March 13, that year to destroy an evil entity that was haunting the celebrated London cemetery. As a result, it was mobbed by would-be vampire hunters, many of whom, no doubt, were fans of Hammer horror films. Also involved was a man who eventually became Manchester's rival, David Farrant, who also claimed he had seen something strange in the cemetery, which "took the form of a tall gray figure, about eight feet tall and it seemed to glide off the path without making any noise," as he explained in his own television interview. Animals were found dead among the graves, and in August 1970, two girls discovered the corpse of a woman, which had been dragged from its coffin, staked, and beheaded. By that time, however, Hammer's *Taste the Blood of Dracula*, which had been partly filmed in the very same cemetery, had been released, further adding to the media storm that was blowing around the place. Manchester and Farrant went on to advertise their participation in an occult duel, which never in fact came to pass, and sustained a rivalry that lasted decades, each claiming to be the one who had defeated the Highgate Vampire.

Because *Taste the Blood of Dracula* had featured the cemetery, which was soon also to appear in the title sequence of *Tales from the Crypt*, and *From Beyond the Grave* (dir. Kevin Connor, 1976), rumor has it that the sensation of the Highgate Vampire had inspired the black magic ceremony in St. Bartolph's Church. In fact, there is no evidence for this, and no mention of it by Don Houghton, despite his story having featured a similarly derelict and overgrown graveyard. However, the Highgate phenomenon, whether it had any basis in fact or not, is undoubtedly a powerful expression of the zeitgeist of the time, which Hammer both reflected and contributed to. An important element of all this is the title of *Dracula A.D. 1972* itself. The working title of the film was *Dracula Today*, which is lame by comparison. When the film was rebranded *Dracula '73*, it lost the resonance of "Anno Domini," which emphasizes the film's Christian context. Manchester believes vampirism to be a perversion of Christianity, and as Hammer's Dracula series progressed, inverted Christian imagery increasingly characterized Lee's portrayal. Dracula's reaction to the crucifix is, of course, consistent, but the Eucharist is later evoked in the bloody resurrection scene of *Dracula: Prince of Darkness*, while the vampire undergoes a kind of crucifixion at the end of *Dracula Has Risen from the Grave*, when he is impaled on a giant cross. (The title of that obviously echoes Christ's resurrection as well.) The tears of blood shed by Dracula as he dies also echo the shortest verse in the Bible: "Jesus wept." The scene in *Taste the Blood of Dracula*, in which the three Victorian libertines are commanded to enact the title of the film, is even closer to the symbolism of drinking Christ's blood during the Eucharist, while Dracula's demise is due to his being overwhelmed by Christian iconography. In *Scars of Dracula*, the vampire desecrates a church before being struck by lightning (with the opposite effect to the one it has on Frankenstein's Monster), which is surely the retributive hand of God.

The occult takes over completely in *Dracula A.D. 1972*, and by the time of *The Satanic Rites of Dracula*, the Count has become the equivalent of Damien in *The Omen*—the Anti-Christ himself, who uses black magic, science, and politics to destroy the world, but who dies wearing a crown of thorns before he can do it.

Six

Cushing and Christopher

> As she grew, my daughter greeted each fresh contract
> with, "How do you die this time, Daddy?"
> —Christopher Lee, *Tall, Dark and Gruesome*[1]

> In *Dracula A.D. 1972* I played my own father—or was it grandfather?
> —in a "flash-back" sequence, but whoever I was, I conked out after a
> ferocious encounter with Christopher Lee's stupendous Dracula,
> which started on the top of a swaying coach and finished up in the mud
> when the coach overturned. One of the wheels had broken in half.
> (Re-reading this list, I'm wondering if there might
> have been easier ways to earn a living.)
> —Peter Cushing, *Past Forgetting: Memories
> of the Hammer Years Years*

THERE IS NO DOUBT THAT *Dracula A.D. 1972* would be far less compelling without its two stars, who by that time had garnered considerable experience in the field of macabre fantasy, as they both preferred to describe the "horror" genre. They had also grown older, becoming even more compelling with age. *A.D. 1972* casts a fond glance at the last Dracula film they made together in 1958, particularly in the prologue set in the 19th century; it is perhaps surprising to realize that they only made three Dracula films together, Dracula's principal antagonists in the other films being played by Andrew Kier, Rupert Davis, Anthony Higgins, and—surprisingly—Dennis Waterman. (In the teasingly entitled *Brides of Dracula*, in which Cushing's Van Helsing also appears, Dracula was replaced by the Baron Meinster of David Peel.) Meanwhile, Cushing went on to specialize in playing Baron Frankenstein, whom he usually played, like Van Helsing, as another kind of hero, though a rather darker one. ("Just a dedicated doctor," he insisted. "There was no evil."[2] Ironically, the least evil of his Frankensteins was in Freddie Francis's *The Evil of Frankenstein* [1964], his most evil and ruthless being in *Frankenstein Must Be Destroyed* [1969].) Even though both Lee and Cushing had, of course, worked together on other film projects during the intervening period, their vampiric reunion 14 years later was a deeply significant occasion—being both retrospective and forward looking. The Van Helsing of *A.D. 1972* is a much softer though no less determined character. He is, for a start, a family man—or, at least he was, having fathered a son, about whom we know nothing. Neither do we know anything about his son's wife, nor what happened to them. All we know is that he is now looking after their daughter, Jessica. Cushing's earlier

Preparing for Combat—Christopher Lee (left) and Peter Cushing preparing to film the prologue for *Dracula A.D. 1972*.

Van Helsings had been bachelors, and while kind to children and patients, they had a steeliness, which Cushing softened for Lorrimer.

One of the contributory factors of this change was the death of Cushing's wife, Helen, on January 14, 1971, just as filming had begun on Seth Holt's *Blood from the Mummy's Tomb*, in which Cushing was to have played the Egyptologist, Professor Julian Fuchs. Helen's death deeply affected his performance in *A.D. 1972*, which began filming only eight months later, on September 27. Astonishingly, by that time he had already appeared in *Twins of Evil* for Hammer and *Tales from the Crypt* for Amicus. The vulnerability of this still grief-stricken man informed his interpretation of Van Helsing. While still spry, genial, and elegant, the contemporary setting required a less mannered approach, and his diction, while as crisp as ever, is adapted to more contemporary rhythms and inflections. There is also less overt theatricality in his gestures. Whereas the period roles for Hammer required conviction, this contemporary role required realism.

The Face of Peter Cushing

With age, Cushing's face increasingly revealed the skull beneath the skin. This aspect was well suited to the macabre; but even before that happened, the face was compelling. His finely chiseled physiognomy was at once beautiful and authoritative, reassuring and yet simultaneously unnerving. It was a curiously chaste face: intellectual and ruthless, ideal for Frankenstein, but also a face of great charm. Kenneth Williams recognized a similarity with his own face:

> Saw myself in "International Cabaret." I look lean and intellectual in the way that Peter Cushing looks ... the voice tends toward the *posh* and the face is often severe & aesthetic when it should be smiling and jolly. The general impression of my performance is someone superior being forced to pander to the inferior; and that is roughly the truth of the situation.[3]

Cushing, of course, never gave the impression of being superior or pandering to the inferior—quite the opposite. Sincerity was his watchword, but Williams's identification of "lean and intellectual" is telling. So, too, the "posh" aspect, in that Cushing was always immaculately turned out and had exquisite manners in his private life. S.S. Prawer compared his performances to those of Barbara Shelley and Jacqueline Pearce:

> Even in their most convincing performances, as in those of Peter Cushing, a fundamental niceness comes through, the aura of hard-working actresses who play their part with conviction but never shed their English middle-class gentility.[4]

Cushing's high cheekbones and increasingly hollow cheeks; the delicately tapered, aquiline nose; the hair invariably swept suavely back from the temples; and the thin lips, often pursed, indicate a pronounced fastidiousness. (Christopher Neame recalled of him: "I'll never forget, he would smoke cigarettes with his white glove on the set. Never wanted to get nicotine on his hands. Just put a white glove on, smoke a cigarette very calmly and with great elegance, take his white glove off and go and do the scene."[5]) The steely light-blue eyes convey intelligence and determination, but also that "niceness" Prawer identified. There is nothing effeminate here, but neither is there anything overtly masculine. Neither is it androgynous, but rather ascetic, which is perhaps why on the few occasions when Cushing was asked to perform sexual violence on screen, no matter that he did it with conviction, it somehow always felt wrong. In an NBC discussion on June 18, 1976, chaired by Tom Snyder,[6] Cushing was adamant in refuting Leonard Wolf's sexual interpretation of *Dracula*. It is rather an uncomfortable exchange, despite Cushing's laughter, because Wolf, who wanted to "do scholarship," obviously felt that Cushing had got the wrong end of the stick:

Greta Garbo in the title role of *Queen Christina* (dir. Rouben Mamoulian, 1933).

> I honor you for being one of the great interpreters of Dr. Van Helsing, but Dr. Van Helsing in Stoker's novel is teaching a little squad of young men how to deal with pale, red-lipped, bosomy young women who put their arms out and say, "Come to me, Arthur." You remember that? [Cushing nods.] And what is he teaching them to do? Each of the people in that novel carries a little pointy instrument: Dr. Seward has a scalpel; the Texan carries the Bowie knife; Jonathan Harker carries the Kukri knife; and the priest of them all, the man who is teaching them how to deal with women, carries the big stick.

"Dear boy," Cushing replies, obviously not convinced, "I carry a fountain pen—all that's for is to sign autographs with! I think sex is talked about far too much. The reason for staking Dracula is to get rid of him; it's not to give anyone kicks." That Cushing could have remained so completely at odds with the symbolically sexual aspect of what is going on in *Dracula* (though he does admit that Dracula is sexually attractive to women) says much about the nature of his appeal. There is an innocence here, which, rather like Stoker himself, channels the psychological implications of the story without being fully aware of them. This conceivably makes the implications all the more powerful. Deconstruction is, as the word implies, destructive. The power of Stoker's novel lies in its similar unawareness. Only an unawareness (perhaps caused by fear) could cause the man who wrote *Dracula* to argue, with regard to "The Censorship of Fiction": "A close analysis will show that the only emotions which in the long run harm are those arising from sex impulses, and when we have realized this we have put a finger on the actual point of danger."[7]

Peter Cushing as Gustav Weil in *Twins of Evil* (dir. John Hough, 1971).

Cushing was an athletic actor but not an erotic one. His power was that of the rapier rather than the battering ram, and the impression of intellectual power informed the physical aspects, propelling his seemingly frail body to acts of extreme physical heroism. However, his body was rarely revealed. In *A.D. 1972*, he does expose a wounded arm, which is quite devoid of overt musculature, even though the fight with Christopher Neame's Johnny Alucard, which causes this wound in the previous scene, is violently energetic (Cushing had played rugby in his youth). Neame was particularly impressed by this aspect of Cushing's performance: "He was very tough and very fit for a man of his age. I would do a lot of the stunts with him, grappling and so on. He was in very good shape. And he did a lot of his own stunts, falling off wagons, and things like that. Extraordinary man and very agile."[8]

At this stage, it might be illuminating, if perhaps at first surprising, to quote what the great French semiotician Roland Barthes had to say about the face of Greta Garbo:

> Garbo offered to one's gaze a sort of Platonic Idea of the human creature, which explains why her face is almost sexually undefined, without however leaving one in doubt. It is true that this film [*Queen Christina* (dir. Rouben Mamoullian, 1933)] (in which Queen Christina is by turns a woman and a young cavalier) lends itself to this lack of differentiation; but Garbo does not perform in it any fear of transvestism; she is always herself, and carries without pretense, under her crown or her wide-brimmed hats, the same snowy solitary face.[9]

Indeed, one may usefully compare Garbo in her wide white collar and broad-brimmed hat in *Queen Christina* with Cushing dressed as the Puritan Gustav Weil in *Twins of Evil*.

Admittedly, Cushing does not share the marble sheen of Garbo's flesh, but the intensity of the eyes, the pursed lips, the sweep of the nose, and the aura of chastity, which accounts for the androgynous quality of both actors, is worth considering. The contrast between Cushing's screen persona and his private life are extreme. Privately, he was a man of devout Christian faith, but was often cast as medical men who played at being God themselves. The opposite of an "intellectual," he always made a convincing academic. He was also a film star who remained self-effacing (in interviews couldn't quite recall the titles of some of his films), and stranger still, he was a "horror star" who did not personally enjoy watching horror films or reading horror stories. "I'm not a horror freak," he once said on television,[10] and he regarded the word "horror" as "the wrong adjective as applied to the films I do, because horror, to me, is, say, a film like *The Godfather*, or anything to do with war, which is real and can happen and no doubt will happen again at some time. The films that dear Christopher and I do are really fantasy, and I think 'fantasy' is a better adjective to use. I don't object to the term 'horror'—it's just the wrong adjective."[11]

A rugby fan and an enthusiast of toy soldiers and model theaters, as well as a watercolorist of delicate landscapes, it was significant that in his first volume of autobiography, Cushing doesn't begin to discuss his association with Hammer until page 126 out of 143. Concentrating on his earlier career (Hollywood with Laurel and Hardy, Shakespeare with Olivier, his time in television, etc.), he reveals that the character of Stanhope in R.C. Sherriff's First World War drama, *Journey's End*, was his preferred type of role[12] and his favorite play.[13] It is also significant that he recorded his wife's concern that he would be typecast in "so-called 'horror' films." The reason for appearing in them wasn't the result of any particular taste for the genre, but "there had been so many lean years and, much as I disliked going against her wishes, I was desperately anxious to make provision for our old age together, and to ensure she lacked for nothing in the meantime."[14] Unaware at the time of what his many fans had been expecting, who were disappointed by the lack of Hammer reminiscences, he brought out a sequel, *Past Forgetting*, two years later to redress the balance. This does nothing to suggest that he personally thought of himself as "a king of horror" any more than Christopher Lee, who liked to claim that he had really only made one genuine horror film (*The Curse of Frankenstein*; the rest Lee described as merely "playing with the audience"). Unlike Lee, however, Cushing graciously accepted the accolade when it was proffered. "I don't mind being a horror film star," he confessed. "To object would be like socking a gift horse in the face."[15]

"Horror"—or "fantasy"—haunted Cushing's career, and he brings to *Dracula A.D. 1972* extremely important associations forged in that Gothic past. Prawer is very illuminating with regard to this kind of cinematic phenomenon:

> The aura of his previous roles clings to an actor.... The bald-headed, club-footed executioner who carries out the behests of Richard III with such obvious relish in *The Tower of London* (1939) is played by the same Boris Karloff whom we have seen as a monster or a mad doctor in earlier movies; this makes him all the more demonic, makes us all the more ready to credit him with evil intents that match those of his master, and weaves an additional aura of terror around a king who commands the allegiance of such creatures. ... Walter Benjamin has told us that in the age of mechanical reproduction the individual work of art loses the "aura" that was once inseparable from its mode of existence; but the star-system, and studio casting policy, created an aura of their own around certain actors and their films to which most cinema-goers would respond. ... [In] *The Man with the Golden Gun* (1974) the presence of Christopher Lee ensures thrill that must be credited, not just to his handsomely threatening presence in this James Bond vehicle, but also to his long reign as the Hammer Studios' principal terror-star.[16]

Lee insisted that "at the age of fifty, I took the firm decision to Draculate no more.... I reached my irrevocable full stop. Thereafter I flung myself out in the snow for the wolves to gorge themselves on, leaving the thing to carry on without me."[17] However, he never left his horror past: he was simply too associated with it. After receiving his knighthood, he vociferously and rather embarrassingly argued with a television reporter that he was "not the King of Horror," but that was precisely what he was. His role as Count Dooku in episodes II and III of *Star Wars* is evidence enough of that. In those two films, he plays a villainous count who wears a cloak, and whose very name echoes the syllables of Dracula.

Prawer again:

> The tone, timbre, and resonance of an actor's voice, his habitual cadences and verbal gestures, the play of his features, the movements of his hands and body, become familiar to us and make us watch for variations as well as repetitions. The aura of previous performances enters, as we have often seen, into our conception of his personality—and so, very often, does what we know or surmise of his off-screen life and personality.[18]

When Cushing looks up at the portrait of himself as Lawrence Van Helsing in *Dracula A.D. 1972*, he is evoking not only the character he plays in the prologue of that film but also his entire past career at Hammer. Another actor in this role would consequently have depleted its effectiveness to such an extent that the film might not be worth looking at, excellent though it is from a technical point of view, as we shall be exploring later. What makes Cushing's performance so fascinating here is his minute and meticulous attention to detail, and the many gestures that illuminate often very short lines. As he sits in the chair behind his desk during the visit from Inspector Murray, Van Helsing smokes a cigarette and looks reverently at the portrait of his grandfather, explaining as he does so the events of 1872. When Murray quietly scoffs at Van Helsing's insistence that his grandfather collected proof of Dracula's insistence, Cushing changes his delivery from wistful reminiscence to quiet, unblinking defiance as he stares at Murray.

"Oh no, there was nothing ludicrous about it. He was a scientist. His evidence was conclusive," he insists. He then looks at the cigarette, which is smoldering in his right hand, as he explains, "There is evil in this world." He then gently rolls the cigarette around his fingers while ruminating on the "dark, awful things" there are in the world. "Occasionally we get a glimpse of them, but there are dark corners and horrors almost impossible to imagine—even in our worst nightmares. There is a Satan." Throughout all this, Cushing doesn't blink once, and his lines carry even greater conviction because we also know that Cushing personally believed them. As he often liked to point out, "Subtract an 'o' from 'Good' and add a 'd' to 'evil,' and you have the two greatest antagonists the world has ever known, or ever will know."[19]

"Professor, I don't know what I expected to hear when I came here today...." Murray remarks.

"But not this?" Van Helsing asks.

"No."

At which point Cushing delivers a marvelous combination of subtle gestures. First, he smiles and closes his eyes, emitting a restrained snigger at his own expense, turning his head slightly down to the right of the screen. He then breathes in a mouthful of smoke from the cigarette, raises his head, and looks to the ceiling, before turning his head to the left and touching his forehead with the middle finger of his other hand, looking down with a self-deprecating smile.

"You think I'm a crackpot," he suggests, holding his middle finger against his forehead, raising his eyebrows on the syllable "crack" and closing his eyes before lowering his face while maintaining the smile in a wonderful ballet of expressions. Altogether it is the most marvelous constellation of gestures, which conveys far more than the line, "You think I'm a crackpot" could achieve without them. Here we have a master class in how to make the unbelievable believable, an ability Cushing was particularly proud of, realizing that audiences "love the unbelievable being made believable, and above all, the fact that good always prevails over evil."[20] If Van Helsing had merely stated that the evidence of the murder Murray has come to talk to him about indicates that the true cause of death is vampirism, he might well have been taken for a crackpot; but by acknowledging that such a theory sounds absurd, by showing that Van Helsing has obviously had to fight this kind of prejudice many times in the past, and most of all by expressing his own vulnerability through such self-deprecation, the audience, already on his side (as this is, after all, Peter Cushing),

Six. Cushing and Christopher 99

Taking Direction—Peter Cushing (left) and Alan Gibson on the set of *Dracula A.D. 1972*.

is much more willing to suspend its disbelief. He looks up, the smile still on his lips, and maintains his sapphire blue gaze at Murray, as if testing that the policeman is sincere in his assurance that he doesn't think he's a crackpot.

Van Helsing then asks what else Murray has come to speak to him about. To relieve the tension of the scene, he stands up and moves over to the other side of the room, smiling, but when he hears that Murray wants to talk to Jessica, Cushing again gives a facial road map of Van Helsing's thought processes. First, the revelation sinks in after he has taken another puff from his cigarette. Then, he arrests his arm as it carries the cigarette away from his lips, and his expression changes to one of bewilderment.

"I beg your pardon?" Van Helsing's body freezes as he stares with concern at Murray.

"Your granddaughter—Jessica Van Helsing?"

Then Van Helsing offers a weak smile, in an attempt to reassure himself that this is unconnected to the murder.

"Yes, but why?"

"To ask a few questions," Murray explains, making light of it. Van Helsing's smile drains from his face as he steps toward Murray.

"In heaven's name, about this?" he asks softly, in a darker, far more serious register of his voice. The mood has now completely changed from an academic and theological discussion to one of personal involvement.

Cushing's ability to time his actions to the demands of the script is nowhere shown more effortlessly than at the end of his later scene with the inspector in

Murray's office at Scotland Yard. He sits in three-quarter profile on the opposite side of Murray's desk, dressed in a contemporary take on his grandfather's Victorian attire: a blue shirt, which matches his eyes, with a diagonally striped tie. The pinstripe suit is cut with a high lapel over a red waistcoat complete with watch chain, which on Cushing never looks antiquated. He makes very few movements in this position, which immeasurably aids his explanation of vampire lore. This is, in fact, far more compelling than it was in 1958; Cushing's greater age and experience, the contemporary setting, and the far more naturalistic approach he brings to the role is enough to convince anyone. The famous "Cushing finger" appears when delivering the line, "This monster is strong again: it has drunk blood. Now, it will infect others; may have infected others already." He then leans forward, closer to Murray. "Unless it is stopped, it will continue to infect others." With his utter seriousness here, he could easily be discussing the dangers of the very real horrors that have plagued us more recently such as the Novichok nerve agent used to poison the Russian double agent Sergei Skripal, which endangered the whole of Salisbury in the U.K., or the global Covid-19 pandemic.

As he walks to the back of the room to collect his raincoat, Van Helsing asks Murray to let him know the moment he finds Johnny Alucard.

"Don't let your men arrest him," he adds as he takes up his coat. "Have him followed"—he puts his right arm in the sleeve—"and let me know immediately"—the left arm slides in. He then adjusts his coat collar and fastens one of the buttons, as Murray explains that the Cavern Club has been closed.

After Van Helsing says, "That's a pity; it may have been a good starting off point," he takes his gloves out of the coat pocket. "Never mind," he continues, pulling on the left-hand glove. "Let's hope I'm right about St. Bartolph's." He then shakes Murray's hand with his right, ungloved hand.

Murray adds, "I just hope you're wrong about this entire business, Professor."

"I wish to God I was, Inspector," Van Helsing replies, looking down for his other glove. "I wish to God I was." The emphasis he places on "God" suggests more than merely Van Helsing's belief in the Almighty, but also Peter Cushing's own strongly held personal belief.

To deliver these lines and time everything so that he is ready to shake Murray's hand before walking out and closing the door behind him would be a joy to watch in any film, and is evidence if any were needed of how immeasurably Cushing's presence lifts this film into the quite different league, to which the script alone might have consigned it. Similarly, after his confrontation with Johnny Alucard, he really does look as though he's been fighting for his life.

Lorrimer Van Helsing is an academic like Stoker's Abraham Van Helsing, but with a difference. Abraham is a polymath, being a philosopher and metaphysician, as well as a medical man. His qualifications are "M.D., D.Ph., D. Litt, etc., etc."[21] Lorrimer's interests are more specific, however, being an anthropologist with an interest in the occult—specifically, in his own words, "psychic phenomena as related to history." Indeed, Lorrimer's grandfather, Lawrence, was also quite a different person from Stoker's Abraham, whom Cushing described as speaking in "double Dutch." Lawrence has no lines to deliver, so we never find out what he sounded like, but we can be pretty certain that he would have sounded the same as Lorrimer, as he's played by the same actor. There is, in fact, an argument that Abraham was based on a Polish cleric named Georg Andreas Helwing. This Lutheran pastor, born in the devilish year of 1666, spoke and wrote in German, as the district of Poland in which he was born and lived—a fief of the Crown of Poland—was part of a Prussian dutchy. Adam Weglowski mentions Helwing's involvement with the case of an "upierz"—a Polish version of the vampire—which was held responsible for an outbreak of bubonic plague in 1710. Helwing explained the "upierz" along rational grounds, arguing that when anyone is buried alive, they bite whatever is nearest to them, which is usually their own body. It could be that Arminius Vambery, the celebrated explorer from whom Stoker learned about Vlad the Impaler, told Stoker about this obscure cleric, whose name is, after all, only one letter away from Helsing.

Houghton's Lorrimer, however, is a mix of more recent models, notably Montague Summers, who was similarly convinced of the reality of vampirism, admitting, "To the feather-fool and lobcock, the pseudo-scientist and materialist, these deeper and obscurer things must, of course, appear a grandam's tale."[22] Compare the following passage from Summers's *The Vampire in Europe* with Lorrimer's assertion that his grandfather had collected "positive proof" of a vampire living in London. Summers was equally credulous:

> Of recent years the histories of Vampirism in England are perhaps few, but this is not so much because they do not occur as rather that they are carefully hushed up and stifled. In 1924 the Hon. Ralph Shirley wrote: "It may be doubted, indeed, in spite of the lack of records, whether vampirism in one form or another is quite as absent from the conditions of modern civilization as is commonly supposed. Although we are not to-day familiar with the Slavonic type of vampire that sucks the blood of its victims, producing death in two or three days' time, strange cases come to light occasionally when people are the victims, by their own confession, of something of a very similar nature, the vampire in these cases being an entity in human form who indulges in intercourse with someone of the opposite sex." ...Such cases, in truth, are happening every day and I have met with not a few instances in my own experience.[23]

Lorrimer is also a descendant of those psychic investigators, John Dyson and Thomas Carnacki, created respectively by Arthur Machen and William Hope Hodgson. He has even more in common with J. Sheridan Le Fanu's Martin Hesselius, the German physician who guides the reader through Le Fanu's collection of supernatural short stories, *In a Glass Darkly*. This contains the famous vampire story, "Carmilla," which so deeply influenced Stoker when writing *Dracula*. Like Abraham Van Helsing, Hesselius is described as a physician: "His knowledge was immense, his grasp of a case was an intuition."[24] Hesselius corresponds with a friend named Professor Van Loo of Leyden ("The professor was not a physician, but a chemist, and had, in his day, written a play."[25]). This correspondent may have provided Stoker with the "Van" that precedes "Helsing."

Even more pertinent to Lorrimer's career is the Society for Psychical Research. As an academic anthropologist at London University, he would no doubt have belonged to this august institution, founded in 1895 by three Cambridge professors from Trinity College: Henry Sidgwick, W.F. Barrett, and F.W.H. Myers. Its celebrated members included Sir Oliver Lodge, a convinced advocate of reincarnation.

One can imagine Lorrimer agreeing with early reports of the Society from 1897 that investigations had "yielded solid evidence for survival and communication" with the dead. According to Renée Haynes, a student of the Society's history, the levitation of the human body might occur "as an involuntary by-product of prayer, among contemplatives, notably Philip Neri ... and Teresa of Avila—who found it extremely embarrassing, and clung on one occasion to the iron bars of a window in a vain attempt to prevent herself rising."[26] Having made the study of "psycho-phenomena" academically respectable, the Society gave rise to several university departments devoted to this controversial subject, the most famous of which is the Koestler Parapsychology Unit at Edinburgh University, funded by the writer Arthur Koestler in the wake of his suicide in 1983; there are also departments of parapsychology at the University of Surrey at Guildford and the North London Polytechnic. Earlier, in 1967, an "Institute of Psychophysical Research" had been set up by Celia Green at Oxford.

The Society also reported evidence of telekinesis, "despite ingenious trickery on occasion."

> The unexplained movements of objects, strange and unaccountable noises, vivid lights, streams of cold air, did indeed occur quite genuinely from time to time, and could not invariably be dismissed as deliberate fraud on the part of the mediums involved; or as conscious or unconscious suggestion producing hallucinations among the sitters—as Sir William Barrett once hazarded; or even as plain lunacy on the part of all concerned.[27]

One Eusapia Paladino, an "almost illiterate Italian peasant woman," claimed and appeared to demonstrate that she could perform extraordinary feats, including levitation, producing notes from musical instruments without touching them, and, most bizarrely of all, exuding "pseudo-pods"—ectoplasmic protuberances resembling the arms of an octopus. Professor Charles Richet, a later president of the Society, was convinced the phenomena were genuine.

Jessica's nightmare, in which she "sees" Dracula's attack on Gaynor in St. Bartolph's church, is the kind of phenomenon once experienced by H. Rider Haggard on July 9, 1904, in which he felt he was drowning, "and then that his black retriever Bob was trying to tell him it was drowning."

> On Sunday 10th Bob did not turn up for dinner—nor ever again. He seems to have been a free-ranging dog who slept outside the house. On the morning of 11th two platelayers on the local railway found a dog collar and dog hairs on the track, and as there were no Sunday trains concluded that on the Saturday night some dog must have been struck by an engine and knocked off the line into the stream below. This flowed towards a weir, under which Bob's body was found the following Thursday.[28]

When *Dracula A.D. 1972* was being filmed, the presidents of the Society for Psychical Research were Professor W.A.H. Rushton, FRS, ScD, MRCS, LRCP (1901–1980), who was president between 1969 and 1971, followed by Professor C.W.K. Mundle (1916–1989). Rushton was a psychologist, who put forward natural explanations of so-called paranormal phenomena. Mundle was a philosopher, who held that such phenomena had as yet uncomprehended natural and material origins. These perspectives contrast with Van Helsing's much more supernatural beliefs. Indeed, the books in his library reflect the occult and magical theories that were fashionable among the hippie generation rather than the more sober investigations of the Society, despite insisting that his grandfather was "a scientist" and that there was "nothing ludicrous" about his belief in vampires.

Christopher

Cushing was an actor first and a film star second. Lee was the opposite, and their styles of performance strongly reflect this difference. Lee's main asset was his remarkable face, imposing height, and rich patrician voice, whereas Cushing's was his equally remarkable ability to inhabit a role. Film was both performers' preferred medium, but what distinguished Lee was his immensely photogenic persona, which, of course, cinema can magnify by means of the close-up. This quality was fully recognized by the Spanish avant-garde director Pere Portabella, who concluded his film *Umbracle* (1972) with a "a long, silent, motionless close-up" of Lee, which the actor remembered as lasting "one and a half minutes and for which I never received full credit, as people supposed it to be a still."[29] In fact, the shot lasts just over 40 seconds, but is no less impressive for that, demonstrating that his face was his fortune. Lee has to do very little to command the screen, but what fascinates us about Cushing is how much he puts into his performances (his famous ability at handling props and his immaculate timing).

One of the greatest regrets of Lee's life was that he never became the opera singer he so longed to be. He did indeed possess a powerful singing voice, as Jussi Björling, the great Swedish tenor, once recognized, but at the time Björling spotted Lee and invited him to study at the Stockholm Opera, Lee didn't have the funds to support himself, and so was forced to decline the offer.[30] When auditioning for Noël Coward, Lee sang the Serenade from *Don Giovanni*. "Do you know, you have a voice?" Coward told him afterwards. "It has a baritone quality. You might even turn into a tenor."

> I saw several meanings behind that remark and said nervously, "Oh, really? That would be good, wouldn't it?"
> "Oh," he said, putting his head back and staring at me in a puzzled way. "Why?"
> "They always get the best parts."
> "Ah," he said, "true." Half-way back up the aisle, he turned and looked back at me. "But not this time," he said with a smile.[31]

In many ways, Lee was better suited to being an opera singer than an actor, for his screen presence is indeed very operatic, being much more mannered than Cushing's and ideal for the more gestural, exaggerated requirements of operatic delivery. He would have excelled in the Wagnerian villains, Hagen (in *Götterdämmerung*) and Klingsor (in *Parsifal*), who are in many ways the operatic equivalents of the kind of "heavy" that Lee so often played. Even in contemporary roles, such as Colonel Bingham in *Nothing but the Night* (dir. Peter Sasdy, 1973), there is a certain stylization in his approach, which Cushing's pathologist, Sir Mark Ashley, in the same film, entirely lacks. Lee was at his most relaxed in *The Wicker Man*, which was an exception that proved the general rule—not that his performances were not compelling, but they were so in an entirely different way from Cushing's, emerging as they did from his screen persona rather than Cushing's detailed approach to character as an actor. Lee's height, which had always been a handicap in the early years of his career, made him the ideal choice for Dracula, along with the "otherness" of his face. This was, of course, very good looking, characterized by deep brown eyes, which often looked black, and were reminiscent of the unnervingly obliterated eyes of Tom Tyler's mummy, Kharis, in Universal's *The Mummy's Hand* (dir. Christy Cabanne, 1940). They also had the ability to remain fixed and penetrative even when he was smiling. His very long, aquiline nose meant that his mouth was quite low down in relation to his eyes. The relation between the two was thus rectangular, whereas Cushing's mouth and eyebrows formed the top and bottom of a square. All these aspects combined to create the opinion that Lee was "too tall and too foreign"[32] for good parts in British pictures—before, that is, he cornered the market in Gothic villains.

With one exception, Lee's Dracula was not the Dracula described by Bram Stoker. That exception was Jess Franco's *El conde Dracula*, made in 1970, in which Lee adopted the military mustache we read about in the novel:

> Within, stood a tall old man, clean shaven save for a long white moustache, and clad in black from head to foot, without a single speck of colour about him anywhere.[33]

Lee felt that Stoker's Dracula was "not at all like me in physical character, but there were aspects of him with which I could readily identify—his extraordinary stillness, punctuated by bouts of manic energy with feats of strength belying his appearance; his power complex; the quality of being done for but undead; and by no means least the fact that he was an embarrassing member of a great and noble family."[34] Lee certainly conformed to Dracula's bone structure, however:

> His face was a strong—a very strong—aquiline, with high bridge of the thin nose and peculiarly arched nostrils; with lofty domed forehead, and hair growing scantily round the temples, but profusely elsewhere. His eyebrows were massive, almost meeting over the nose, and with bushy hair that seemed to curl in its own profusion. The mouth, so far as I could see it under the heavy moustache, was fixed and rather cruel-looking, with peculiarly sharp white teeth; these protruded over the lips, whose remarkable ruddiness showed astonishing vitality in a man of his years. For the rest, his ears were pale and at the tops extremely pointed; the chin was broad and strong, and the cheeks firm though thin. The general effect was one of extraordinary pallor.[35]

As Stoker had based his description on images of Vlad Tepes, it was appropriate that Lee should have been asked by Calvin Floyd to make a television documentary about the Romanian hero. He dressed up for the part, complete with mustache and long curly hair, and wandered through Castle Bran, raising Vlad's ghost. He did, indeed, look remarkably like Vlad, as well as sharing much in common with the features of Sir Henry Irving, on whom Stoker also based his description of Dracula. If anyone was born to play the part, it seems that Lee was that man, but the Hammer incarnation was also influenced by earlier Draculas, particularly Bela Lugosi, who not only dispensed with the mustache but also looked even less like Stoker's description. Lugosi's image of Dracula was so pervasive, the BBC's otherwise extremely faithful adaptation of the novel in 1977 cast Louis Jordan as another clean-shaven Count, who was also cloak-less. Lee opined that Stoker made no mention of a cloak, which is certainly the case when Dracula first introduces himself to Harker, but a cloak does appear when Harker observes him climbing up the wall of the castle "*face down*, with his cloak spreading out around him like great wings."[36] The cloak was thus not the invention of subsequent adaptors and actors, so Lee had no need to object to the adoption of this item of clothing—not that he did, originally; as we have seen. When Lee played count Dooku in *Star Wars Episode II—Attack of the Clones* (dir. George Lucas, 2002) he described his character as "the most malignant, dangerous and lethal force in the entire story, possibly in the entire galaxy."[37] He again wore a black cape, which billowed out behind him in a distinclty Draculine manner.

In 1971, he confessed:

> Obviously, I feel a sense of imprisonment at times but at the same time I'd never turn my back on Dracula. After all, he has been bread and butter to me and I'm grateful to him—any of us has to be glad just to be in work with the film industry in the uncertain state it is in at the moment.
>
> You have to immerse yourself completely in the character and forget your own personality. The portrayal from start to finish must be straight, honest and sincere. A trace of tongue-in-cheek deserves the audience's laughter.
>
> Obviously, whoever plays Dracula makes the picture. I was fortunate enough to give an interpretation of a character which was a purely personal one and which paid off.[38]

Lee did, however, eventually turn his back on Dracula after *The Satanic Rites*. Unwilling to play Dracula even in *Taste the Blood of Dracula*, only the prospect of unemployment due to the collapse of several contracts for other films at the time made him agree to *Dracula A.D. 1972*. He nonetheless refused to say many of the lines Don Houghton had written for him, such as, "Do you not know that I was always here? Always. In the air around you. Always. Since the dawn of time. Since the rebel angels descended into hell. Since darkness followed light. I am Dracula, Lord of Darkness, Master of the Walking Dead! I am the curse, the Apollyon, Angel of the Destroying Furies! I am the Apocalypse."[39] It wasn't the first time Lee had cut his own lines. Discussing his performance in *Dracula Has Risen from the Grave*, he said, "I think he should have something to say in these films, though when he does speak it has to be something worth saying. I cut out a lot of my lines and left in what was short and to the point; phrases like 'You have failed me. You must be punished.'"[40]

When Lee was asked to leave the Gothic confines of St. Bartolph's church and occupy a penthouse at the top of an office block in *The Satanic Rites of Dracula*, he masqueraded under a quasi-Russian/Hungarian accent before being unmasked as his characteristically satanic Count. He himself regarded this presentation of "that character," as he always subsequently referred to Dracula, as resembling a Bond villain, which it does. He even says, "Professor Van Helsing, I have been expecting you," in the manner of Bond's archenemy, Blofeld. It would have been interesting to see his Dracula as a houseguest in Johnny's flat, as originally intended.[41] How would he have interacted with his disciple on a sofa, or in a sports car? Despite Lee's yearning for more dialogue ("You see, those of you who have read the book ... you're aware of the fact that to begin with he never stops talking"[42]), it is doubtful that he would have been as convincing in contemporary dialogue as Cushing was. Head of Hammer, Michael Carreras, was particularly insistent that Dracula should remain restricted to the interior of the church, where Lee is undoubtedly magnificent but hardly modern—a combination Robert Quarry managed to achieve to great effect in the Count Yorga films.

Notwithstanding, Lee's performance as Dracula in *A.D. 1972* is arguably his best portrayal of the vampire count, aided immeasurably by Alan Gibson's fluid direction and the considerable improvements that had been made in makeup since 1958. Lee increasingly complained that he had less and less to do, but his previous Draculas had always spent most of their time off-screen. Dracula is also absent for much of Stoker's novel. In fact, Lee has no less to do in *A.D. 1972* than he had in 1958. He has a spectacular entrance, filmed from below, which transforms him into a positive monolith of evil and is arguably more effective than his famous entrance at the top of the stairs in 1958. He is even more terrifying when attacking Caroline Munro's Laura than he was attacking Valerie Gaunt in the first film. (Jonathan Rigby describes this well: "Dracula looking skyward after the first bite, blood leaking down over his chin, then resuming his attack with a horrid, mock-coital jerk."[43]) He swirls his cape in the moonlit nave of St. Bartolph's in the epitome of Hammer's Gothic manner, fully expressive of what he himself called the "terrible solitude of Evil,"[44] which Lee was always so keen to capture. The way in which Gibson films the apparent dream sequence experienced by Jessica, which turns out to be a genuine assault on Gaynor, is truly hypnotic, while his subsequent scene with Christopher Neame is, as we shall see later, perhaps his most commanding incarnation of the Count. The final confrontation with Van Helsing is a lot bloodier than it was in 1958 and no less athletic, and Lee even manages to insert a line from Stoker's book, which is, again, more than he was able to do in 1958.

The action echoes various aspects of previous confrontations. In 1958, Dracula hurls a candlestick at Van Helsing, which he repeats in 1972. In *Dracula Has Risen from the Grave*, Dracula removes the stake that Barry Andrews's Paul has thrust into him. In *A.D. 1972*, Jessica removes the silver-bladed dagger Van Helsing has plunged into Dracula's chest. The effect in the latter film is visually less spectacular but in fact more unnerving due to Gibson's presentation of the hypnotized Jessica, who stands in the background holding the weapon, while Dracula stares at Van Helsing with malevolent triumph. The hiatus that follows also echoes the standoff in the 1958 finale.

Intriguingly, *A.D. 1972* was in fact only the second time Lee's Dracula had been impaled in the traditional manner by means of a wooden stake—or, in this case, several wooden stakes. Previously, he had been overcome by religious iconography, transfixed by a crucifix, drowned, struck by lightning, and disintegrated by sunlight. A stake was thrust into him in *Dracula Has Risen from the Grave*, but he was able to remove it, as his atheistic assailant didn't utter the required prayer. Gibson also gives Lee far more close-ups than he had had in prior films, giving him an opportunity to register the Count's thought processes. In his scenes with Johnny Alucard, he expresses disappointment that Gaynor, whom Johnny has brought to be the vampire's next victim, "is not the one. You have not learnt to obey. She is *not* the one!" Later, when Johnny demands the power of immortality, Lee has his finest moment of the entire Hammer Dracula canon, when he spins around, shouting, "You demand!" before pointing at him and snarling, "I have returned to destroy the House of Van Helsing forever, the old through the young. You, and your line, have been chosen." Lee is able to convey what is needed with regard to the disposal of Gaynor's body by means of a single expression, before he agrees to Johnny's demand. Christopher Neame's memory, that Christopher Lee "got a little carried away and drew blood," is not supported by evidence on screen. He does, however, quite rightly regard the camerawork as "superb and very revolutionary."[45] Johnny is also Dracula's first male initiate in a Hammer film, a fact that finally addresses Stoker's latently homosexual line, "This man belongs to me," spoken by Dracula when his brides are about to sink their fangs into Jonathan Harker's neck.

Slaked—Christopher Lee as Dracula with Caroline Munro as Laura in *Dracula A.D. 1972*.

Gibson loses no opportunities for close-ups of Lee in the finale. He makes a priest-like entrance as he advances toward Jessica, who is lying on the altar; we see the almost imperceptible smile of anticipation as he looks down at her, which is followed by his reaction to her crucifix, and the pain it causes when it burns his hand. He then expresses both fury and bewilderment when Van Helsing shouts his name, and marvelously evokes Dracula's gradual realization that this is the ancestor he has returned to destroy. Dracula's smile here seems to echo the unnerving grin of Gwynplaine, as played by Lee's favorite actor, Conrad Veidt, in Paul Leni's *The Man Who Laughs* (1929). As he pursues Van Helsing up the spiral staircase to the choir gallery of St. Bartolph's, he seems to glide rather than climb, and as Van Helsing unsheathes the dagger, Dracula's expression subtly changes from demonic triumph to the realization that he is now in very real danger. He repeats this emotion a short while later when confronted by the stakes that Van Helsing has hidden beneath brushwood in the cemetery. Lee had only once before fallen into a grave as Dracula. This was on the set of the 1958 *Dracula*, when "the unexpected weight of a tubby stunt double I had to cast into an open grave, had caused me to tumble in after her."[46] Despite the critics' revulsion at Hammer's first Dracula film, there was relatively little blood, but in *A.D. 1972*, it gushes ghoulishly from Dracula's impaled body along with gruesomely gurgling sound effects.

It is significant that a still from this film was chosen to adorn the *Hammer Presents Dracula with Christopher Lee* LP in 1974, the reason being quite simply that Lee had never looked more impressive. (The picture credits failed to recognize Caroline Munro, however, who swoons in his arms.) The story that Lee narrates on the LP is actually set at the turn of the 19th century, so in that respect the still is inappropriate, but it would be hard to find a more impressive manifestation of the Hammer Dracula in full bloodlust. Far from being a nadir in Lee's presentation of "that character," *A.D. 1972* in fact gave him far more opportunities than before, which he grasped with even greater conviction, despite his personal misgivings. As Neame more correctly relates:

Dracula on Disc—the EMI *Dracula* LP, prod. Don Norman, 1974 (photograph by David Huckvale).

He was very professional. Wonderful to be with because he was ... he was absolutely the part. You couldn't imagine anyone being better than him. Or being more impressive than him. Just his presence alone helped you get into the role. He didn't say anything to me at all. He would sing opera in his dressing room and be very frightening on the set, and a dear man.[47]

Even more than Cushing's Van Helsing, Lee's Dracula in *A.D. 1972* is both a retrospective and a summation of his association with that role. *The Satanic Rites of Dracula* took the character in a different, potentially more invigorating direction, which Lee was unwilling to pursue any further, but in *A.D. 1972* his traditional Gothic characterization reaches its peak, and is really only equaled by the 1958 incarnation, which obviously made a much bigger impact at the time as it was so very different from anything that had come before it. Lee remained consistent in his commitment to the role, and was only constrained by factors over which he had no control. Gibson's direction and Dick Bush's photography served Lee better than anyone else had since Terence Fisher and Jack Asher, vastly contrasting though those styles were.

Seven

Cast and Crew

After the disappointing response to *Scars of Dracula*, Sir James Carreras pitched Anthony Hinds's outline for a Dracula film set in India to Warner Brothers. This was originally called *Dracula—High Priest of Vampires*, later retitled *The Unquenchable Thirst of Dracula*. One of the reasons it was set in India was that Warners had money tied up in India, and this film would be a way of releasing those funds. The exotic location was also seen as a way of invigorating the increasingly anemic Dracula franchise. The story concerns Penny Woods, who travels to India to find her sister. The sister has become a victim of Dracula, who now resides in a lavish palace in a fictional place called Mahabad and would eventually to be attacked by vultures. When Hinds retitled his idea, he set the proceedings in the 1930s, but though Warner Brothers wasn't tempted by the changes it did see the potential of what eventually became *Dracula A.D. 1972*. Various titles were floated: *Tomorrow Dracula*, *Dracula Now*, *Mood Dracula*, *The Dracula Trip*, *Draculalucard*,[1] and what eventually became the working title of *Dracula Today*.

Don Houghton became involved as screenwriter because of his connection with the producer, Josephine Douglas. Douglas had started her career as an actor and had appeared in several British films: a small part in Alfred Hitchcock's *Stage Fright* (1950), and as a receptionist to James Hayter's bumbling doctor in Michael Anderson's *Will Any Gentleman...?* (1953), before moving into television production. In 1956 Douglas had her first encounter with Peter Cushing when she invited him to talk about his toy soldier collection for a television show called *House*. She also appeared on TV panel shows such as *Find the Link* and *The Name's the Same*, and it was this association which led to her briefly playing herself as a panelist on a fictional show, hosted by Eamonn Andrews and called "What on Earth Was That," in the Sidney Gilliat comedy, *Left, Right and Centre* in 1957. This, of course, was the year in which Hammer began its Gothic career with Terence Fisher's *The Curse of Frankenstein*. In the same year, she also became coproducer and cohost of the first "teenage" pop show, *Six-Five Special*, appearing as herself alongside Pete Murray and many pop acts of the day in Alfred Shaughnessy's 1958 film of the same name; it was this association that ultimately led to her involvement with *Dracula A.D. 1972*.

James Carreras had received his knighthood in the New Year's Honors of 1969 for "services to youth" and was aware of Douglas's reputation with youth programming. As pop music was to feature in the modernization of Dracula, Douglas seemed to be an ideal candidate to produce it. Having secured her services, Carreras then asked her if she knew anyone who would be willing to write a script. Douglas suggested Don Houghton, with whom she had worked on the hospital soap opera, *Emergency Ward 10*, which she had produced at a time when it was highly unusual for a female producer to work in British television.

Star and Producer—Christopher Lee and Josephine Douglas on the set of *Dracula A.D. 1972*.

Douglas, as one would expect, promoted the general idea of a modern Dracula with enthusiasm: "It seems to be an apt moment for bringing Dracula up to date. At a time when there is such a pronounced interest in the occult amongst the kids, the blending of the traditional theme and modern setting is a subject I very much wanted to make."[2] Though she was pleased with the result, the process of producing it took its toll. Philip Martell, who became very friendly with her, told me that after her only experience with Hammer, she vowed she would never make another film again, which was indeed the case.

Houghton had had two horror stories published when he was a teenager, and after leaving the Royal Navy in 1949, he settled for a while in Australia, where he worked in the film and television industry. Disillusioned by the Australian media business, he returned to England in 1965 and became the scriptwriter for *Emergency Ward 10*, during which met his wife, actor Pik-Sen Lim. Later he wrote two scripts for *Doctor Who*, having previously known Jon Pertwee, who was performing the title role at the time, when they had both served in the navy. He was also a script editor for the long-running soap opera *Crossroads*.

Cinematographer Dick Bush was well qualified to film Hammer's latest Gothic project, having previously photographed Jonathan Miller's seminal adaptation of M.R. James's ghost story, "Oh, Whistle and I'll Come to You, My Lad" (1968), Piers Haggard's *Blood on Satan's Claw*, and John Hough's *Twins of Evil*. He brought a polished and painterly quality to Gibson's direction. Several shots leap to mind: the bridge over which the coach thunders in the prologue, framed by overhanging trees; Johnny Alucard Senior leading his horse over a grassy meadow on his way to bury Dracula's ashes in St. Bartolph's churchyard; the highly evocative composition of the assembled mourners in their top hats, filmed through a screen of willow trees and teasel heads; and the close-up profile of the mourning widow behind her veil. All these would grace a film with far more intellectual pretensions. Bush's experience on *Twins of Evil*, which features a Black Mass, doubtless influenced the way in which he filmed the Black Mass scene in *A.D. 1972*, in particular the shimmering glow of the candles, which both films share. Gibson also opted for a considerable amount of handheld camerawork, which considerably intensifies the audience's involvement with the intimacies and terrors being played out before them. Bush also helped to make Lee and Cushing look better than they had ever looked before in a Dracula picture, and cast an unnecessarily flattering soft light over Stephanie Beacham's Jessica. Even the milk bottles in the street glitter moodily in the moonlight behind her grandfather when he investigates the rickety fence of St. Bartolph's; and by filming Christopher Neame from below during his invocations as Johnny Alucard, his face is given an unearthly quality, foreshadowing the much more monolithic manifestation of Dracula a little later on.

All the actors who played what Inspector Murray refers to as "spaced-out teenagers" in *Dracula A.D. 1972* were actually in their twenties at the time. Caroline Munro was the youngest of the eight, being only 22, but William Ellis, who plays Joe Mitcham, was 28. This undeniably sits awkwardly with Murray's classification of them. These so-called teenagers are also fairly affluent and mostly middle-class. They may employ hippie-speak of doubtful relevance to the time, but they do so with Received Pronunciation, slightly modified in the case of Philip Miller's Bob and Ellis's Joe, but their accents still don't place them very far from the middle of the King's Road. Expensive drugs are available to them all (Inspector Murray later points out that the Cavern Coffee Bar is being used "as a distribution center for pot and LSD," while Johnny later invites Gaynor to help herself to "smokes" in his flat. Ironically, a newspaper A-board outside the Cavern advertises the headline, "How China Fights America with Drugs"). Bob drives his own car, as does Janet Key's Anna and Neame's Johnny Alucard. Jessica, meanwhile, lives with her academic grandfather amid highly respectable and affluent surroundings. Beacham was 24, and of all the "teenagers" she has the most middle-class voice, which suits her character's background. The fact that she is living with her grandfather emphasizes the film's intergenerational conflict, especially in the scene between them in which Jessica calls their home a "mausoleum" and confesses that she's "never dropped acid" and is not "shooting up" or "sleeping with anyone just yet." Cushing responds to this litany with mild but affectionate bewilderment. (The description of the house as a mausoleum also provides a nice balance with Dracula's eventual *pied à terre* at St. Bartolph's: Van Helsing and Dracula are united by their opposition, like Wotan and Alberich in Wagner's *Ring* Cycle, in which Wotan is called "Licht-Alberich"—light Alberich—as opposed to the dark Alberich of the evil dwarf. To destroy Dracula, Van Helsing must be just as brutal and cunning as his adversary.)

Christopher Neame was 24 when he became Dracula's disciple. He was unsure why he was cast in the role, but explained that people had long told him that his eyes were "always fairly intense, so I've always been cast as villains." He assumed that he had secured the role on the strength of having previously appeared as a prisoner of war in the BBC TV series *Colditz*,[3] though his first part for Hammer (and his first film role) was as a peasant in *Lust for a Vampire*. Neame's Johnny Alucard lives in a swanky, and presumably rather pricey, bachelor pad. No one seems to know where he came from. "Met him at a party one night" is all Jessica can recall. His surname derives, of course, from the pseudonym used by Lon Chaney, Jr.'s Count in *Son of Dracula*. Like Lorrimer's grandfather, Johnny's ancestor is a dead ringer for his descendant. Johnny obviously has plenty of money, but in other respects he conforms to the early seventies type of modish occultist, whom we see at work in such documentaries as Derek Ford's *Secret Rites* (1970), in which everyone gets alternately naked or dressed up in robes and Egyptian masks during the Wiccan rituals of Alex Sanders, and Kenneth Anger's occult fantasy, *Lucifer Rising*, in which Mick Jagger's brother, Chris, has a portrait of Crowley in his bed sit, much as Johnny has one of Dracula in his.

Less is known about the other characters. Michael Kitchen's Greg Pullar is the most enigmatic. He has the privilege of unzipping and snogging Jane Anthony's startled debutante at the opening party before explaining to her that "the whole idea, baby, is that we get out one minute before the fuzz get here." After that he has nothing much more to do, and disappears completely after the Black Mass scene. (Kitchen has remained notoriously reluctant to discuss his involvement with the film.) The last we know of Greg is when Murray is forced to let "the kids" go after having rounded them up (off-screen) at Joe's party on a drugs charge: "An army of angry lawyers and parents descended and bailed them out." Houghton then gives Van Helsing a delightfully mordant line: "They would all be safer in jail."

According to David Gee's exhaustive analysis of the evolution of Houghton's screenplay, we were originally to have been shown Joe's party in full swing:

> Joe Mitcham's flat is in a street of fairly dilapidated terrace houses, probably off the Fulham Road. Murray arrives in his Cortina, followed by two police Panda cars. Inside Joe's flat a swinging party is in progress. A boy spouts way-out poetry, a blonde girl pulls the newly arrived Bob off for dancing; Joe, the host, who has a wine bottle, is with a girl named Maureen, who lets him fall flat on his face and takes up with another boy. When the police raid commences, Gregg shouts, Fuzz. The Sergeant pulls Joe to his feet. The group finds out about Laura's death, but a defiant Anna doesn't want them to cooperate with the police.[4]

Houghton also intended us to see the "army of angry lawyers and parents" alongside pressmen outside Chelsea Police Station "trying to get statements and taking photos." He also had the idea of showing us the father of Janet Key's Anna Bryant, a certain General John Bryant, pushing his daughter into a waiting Rolls-Royce (further evidence of the well-heeled background of these trendy hippies), while Joe's

Party Animals—on the set of *Dracula A.D. 1972*, Maureen Flanagan in silver hot pants dances next to Christopher Neame's Johnny Alucard. Behind Neame stands Ernest Blyth as one of the party guests. Blyth stands with his back to William Ellis' Joe Mitchum, who is looking toward the mirror. Sitting at the piano is Stoneground's Cory Lerios. Dancing on top of the piano is Glenda Allen. Directly in front of her, Stephanie Beacham as Jessica Van Helsing, is dancing opposite Philip Miller's Bob Tarrarnt. Behind him stand members of Stoneground: Tim Barnes (guitar and vocals), Annie Sampson and Lynne Hughes (backing vocals), and, in the corner, Sal Valentino (vocals and guitar).

"beefy parents bundle him away; Greg comforts his sobbing mother. Bob, alone, thoughtfully, walks towards King's Road."[5]

Janet Key's Anna Bryant has considerably less to do in the finished film, but is nonetheless a necessary cog in the wheels of the plot, for it is she who spots Van Helsing running down King's Road (rather a coincidence) and gives him Johnny's address. Having visited him "for kicks" some time before, she found Johnny "so weird"—though what happened during their encounter is left to the imagination. In a still of a scene that didn't make the final cut, we see her at the wheel of her car, having dropped Van Helsing off outside Johnny's flat. Having previously appeared in *The Vampire Lovers* as Gretchen, Key would appear in two more horror films: first as the chambermaid Bridget in Roy Ward Baker's *And Now the Screaming Starts* (1973), alongside Beacham, and then, in 1975, as Jill Fletcher in Peter Sasdy's *I Don't Want to be Born* in 1975.

William Ellis, who played the Dodo in William Sterling's *Alice's Adventures in Wonderland* in the same year as *Dracula A.D. 1972*, appears here as Joe Mitcham. He has more to do than the rest of the group, wandering around in his white monk's habit, playing the fool. He obviously finds Johnny unnerving, and is unwilling to stay as long as Johnny suggests he should before the police arrive during the opening party scene. He also delivers one of the film's key shocks when he startles Jessica and Bob, suddenly appearing from behind the grave of Lawrence Van Helsing wearing a skull mask. Another curious parallel might usefully be made between that prank and the monkey mask that was left behind in the party that starts off *Father, Dear Father*. In the latter instance, the monkey mask is, of course, played for laughs:

Scary Skull—Alan Gibson examining Joe Mitchum's disguise in *Dracula A.D. 1972*.

The girls' nanny (Noel Dyson) puts it on and "monkeys around." Patrick Cargill then enters and doesn't register that she's wearing it. "God, what a mess these kids have made," he complains. "Just look at this room, Nanny. I mean, why is it that the kids can't have a party without making such an appall...." By now the mask is off. "Nanny," he adds, staring at her again, "you look quite strange."

Joe Mitcham's mordant prank nearly ruins Johnny's elaborate preparations, as Bob is on the point of taking Jessica back home, agreeing with her that "the whole thing was a nothing idea." He brusquely informs Joe that the grave belongs to one of Jessica's ancestors. "Well how was I to know?" Joe replies. "I haven't read any good tombstones lately." He then persuades them both to stay, as "Johnny's gone to an awful lot of trouble," before skipping into the church while humming a snatch of Mungo Jerry's song "In the Summertime," which, at the time of filming, was still a relatively fresh hit, having been released only the previous year.

Caroline Munro's Laura Bellows is the youngest and also the most naïve of the group, who all too willingly throws herself upon the sacrificial altar at St. Bartolph's after Jessica hesitates to do so. Having risen to Hammer stardom on the strength of her billboard ads for Lambs Navy Rum, Munro provided much of the sex appeal in the film, as well as becoming one of the most publicized of Dracula's victims. However, she definitely felt that the dialogue was "a little bit out of touch."

> I think that had been a few years before, quite honestly. I would say, it would have been, maybe, the mid–60s, you know, with the dialogue and stuff. It was changing, you know, the "mod scene," although it was the beginning of the 1970s. ... Looking back on it, it was quite fun, but quite hard to say some of it, really.[6]

The fact that Laura is excited by the shrouds, which Johnny has brought for the Black Mass, subtly sets up her imminent eagerness to become Johnny's victim. When the blood begins to flow, however, she changes her tune, and breaks down in a very convincingly acted scene of sheer terror and despair. Dracula then attacks her, after which Munro had to endure being buried up to her chin in dirt to play her own severed head. During the filming of this scene, she was left under a tarpaulin (it had begun to rain) while the crew broke for tea. All we know about Laura is that she came from Watford, though Johnny makes up a shaky story about her parents living in Ramsgate.

Marsha Hunt, who plays Gaynor Keating, brings perhaps the strongest and most authentic connection to the '60s hippie scene, having had relationships with both Mick Jagger and Marc Bolan, been on protest marches against the Vietnam War, and appeared as an extra in Antonioni's *Blow-Up*, as well as the hit musical *Hair*. She also has one of the best lines in *A.D. 1972*— "Aren't they always?" delivered with weary nonchalance. Soon after this, she becomes Dracula's second victim, Johnny having softened her up after having taken her to a "Jazz Spectacular" at the Albert Hall. And lest we should laugh at that idea, there really was a Jazz Spectacular in Seattle in 1970, so why not in the Albert Hall as well?

Johnny is an up-to-date version of two archetypes: the sorcerer's apprentice and the devil's disciple. In this respect he is a modern version of Stoker's Renfield, who facilitates the arrival of Dracula to contemporary London. Both Johnny and Renfield call Dracula "the Master,"[7] and we should not forget that Don Houghton's second

Head Start—preparing Caroline Munro for her severed head shot in *Dracula A.D. 1972*.

Doctor Who serial was 1971's "The Mind of Evil," featuring Roger Delgado as the Doctor's nemesis, the Master, who had first appeared earlier that year in immediately preceding serial, "The Terror of the Autons," written by Robert Holmes. (The title of "Master" had been chosen by producer Barry Letts and script editor Terence Dicks, as it was an academic qualification that formed a good parallel with "Doctor.") Houghton was well aware of the connotations of the term when scripting *A.D. 1972*. (Intriguingly, the first line of "The Mind of Evil," accompanying a shot of a grim Victorian prison, is "Looks like Dracula's Castle.")

Johnny also resembles the sorcerer's apprentice of Goethe's poem of the same name (made famous by Disney's use of the tone poem by Paul Dukas in *Fantasia*, which was based on the story). Goethe's apprentice finds himself dangerously out of his depth when the spell he uses to enchant a broomstick gets out of hand. Similarly, Johnny is both excited and frightened by what he has unleashed. At first, he can't wait to get going. He rushes into his flat and darts to his Dracula shrine, where the ring and dried blood are kept below the Dracula woodcut. When the ceremony is complete, he is exultant, "I did it!" he shouts. "I summoned you!" but he is soon put in his place by Dracula, who reminds him, "It was my will." Johnny then follows his Master into the church and, from behind a column, watches Dracula attack Laura, wide-eyed with terror and biting his fingernails. However, by the time it's Gaynor's turn, he smiles as he watches.

His own death scene is highly effective: Having been overcome by light reflected from a shaving mirror by Van Helsing (Neame hurls himself over a chest of drawers and unsets a potted palm to great effect), he is melted by the clear running water

"*No sweat*"—Philip "Pip" Miller as Bob Tarrant stands over Stephanie Beacham as Jessica Van Helsing, while Christopher Neame's Johnny looks on in *Dracula A.D. 1972*.

of his own shower, in a scene to which we will return later. (Vampires, presumably, stink.) Houghton's original idea, however, had been for Johnny to fall from a window and be impaled on iron railings below.[8]

Philip Miller's Bob was also to have had his own death scene, after having been turned into a vampire (off-screen, alas) by Johnny. Whereas we see Dracula at least *prepare* to vampirize Johnny earlier on, we never see Johnny getting intimate with Bob, which would no doubt have been a little too suggestive for Hammer at the time. Homosexuality, we must remember, was still only partially decriminalized in the U.K. by 1971, and was still very much a taboo subject. The only other reference to homosexuality made by the company had been in *Dr. Jekyll and Sister Hyde*, in a scene of transgender implication. (Ralph Bates's Jekyll, who has been transforming into an evil woman, encounters Lewis Fiander's Howard Spencer, who has earlier enjoyed an amorous encounter with "Sister" Hyde. Jekyll, confused by the memory, reaches out to touch Howard's face, breathing his name amorously, while Howard ponders the implications in the light of the dress Jekyll has just bought at a French corset maker.) It is a pity that Hammer didn't have the courage to dwell on the two same-sex encounters in *A.D. 1972* in more detail. Even more unfortunate was the editing out of Bob's death scene, which was indeed filmed, as a surviving still proves: Bob is shown reacting to the sunlight in St. Bartolph's churchyard, where Van Helsing later discovers his corpse.

Miller (as Pip Miller) later appeared in Richard Marquand's *Star Wars Episode VI—The Return of the Jedi* (1983), and as Sergeant Ross in David Drury's 1985 *Defence of the Realm*, but has made few film and television appearances since then. In 2018, he decided to make a sea-voyage pilgrimage to Santiago with his border collie, Buck, to help atone for a sense of guilt he felt at not donating one of his own kidneys to his brother, Kit, when Kit was diagnosed with kidney disease.[9]

The other major members of the cast are the police. Their presentation here is particularly interesting in the context of how policemen were being portrayed on British television at the time. The friendly image of the bobby-on-the-beat in the long-running TV series *Dixon of Dock Green* (also set in London) starred Jack Warner in the title role from 1955 to 1976, but a more realistic and rather grittier series, *Z-Cars*, set in a fictional town near Liverpool, changed the tone considerably. Jack Warner's character had been shot and killed by Dirk Bogarde's Tom Riley in Basil Dearden's *The Blue Lamp* (which inspired the *Dock Green* series), as far back as 1950, and Warner became Hammer's first "horror" copper when he was promoted from Sergeant Dixon to Inspector Lomax in Val Guest's *The Quatermass Experiment* in 1955. Hammer's subsequent policemen, until *A.D. 1972*, remained confined to the past, and usually played a distinctly functional role. Eddie Byrne's Inspector Mulrooney in *The Mummy* is a thankless role; most police roles in horror films are, as they are merely investigating crimes the audience has already solved. Police usually compete with the hero, and thus have to be kept in the background if they can't be avoided altogether. In the Sherlock Holmes stories, the police are represented as incompetent, to provide a foil to Holmes's genius; no one wants the police to defeat Dracula instead of Van Helsing. A policeman does appear in the 1958 *Dracula*, played by George Merritt, who like Jack Warner specialized in police roles, but his function is merely to inform us about the little girl, Tanya, encountering the vampiric Lucy. There are no police in *Dracula: Prince of Darkness* or *Dracula Has Risen from the Grave*, but once the vampire was placed in Victorian London in *Taste the Blood of Dracula*, the police became necessary in the form of Michael Ripper's Inspector Cobb. Cobb is played as a comic character wrapped up in a voluminous scarf, who leaves the heroism to Anthony Corlan's Paul Paxton. Two unattractive and virtually redundant officers played by Richard Durden and David Leland appear in *Scars of Dracula*; their only function is to allow Michael Gwynn's priest to overhear information necessary to the plot. They soon lose interest when they discover that the man they are searching for has gone to Dracula's castle, which is outside their territory, "as you might say."

The police in *Dr. Jekyll and Sister Hyde* and *Hands of the Ripper* are again largely redundant in terms of the plot, but necessary, as one can hardly have stories about Jack the Ripper without the police being involved in some way. Michael Ripper played another policeman in *The Plague of the Zombies* (dir. John Gilling, 1966) but similarly has no real part in the plot. Thorley Walters's Inspector Fricke in *Frankenstein Must Be Destroyed* is another amusingly incompetent comedy character, characterized by the habitual taking of snuff and a vituperative relationship with Geoffrey Bayldon's police doctor, but Windsor Davis's police sergeant in the same film does provide some real tension when he searches the guesthouse in which Frankenstein has performed his latest experiment. It is usually best if the police can be avoided altogether in supernatural stories, which is why they don't clog up *Blood from the Mummy's Tomb*, as Mulrooney had clogged up *The Mummy*. Professor Fuchs has left strict instructions that the police should not be involved and that his doctor (Aubrey Morris) and daughter should "take decisions on his behalf."

Dracula A.D. 1972 revitalized the role of the police in Hammer films. Here they play an integral part in the narrative as well as helping to provide the sense of contemporary realism. Not only are Michael Coles's Inspector Murray and David Andrews's Sergeant Pearson prototypes of John Thaw's Regan and Dennis Waterman's Carter in *The Sweeney*, but the way in which Gibson films them also foreshadows the highly cinematic approach taken by the TV series, which, unlike most British television of the time, was filmed entirely on location. The horror elements of their investigations include Laura's severed head, the dead bodies of Gaynor and the woman Johnny attacks when she leaves the laundromat, and, in the aftermath of the fight between Van Helsing and Johnny, Van Helsing's bloody arm, which Sergeant Pearson binds. He makes a tourniquet from the professor's shirt and advises him to "get this looked at at St. Stephens" before doing anything else. These horror elements are tame by comparison with what Regan and Carter were to encounter in the second Sweeney film, *Sweeney 2*, directed by Tom Clegg six years later in 1978. In that film, there are so many casualties, even at the beginning, that Regan says, "I've never seen so many dead people." A dedicated hit-and-run team are targeting banks and killing any of the team who get injured. Actors are consequently drenched in far more Kensington Gore than Laura ever was on the altar of St. Bartolph's. A police driver has his foot amputated (not that we actually see that), and in the finale, the leader of the gang shoots his girlfriend before shooting himself in the mouth, leaving mortal remains that make Laura's severed head look positively decorous.

Significantly, the first thing we see of the police in *A.D. 1972* is when Artro Morris's police doctor pulls a red blanket over what remains of Laura's body in the derelict graveyard. He explains that the body has been "shockingly mutilated. Work of a maniac, I'd say. Must have gone completely berserk." He adds that the whole body has been drained of blood, but we don't actually see the carnage, which is effectively left to the audience's imagination. Murray, protected against the cold by the trendy fur collar of his overcoat, speaks with no trace of Regan's cockney accent, but the speech patterns are just the same: "It's a grim setting. Body might not have been discovered for weeks—crude attempt to bury it—lonely place yet right in the heart of London. Could be a cult murder ... had a spate of them in the States a time back.... Well, you boys have been saved some trouble anyway: she was already wearing a shroud."

Dixon of Dock Green had never experienced such Hammeresque horrors, and despite the increase of violence in *Z-Cars*, the BBC was reluctant to go so far. *Dracula A.D. 1972* thus pointed the way in which police dramas were soon to evolve. Indeed, *The Sweeney*, especially in its two film incarnations, could be seen as a secularized version of Hammer's last two Dracula films. Instead of vampires, there are human monsters aplenty, together with comparable office scenes and police visits to private residences. One of Gibson's many skills was his ability to stage these scenes in such a compelling way. They are, after all, potentially rather dull affairs: basically the impartation of information, but combined with the chemistry between Coles and Cushing, Gibson's direction, as we shall see later, makes them highlights of the film.

Coles had worked with Cushing before on *Doctor Who and the Daleks* (dir. Gordon Flemyng, 1965), in which Coles had played a blue-faced alien—the antithesis of his role in *A.D. 1972*—and after playing Inspector Murray again in *The Satanic Rites of Dracula*, he went on to play a violent gangster in the first Sweeney film, directed by David Wickes in 1977. Like all up-to-date executives in the 1970s, Inspector Murray has several executive toys on his desk, including a Newton's cradle, which he sets in motion while pondering the case. It is in this scene that Don Houghton inserts his first expletive, when Murray responds to a call about the press requesting information. "Gruesome bastards: they love this sort of thing." Again, *The Sweeney* would take this kind of language as read, but *A.D. 1972* got there first.

Sergeant Pearson is always hungry, like Dr. Watson in the Sherlock Holmes stories. When he enters Murray's office at Scotland Yard with information about Laura's associates, he brings sandwiches and coffee with him. After their visit to Van Helsing's home, he asks Murray if "there's any chance of a cup of coffee [and] cheese roll, sir: I'm starving."

During that latter scene, Cushing and Coles complement each other perfectly. Coles's voice is slightly higher pitched than Cushing's, and this helps us, subconsciously, to identify that Cushing has the higher authority. Rather than Van Helsing assisting the police, it is actually the police who help Van Helsing solve the mystery and defeat the vampire.

As we have already seen, Houghton was capable of coming up with very arresting lines. Most famously, in *The Satanic Rites*, Van Helsing observes, "Things do go bump in the night—quite often." In *A.D. 1972*, Murray asks him if there are people who get their kicks by draining bodies of blood, to which Van Helsing replies, with doom-laden pauses in all the right places: "No. Not people."

Supernatural films set in the present day of course have to confront the skepticism of the police, which Houghton also effectively negotiates here. He has Murray being open-minded to the possibility, though at first he asks Van Helsing if he is joking. When Van Helsing asks if he dismisses the possibility (a very good way of addressing such a fantastic subject), Murray replies, "I don't know. I've been a policeman too long. I don't know."

Later, when Jessica arrives and is asked about her movements the night before, she lists the names of the people she was with; a significant glance between Murray and the sergeant confirms their suspicions. When she becomes vague about where they went, Coles delivers the word "specifically" with marvelously controlled impatience. The following morning, Van Helsing visits him in his office at Scotland Yard, where his frustration breaks loose: "I'm just a plain, run of the mill copper," he explains. "Put me up against a villain and I'll run him down: Thief, conman, thug, murderer—sooner or later I'll nobble them because that's what I'm trained to do. I know the way they work." Vampires, however, are out of his line. He admits that if any of his superiors thought he was going to take Van Helsing seriously, they'd have him certified, but he's sufficiently impressed by Van Helsing's "background and qualifications" to do just that. Cushing's immaculate performance makes this scene work as well as it does—his complete sincerity (the actor's watchword for all his performances) allows Murray (and the audience) to have complete faith in Van Helsing.

After Murray's meeting with Van Helsing in Johnny's flat, we see no more of him. Houghton had toyed with the idea of having him turn up after the final confrontation, after which a bat would flit over the graveyard.[10] Instead, Murray merely says he will look in at St. Bartolph's later, but by that time, the film has come to an end. Dracula is dead, and the appearance of a policeman would have been dramatically redundant.

Coles's return in *The Satanic Rites of Dracula*, along with Cushing and Lee proved to be their final vampiric adventure. It is a great pity that Hammer was unable to continue this new approach to their old characters, but many factors came together to prevent that, the parlous state of the British film industry being one, Lee's refusal to Draculate any longer being another. The lackluster reception of these two films, which were so negatively received by Hammer's fan base at the time, put an end to the saga. Distance now reveals what expertly crafted films Gibson's two modern-dress Dracula films are. As well as providing a fascinating time capsule of the period; they also register the changes that were taking place in British popular culture in that transitional period.

Finally, there are one or two other performers who also deserve our attention. A particularly intriguing one is the "Crying Matron" in the opening party scene, played by Jo Richardson. Being officially credited suggests that she may originally have been given more to do, but in the final cut all we see is her being very distressed in the arms of a distinguished dinner-jacketed man vaguely reminiscent of Christopher Lee. She wears a lime-green evening gown and cowers from Johnny as he passes her. Richardson was, however, much better known as Mrs. Witton in *Crossroads*, the long-running TV soap opera on which Houghton had also worked. Also present at the party is the chief "Matron," played by Lally Bowers, and she does have lines. She also has the privilege of throwing a glass of wine in William Ellis's face when he says she reminds him of his father. Most of the time, however, she has simply to stand with an expression of horrified distaste at the chaos that has been visited upon her drawing room by her son Charles, who in his bow tie and dinner jacket seems a very unlikely fan of Stoneground.

Several of the background actors who make up the party guests have been identified as well. These include Philip Stewart, who is given a close-up immediately after Charles phones for the police. Gibson wanted as many elderly faces as possible to contrast with the so-called teenagers, and the bespectacled Stewart, who by then had a very lived-in face and teeth that resembled a row of gravestones, was ideal, having appeared in the background of over 100 films, beginning in 1937 in the musical comedy *Let's Make a Night of It* (dir. Graham Cutts). Three of his subsequent appearances were in Hammer titles. The first was *Never Take Sweets from a Stranger* (dir. Cyril Frankel) in 1960, in which he can be seen sitting in the corner behind Felix Aylmer in the courtroom scene, posing as an official. He turned up next, in yellow-face, behind Geoffrey Toone in the saloon run by Christopher Lee's Chung King in *The Terror of the Tongs* (dir. Anthony Bushell, 1961), while in *Dracula Has Risen from the Grave*, he has his sleeves rolled up, smoking a cigarette in George A. Cooper's Transylvanian tavern. After his close-up in *Dracula A.D. 1972*, we observe him discussing the situation with the police when they eventually arrive.

Another prolific background artist at the party is Ernest Blyth, who can be seen behind Charles talking to a lady in red. His even more prolific career as a background actor also began in the 1930s with the fantasy, *Alf's Button Afloat* (dir. Marcel Varnel, 1938). He chalked up nearly 200 film and television appearances, including a man reading in the British Library opposite Dana Andrews in Jacques Tourneur's *Night of the Demon* (1957). In Hammer's *The Revenge of Frankenstein*, he wears a very large white cravat in the musical soirée scene, and says "Certainly" when Cushing's Baron asks if he will excuse him. In *The Snorkel* (dir. Guy Green, 1958), we see him smoking, in conversation with a lady in a hotel lobby. He also turns up in Terence Fisher's *The Mummy* (1959), in which he sits beside Raymond Huntley during the short inquest scene. Hammer also called on his services for *The Ugly Duckling* (dir. Lance Comfort, 1959). Like Philip Stewart, he too appears in *Never Take Sweets from a Stranger*, as a juror (back row, wearing glasses), while in *The Two Faces of Dr. Jekyll / U.S.* title *Jekyll's Inferno* (dir. Terence Fisher, 1960), he wears a military uniform as one of the patrons of the Sphinx Club, where he applauds Norma Marla's Lady with a Snake. He was also a funeral mourner in Jimmy Sangster's lackluster *The Horror of Frankenstein* (1970), a dinner-dance party guest in *That's Your Funeral* (dir. John Robins, 1972), and in *10 Rillington Place* he provided a copiously note-taking barrister during the trial of John Hurt's Timothy John Evans.

Lewis Alexander was another highly active background player with around 150 film and television appearances made throughout the 1960s and up to the mid–1980s. He played a neighbor in Polanski's *Repulsion*, walked out of an auction room in *The Skull*, attended an Edgar Allan Poe exhibition in *Torture Garden* (dir. Freddie

Francis, 1967), dropped in at the Folies Bergère in *The Creeping Flesh* (dir. Freddie Francis, 1972), and visits the opera in *Frankenstein: The True Story* (dir. Jack Smight, 1973). He dined in the background in the café scene in *Hands of the Ripper*, and in *An American Werewolf in London* (dir. John Landis, 1981), he made a late appearance as a "passer by." In *Dracula A.D. 1972*, he is the distinguished gentleman standing next to the two disapproving ladies who, if looks could kill, would have killed the hippies long before Dracula is resurrected.

Even more prolific than Blyth, Stewart, and Alexander was Reg Thomason, who in *Dracula A.D. 1972* is also briefly seen entering the church of Our Lady of Dolours in Fulham Road on Sunday morning, prior to Van Helsing stealing some holy water from the font. Thomason chalked up over 250 appearances between 1947 and 2000, three years before his death. As well as appearing as a reporter in the first *Sweeney* film, he was a party guest in *Madhouse* (dir. Jim Clark, 1974) and played pub customers in *The Creeping Flesh* and *I, Monster*. He was a solicitor in Freddie Francis's *Trog* (1970) and a drunk in Gordon Hessler's *The Oblong Box* (1969), as well as forming

"Just a minute young lady!"—(from left) Stephanie Beacham as Jessica Van Helsing, Philip Miller as Bob Tarrant, and Constance Luttrell as Mrs. Donnelly in *Dracula A.D. 1972.*

part of the resistance in Gordon Flemyng's *Daleks' Invasion Earth 2150 A.D.* (1966), the title of which interestingly foreshadows that of *A.D. 1972*.

John Franklyn-Robbins's uncredited role as "Minister" was, in the end, reduced to a voice-over, which intones the Service for the Burial of the Dead from the *Book of Common Prayer* during the interment of Lawrence Van Helsing.

There are, of course, younger party guests who conform to Charles's dress code of evening wear. Gibson doesn't concentrate on these, but it is important to recognize that they are there, adding a little more realism to the idea of having a rock group as musical accompaniment of the festivities. Among the gatecrashing hippies there are several other background players whom we can identify. Along with Christopher Morris as the boy in the window, who first spots the approaching police car and shouts "Fuzz!" there are the Hippie Girl and Boy, played by Penny Brahms and Brian John Smith, who are amorously engaged under a table. Two go-go dancers were also hired to liven things up, one of whom, Maureen Flanagan, was interviewed by Colin Beardmore for *Little Shoppe of Horrors* magazine:

> I was booked from my Model Agency—"Blondes"—because I could dance and also I brought along three fabulous outfits!
>
> The one chosen was Silver Leather, my sis-in-law made it. How I got into hot pants I don't know! But I think at the time I had everything!
>
> The director remarked on my legs, my hair—no other model in London at the time had better legs and hair. Between takes I was talking to Christopher Neame and Stephanie Beacham.
>
> I also made friends with Caroline Munro who had been a model before acting. I was talking her out of biting her nails!!
>
> The other girl on piano was my friend Glenda Allen, model and actress. We met Christopher Lee and had photos with him but he refused to put his arm round us or smile....
>
> Those were the days, Colin. All girls in mini skirts, hot pants, beads, flowers in our hair, makeup, etc. Not like now when they go out in pyjamas!![11]

Then there is Mrs. Donnelly, Van Helsing's redoubtable housekeeper. After hearing that Friday is her day off, we are given our only glimpse of her on Sunday, though we later hear her voice on the telephone. She is played by Constance Luttrell, who had been a Gaiety Girl in the 1920s and had previously appeared in several British television series, but *A.D. 1972* was her first and only feature film. An amusing photograph survives of her pulling the strings of a corset being tried on by Stephanie Beacham during the shoot. She too is part of the film's fascination with the generation gap, for Mrs. Donnelly would have fitted in well with Charles's superannuated party guests. She shakes her head disapprovingly when Bob, now a vampire, lures Jessica back to the Cavern to be kidnapped by Johnny. This very much echoes the foolish actions of Mrs. Westenra in Stoker's *Dracula*, and Olga Dickie's maid, Gerda, in the 1958 *Dracula*, when she removes the garlic flowers Van Helsing has placed in Lucy's bedroom to protect her from the vampire.

Last but not least, there are the ten members of the rock group Stoneground, who sing "Better Get Through" and "Alligator Man" during the opening party scene: Cory Lerios (piano), Brian Godula (bass), Tim Barnes (guitar and vocals), Sal Valentino (vocals and guitar), Steve Price (drums), John Blakeley (guitar), and Deirdre LaPorte, Annie Sampson, Lydia Moreno, and Lynne Hughes (backing vocals). Stoneground was not Hammer's original choice, however. That was Rod Stewart and the

Faces (who were also under contract to Warner Bros.), but the Faces were unavailable at the time. Stoneground was, however, and having only recently been formed (in San Francisco in 1970), they were still a hot property. The name was inspired by stone-ground bread, which some of the musicians were using at the time to make sandwiches.[12] Sampson recalled that Gibson gave them no specific directions other than "Just have fun!"

> Christopher Lee came to the set, and he was a wonderful man. I talked to him and he was really gracious and kind. He was in his street clothes when I saw him. And I saw Peter

Alligator Man—Cory Lerios (piano), Glenda Allen (on the piano), and Sal Valentino (vocals/guitar) in *Dracula A.D. 1972.*

Cushing there too. It was a wonderful day and a wonderful time getting to meet the actors. Christopher Lee thanked us for doing the movie; in fact, I was talking to him about it because I didn't know if I wanted to be in this movie about the Devil. Because I'm a Christian, you know what I mean? But I said to him because the cross and the Bible win in the end, I think I can do it. And he goes, "Yup, that's right!" But I was really concerned at first…. It really was a party, people were eating and…. I've only seen it once or twice, but that comes across.[13]

Collectively, Stoneground forms the perfect contrast to the environment in which they find themselves: John Blakeley in his Kaiser Cement baseball cap, Sal Valentino sporting a CND badge on the strap of his rather battered electric guitar, everyone with long hair, some with half-grown beards, Steve Price in bright red with matching beret. The music is much rawer than the kind of "classics with a beat" in the *Father, Dear Father* party. There really is nothing "retro" or anachronistic about all this in the context of the time in which the film was made. Nothing could have been more up to date, which perhaps accounts for the animosity toward the film felt by so many Hammer fans when it was first released. Accustomed to lovingly re-created Victorian settings and period costumes, this was a shock indeed. Fifty years later, the patina of age has softened the impact.

There are other briefly glimpsed faces that also deserve our attention, chief among them being the uncredited actor, who plays Marjorie Baynes. The close-up Gibson gives her in *A.D. 1972* shows her looking tired and impassive, smoking her cigarette in the deserted laundromat. Is there anywhere less homely than a laundromat in the middle of the night? She is one of the "lonely people" the Beatles sang about in "Eleanor Rigby," and as she loads her laundry into a blue plastic bag, picks up her handbag, and throws her cigarette into the gutter, she has no idea that Johnny is waiting for her, his newly sprouted fangs ready to bite.

Hammer's screenwriter, Christopher Wicking, can also be glimpsed dancing with the others at the party, but the identity of so many others remains elusive: the man wearing a monocle and smoking a cigar at the party, for example; the man sitting in a chair, who is being teased by Janet Key; and, even more significantly, as he is given such an important close-up, the policeman who smiles at the two hippies under the table, which brings the party to a close.

Eight

Cameras and Choreography

Roy Skeggs, Hammer's latter-day producer, had no doubts about Alan Gibson's talent as a director. "Alan was one of the best and possibly the most underrated directors of those I worked with."[1] Michael Carreras, head of Hammer at the time, admired him for the same reason, even though he didn't like him as a person, though he never said why: "I liked him as a director. He was a good director—I'd sit down with him and say, 'Alan, this is what we have to do today.' And he would do it but without ever rushing it. He would find a way of doing it if it was that important. If he needed something, he would discuss it with you. He was a director without arrogance. It doesn't make you a good director, but it makes you good from a producer's point of view."[2] Hugh Harlow, who was production manager on Gibson's previous film for Hammer, *Crescendo*, recalled, "I found Alan a very laid back and amiable person to know and work with. No airs or graces. Just a simple knuckle down and get on with the project in hand, and I remember he smiled a lot, that I found was a good sign."[3] Gibson's laid-back approach was one he positively advocated:

> You, the director, should appear relaxed and calm ... and make sure it all seems very informal and that apart from some hard work it will be fun. You can't beat a pub lunch on the first day's rehearsal; it breaks down barriers, creates an atmosphere and starts the whole project off with a relaxed and easy feeling of togetherness.[4]

Actors also appreciated the confident yet relaxed approach of this "gentle giant." Nigel Havers, who worked with him on the 1987 TV series, *The Charmer*, remembered "he never put a foot wrong," despite the fact that "he knew how ill he was all the way through the shooting, but never mentioned it to anybody."[5] (Gibson died in 1987.) Sir Michael Redgrave wrote to him after working for him on *Goodbye Gemini*, acknowledging, "I enjoyed working on the film quite enormously and—how can I say this without seeming to gush—especially, particularly and quite definitely, working with you." Joseph Cotton, who he directed in the 1979 TV movie, *Churchill and the Generals*, said, "working with you was a pleasure, as usual," while Sir John Mills (after filming the episode "Operation Safecrack" from the TV series *Tales of the Unexpected* in 1982) wrote, "it was great working with you. In fact, you are so good I think you ought to take it up professionally!"

Gibson's daughters, Sarah and Jessica, who kindly let me know about those letters, also remember that Ingrid Bergman "had a great relationship with Alan, and when filming *A Woman Called Golda* was complete she gave him a framed sketch of herself as Golda inscribed with 'Alan, thank you for helping me be Golda.' She came to our house for a meal, and swapped recipes with our mother. You can see through the photos how closely they worked together."

Cushing admired him too. He went on to work with him on the 1984 TV movie *Helen Keller: The Miracle Continues*, and sent a letter to him afterwards in which he wrote, "It was *such* a pleasure to work with you once again, and thank you for your wise guidance and help with 'the Prof.' What a happy and excellent cast and crew you have assembled." And he attached a photo of them both when they worked together on the *Hammer House of Horror* TV series for the episode "The Silent Scream."

That, of course, was some time after *Dracula A.D. 1972*, which was the first time Cushing and Gibson had worked together. Even then, Cushing sang his (and others') praises from the start: "I think we have a great director in Alan Gibson, who has wonderful ideas, and Dick Bush (cameraman) is doing a magnificent job, and Don Mingaye's sets all round are beautiful, and such a lovely cast, all the young people are so marvelous."[6] It is those "wonderful ideas" and how they combine with Bush's photography that this chapter will explore as we make our way through the film.

Gibson started his career as an actor, but moved into directing in 1965 when acting didn't work out, despite having been accepted by the Bristol Old Vic. His first job was directing two television series, *199 Park Lane* and *Eh, Joe*. He continued to work in television, including for Hammer's TV series *Journey to the Unknown*, which eventually led to the Hammer psychological thriller, *Crescendo*. That was followed by *Goodbye Gemini* (aka *Twinsanity*), which, as we have already seen, in some ways foreshadowed the style and situations of *Dracula A.D. 1972*. It begins, like the main title sequence of *A.D. 1972*, on a motorway. The two protagonists, Jacki and Julian (played by Judy Geeson and Martin Potter), are introduced while traveling on a coach that brings them to London. Both sequences thus share an aesthetic of concrete and movement. The twins arrive at their father's property in Chelsea—another parallel with *A.D. 1972*. This is No. 9, Cheyne Walk—a very grand residence with interiors not unlike those of the *A.D. 1972* party. Gibson starts off the *Goodbye Gemini* party sequence a while later with a stained glass panel of two angels in Pre–Raphaelite style, an image he repeated in *A.D. 1972* when Van Helsing visits the church to collect holy water. The interior of the houseboat in which the *Goodbye Gemini* party takes place has red carpets and white walls, a color scheme that sufficiently intrigued Gibson for him to repeat it in his other contribution to *Hammer House of Horror*, "The Two Faces of Evil."

We are eventually introduced to Freddie Jones's bitter homosexual, David, who languishes on a red hammock like the caterpillar in *Alice in Wonderland*. Jones would, of course, appear in Gibson's second Dracula film as Professor Julian Keeley. David and Michael Redgrave's M.P., James Harrington-Smith, are situated at the other end of the generation gap that concern both *Goodbye Gemini* and *A.D. 1972*. David ironically refers to the dancing twins as "beautiful people," and observes that there are "no holds barred in SW3" when it comes to sexual relations among the younger generation. "You and I should feel like two old tombstones, my dear," he adds. "If we're careful, someone might come up and inscribe us."

The climax of the film features a bloody ritual sacrifice in which the two twins murder Alexis Kanner's bisexual blackmailer, Clive Landseer, who is already in trouble with a gangster over money. This highly effective sequence obviously has much in common with Laura's blood-drenched ordeal in St. Bartolph's Church; there is a consequent police investigation into the atrocity, with Peter Jeffries playing the equivalent of Michael Coles's Inspector Murray. He questions Harrington-Smith, who has become unintentionally involved by shielding Jacki, much as Murray questions Van Helsing. *Goodbye Gemini* thus has rather more in common with *Dracula A.D. 1972* than Gibson's first Hammer film, *Crescendo*, which is nonetheless a very underrated psychological thriller with a musical theme.

Marking a stark contrast with the style of Terence Fisher, who largely eschewed complex cinematography, Gibson begins *A.D. 1972* with a wide variety of differing perspectives, beginning with a low-angle shot of a road supposedly in Hyde Park. As a tribute to Fisher, whose trademark it was, we are shown autumnal leaves blowing across the road as we are informed, in red Gothic script, that this is "A Hammer Production." The authority of such an announcement, in such a font and such a color, is crucial, given the eventual contrast with what will happen a short while later. The lettering suggests that this is a traditional Hammer offering, which it both is and is not. Two horses pulling a carriage appear around the corner; Dracula and Van Helsing are fighting on the roof. A long shot then shows the coach crossing Tykes Water Bridge, also in Aldenham Park, which had been often used before, notably in *Taste the Blood of Dracula*. A brief close-up of the spinning wheels, with their characteristic yellow spokes, then switches to an eye-level shot of the coach advancing over the bridge, as the narration announces, "The year: 1872, and the nightmare legend of Count Dracula extends its terror far beyond the mountains of Carpathia to the Victorian metropolis of London." Midway between this information, another shot takes over, this time from much higher up in a tree, which pans from right to left through a curtain of leaves and branches and follows the coach passing over the bridge. A close-up now focuses on the legs of the galloping horses, before shifting perspective to the rear of the coach, moving up to show Dracula and Van Helsing struggling on the roof before cutting to a view of the leather coupling that is soon to break. A different angle of one of the wheels follows, before we cut back to the top of the coach, and the narration concludes with the words, "the demon-vampire, Dracula." The moniker is of course pertinent to the occult context of his later resurrection. After the red lining of Dracula's cape billows out, Gibson returns to the coach coupling, and another angle showing first the front and then the back wheels.

Until now, we have been watching Eddie Powell and Peter Munt, who play Lee and Cushing's stand-ins, but Gibson now reveals the faces of both his stars fighting to the death. Again, he cuts to a spinning wheel, back to Lee and Cushing, and then to the leather strap of the coupling before another shot of the horses' legs seen from behind, and a shot of the coupling beginning to break. From the driver's seat, we watch the horses break free, then switch back to Cushing's reaction before cutting again to see Dracula push him off. Back on the roof, Dracula raises his hand to his face, realizing that the coach is about to crash, which it does, and a wheel spins off into the water of the lake, just as Gaynor's body will later roll into it not far from the bridge. Thus does Gibson set up another of the many parallels between 1872 and

Eight. Cameras and Choreography

And they're off!—horse wranglers setting off the coach for the prologue in *Dracula A.D. 1972*.

1972. (Intriguingly, Don Houghton would reuse this image in the script he wrote for the LP *Hammer Presents Dracula with Christopher Lee*: "The track was rock strewn and deeply rutted, and before long, one of the rear wheels came spinning off.")

In all, there are 24 cuts in the 70 seconds it has taken to reach this stage, and from this statistic alone, it becomes clear to the audience that Terence Fisher is not at the helm, for he would never have compiled such a kaleidoscope of rapid shots, filmed from so many different angles. The score by Mike Vickers, which I will be dealing with in more detail later, also connotes the difference, for the texture and sonority is very different from the orchestral style of James Bernard, who had scored all of Hammer's previous Dracula films.

The mood now changes, aided by a change in the pace of music. A long shot shows Johnny's ancestor (Christopher Neame) galloping to the scene of the accident on his horse. Gibson reprises the earlier high angle shot from the tree, its yellowing leaves quivering, as we follow Johnny's progress along the road below.

With Van Helsing lying on the ground, Gibson introduces the first of his zooms. Nine shots follow, which are alternately cut between Van Helsing and Dracula. The handheld camera creates a much greater sense of intimacy and urgency. The yellow spokes of the wheels, one of which has impaled Dracula, form the key color element in the passage. It is from behind one of the shattered wheels that Van Helsing watches Dracula disintegrate, and we observe Van Helsing's collapse through the wheel too. Yellow not only complements the color of the decaying leaves of the autumnal park, but also carries suitable connotations of decadence. (Yellow would become the characteristic color of the decade in which Stoker's novel was first published—even though the events in this prologue are set 25 years before that literary landmark.)

Van Helsing Senior has sustained a very nasty head wound. Never before had Cushing's Van Helsing been quite so badly injured, despite having been bitten by a vampire in *Brides of Dracula*. Dracula, of course, has considerable blood on his hands and mouth, but without any of the stylization we see at the end of *Dracula Has Risen from the Grave*, when he weeps bloody tears. This scene is much more realistic, and is really a Victorian Gothic version of what television audiences would see every week in *The Sweeney*. Even in this Victorian prologue, Gibson has updated his approach to Hammer's Dracula.

Alucard Senior now appears on horseback and arrives in time to watch Dracula's body disintegrate and register his horror at the sight. He then picks up Dracula's ring and puts it on, just as his descendant in 1972 will do in his Chelsea flat, as well as at the Black Mass. Why, however, is Alucard Senior here? It appears he knows that Dracula will be turned to dust, as he has furnished himself with a glass vial in which to scoop up the remains; but what would he have done if Dracula had been triumphant? Is Alucard Senior a vampire as well?

We cut to a long shot of a grassy hill, very painterly in its effect, and nicely framed on the left of the screen with the fragile stems of a willow. (Willows symbolize eternal life and the idea of rebirth.) Alucard is leading his horse toward St. Bartolph's Church, where Van Helsing is being buried. We glimpse a gathering of top hats seen at first out of focus, through a screen of leaves. The focus is then sharpened and we hear the minister reading the Service for the Burial of the Dead from the *Book of Common Prayer*.

Gibson cuts to an equally painterly shot of Mrs. Van Helsing's veiled profile. The veil cuts the screen in half, the golden light in the background now revealed to be the yellowing grasses through which Alucard has been walking. As the focus is pulled, he is revealed on the left of the screen (the left being traditionally the "sinister" or evil side).

A shot of the tombstone shows the inscription, "Requiescat in Pace Ultima"—"Rest in Final Peace," which highly unorthodox variant of the term presumably signifies that Van Helsing's family knows he has not been turned into a vampire. (Such awareness of Lawrence's activities is later confirmed by Lorrimer when he tells Jessica, "our family has a long tradition of research into the occult.") The white flowers on top of the coffin gradually sink below the frame in another rather painterly moment, and we then observe the coffin being lowered into the earth.

Alucard, meanwhile, sets about burying Dracula's ashes and inserting a fragment of the yellow wheel spoke into them. Again, he occupies the left of the screen. As he does this, the priest has reached the words: "thou most worthy Judge eternal, suffer us not, at our last hour, for any pains of death, to fall from thee." The main titles now begin, with Christopher Lee's name announced in red Gothic font. By this time in his career, Lee commanded top billing, whereas in the first Dracula film, it was Cushing who had enjoyed that privilege. Cushing's name follows, as the priest rearranges the original order of the Service, inserting its opening lines (taken from the Gospel of St. John) to emphasize the undead context of what is going on: "I am the resurrection and the life, saith the Lord: he that believeth in me, though he were dead, yet shall he live: and whosoever liveth and believeth in me *shall never die.*" (John Franklyn-Robbins, who reads these lines, subtly emphasizes the words I have

---

18   Continued   18

                     MINISTER (NOW O. O.V. AGAIN)
          ... O holy and merciful Saviour, Thou most
          worthy Judge eternal, suffer us not at our
          last hour for any pains of death to fall from
          Thee ...

And by this we are now on a M.S. of the figure - and recognise him to be ALUCARD. We can see that he stands beyond the churchyard boundaries, thus the ground beneath his feet is unhallowed.

                     MINISTER (O.O.V.)
          ... I am the resurrection and the life, saith
          the Lord: he that believeth in me, though he
          were dead, yet shall he live ...

From beneath his cloak ALUCARD takes the broken shaft and pushes it into the ground. On his face there is a cynical, evil smile. For, as the MINISTER's voice is heard to deliver the next lines, ALUCARD sprinkles the grey dust of Dracula's body onto the earth in front of the shaft.

                     MINISTER (O.O.V.)
          ... And whosoever liveth and believeth in
          me, shall never die.

Finally, the CAMERA moves in CLOSER STILL on ALUCARD, and we see that he has the medallion about his neck and the signet ring on his finger. And we MOVE FROM him to the shaft. HOLD ON THIS and

<u>SUPER OVER THE SHOT THE MAIN TITLES AND CREDITS, ETC.</u>

But as each CREDIT is shown, the shaft seems to age a little more, until, at the last CAPTION it is little more than an aged and rotting piece of wood.

As the last CREDIT fades ...

19   W. S.   CHURCHYARD   19

The SHOT is WIDENED to show the area near the grave. Everything has aged and is overgrown. There is an old tombstone on the site. On it is carved the inscription: TO THE MEMORY OF LAWRENCE VAN HELSING; BORN 1814. DIED SEPTEMBER 18th 1873. REQUIESCAT IN PACE ULTIMA'.

Houghton's Titles—the scripted version of the main title sequence for *Dracula A.D. 1972.*

placed in italics.) Alucard looks up and smiles, making the words even more significant. The title of the film is then presented in two parts. "*Dracula*" shares the red Gothic font of the two stars, as the camera pans from the gravestone to the sky (in fact passing the demolished stones of St. Bartolph's churchyard as it will be in 1972 rather than the Victorian cemetery as it was in 1872). A plane then appears from nowhere in the middle of the blue sky, center-screen, and "*A.D. 1972*" appears below "*Dracula*" in Roman capitals, which signify modernity in contrast to the historicism of the Gothic font.

This inspired way of suggesting the passage of a century was probably Gibson's own idea, as the draft scripts don't mention it. It is also yet another way in which Gibson references Hammer's sole previous coupling of Dracula and Van Helsing 14 years earlier, in 1958. Terence Fisher had begun that film with an imposing shot of a stone eagle outside Dracula's castle, around which the camera solemnly rotated to the accompaniment of James Bernard's celebrated "Dra-Cu-La" theme. The plane, therefore, should also be interpreted as a modernized version of that eagle, especially as the film itself has already been introduced with a snatch of Bernard's theme over the Warner Bros. logo, again summoning memories of Hammer's past Gothic glories. Mike Vickers's score immeasurably aids the intended shock of the time shift, while the imagery of the main titles picks up on the kind of irony Hammer had only used in their later posters for Dracula films ("Dracula Has Risen from the Grave—Obviously" and "You Can't Keep a Good Man Down," etc.) rather than the films themselves: The gantries of a crane form a cross, while a footbridge crossing a motorway, again suggests a crucifix. As we are now in the 1970s, nothing connotes that period better than brutalist concrete, which forms the walls of the underpass down which the camera now travels. We then cut to a shot of congested traffic in Chelsea, with London cabs and transit vans jostling for space, and then ride along a road lined with plate glass windows, which, unlike vampires, *do* cast reflections. Gibson concentrates on red objects: the scarlet triangle of a Bass Charrington beer logo outside a pub, a red London Transport double-decker, and the blood-red letters advertising a London Steak House, "Steak" suggesting its homophonic twin. Finally, a red No. 19 double-decker bus to Finsbury Park travels toward us behind the name of producer Josephine Douglas and eventually forms a suitably sanguine background for Gibson's director credit. We are thus prepared for the unfocused red background of a foregrounded wine glass. Pulling focus, the redness is revealed to be the clothing of Steve Price, the drummer of Stoneground. The glass is kicked over by a dancing shoe, and we find ourselves, *in medias res*, at the party.

Gibson sensibly uses the party to introduce us to the group's dynamics. We observe Laura dancing energetically with Johnny, demonstrating her obvious attraction to him, which explains her later enthusiasm for lying on the altar at St. Bartolph's. There are as many generational juxtapositions as Gibson can contrive: The Go-Go Dancer in silver hot pants, for example, has her legs foregrounded against the Crying Matron, who sits uncomfortably on the sofa in the background. Below the buffet table, the Hippie Girl and Hippie Boy are "still at it," as Joe puts it, while the bored Girl is shown munching nonchalantly on an apple, like Eve. Behind Joe, leaning against some furniture with his leg crossed in front of him, stands a *younger* dinner-jacketed party guest, which is an important detail, as this makes the booking of Stoneground in such an environment a little more plausible: there are younger, if admittedly still upper-class, guests present.

The camera zooms in to Johnny's face, establishing his importance, and later, when there is a close-up of Jessica, we observe him looking at her (with obvious intent). Again, he appears on the left-hand side of the screen. Before that, however, Joe snatches a tray from a waiter and begins to dance with Gaynor. Another shot of the Crying Matron and her husband is then juxtaposed with the active cymbals of the drum kit.

As it weaves among the dancers, Dick Bush's handheld camera makes us feel that we are part of the party ourselves. When Jessica and Bob smile at each other, and are on the verge of kissing, the camera tilts to the right (appropriately so, as these are "good" characters); after we are shown Laura still dancing wildly with Johnny, it then rights itself before moving between them to rest on Sal Valentino singing "You Better Come Through."

Charles now calls the police, and the teenagers discuss how long it will take for them to arrive. During this discussion we find out that the party is taking place on a Friday night. Unfortunately, this information somewhat muddles the rest of the film's chronology. For the succeeding events to tally, the party should really be taking place on a Thursday evening. The following morning, on which the teenagers meet up at the Cavern, would then be a Friday. Johnny suggests that they perform the Black Mass that night (the Feast of Belphegor, which is apparently "significant"). Laura's body is discovered the following day (Saturday), and Murray and Sergeant Pearson visit Van Helsing that evening. Gaynor is killed later on Saturday night, which brings us to Sunday morning, when Van Helsing visits Murray at Scotland Yard, and later than night dispatches Johnny in the early hours of Monday morning, later destroying Dracula on Monday night; but this chronology is disturbed by a Friday night party. If we correct this to Thursday, we realize that Dracula is actually only active for a mere three days.

When Johnny pushes a Chinese porcelain statue off the table on his exit, we cut to the bass player John Blakeley, smiling below his "Kaiser Cement" baseball hat, just as the helmeted policeman will do in response to the Hippie Boy's greeting of "Peace, man!"

Walking down King's Road in Chelsea, the group make their way to the Cavern coffee bar, which at the time of filming had been a restaurant called La Bersagliera ("The Ponte Vecchio," where Van Helsing will later propose to Jessica as a place to eat out together, is entirely fictional). Amid the purple light of the Cavern's interior, Johnny suggests they all try "something new but as old as time." Laura is wide-eyed with interest in what Johnny calls "way, way out." He stares directly at the camera in a close-up to explain what he has in mind: "A date with the Devil." It is unclear what he means by "a bacharel with Beelzebub," as "bacharel" is a Portuguese word for "bachelor," but Laura thinks all this "sounds wild!"

Once again, Houghton demonstrates his ability with terse dialogue:

"They do say it's dangerous … don't they?" Jessica says demurely.

"Yes, I believe they do," Johnny replies. He cuts a rather ironic figure here,

Cavern Coffee Bar A.D. 2024—372 King's Road, Chelsea (photograph by David Huckvale).

somewhat like Anton LaVey, the founder of the Church of Satan, though unlike LaVey, Johnny really does believe in the Devil as a supernatural entity rather than a mere metaphor.

"Do you really think it will work, Johnny?" Joe asks.

"No harm trying," Johnny assures him.

"Isn't there?" Jessica wonders.

Johnny then drives his sports car to his flat at the junction of Hillgate Place and Farm Place W8, which is actually in Kensington rather than Chelsea. On the journey there, Gibson includes a shot of another red double-decker bus, Johnny's Triumph Stag contrasting favorably with a passing Ford Anglia.

After we see Johnny enter his flat and place Dracula's ring on his finger, Gibson articulates the somewhat perfunctory but necessary conversation that follows between Jessica and Bob (necessary because it establishes Jessica's relation with Van Helsing, and that he is an academic anthropologist) by setting it in a car wash. The green light of the machine changes, significantly to red, and at first we don't know quite where we are. Gibson thus creates mild tension. We cut to an aerial shot looking down at the car entering the machine before Gibson takes us inside the car, looking at Jessica and Bob from the rear seat. An exterior shot confirms that this is a car wash before we return to the interior as Jess and Bob kiss. David Cronenberg would eroticize this environment in his controversial 1996 adaptation of J.G. Ballard's novel, *Crash*, in which Elias Koteas's necrophiliac Dr. Robert Vaughan has troubling sex with Deborah Kara Unger's nymphomaniac Caroline Ballard, surrounded by suggestive soap suds frothing up and surging against the windscreen and windows. Bob and Jessica's kiss under similar circumstances in *Dracula A.D. 1972* is innocent and affectionate, but nonetheless, the car wash could suggest the sexual encounters they might be having off-screen.

Bob then drives off, and the camera pans to follow his progress, stopping at the exit of the garage to indulge in a close-up of Jess's profile—on the *right* hand side of the screen. We also pass the arrow of a road sign pointing to the *left*—their direction of travel—both literally and in a metaphorical sense too—toward the Devil. As they move down Fulham Road, Gibson manages to include various other red objects in a single take: another double-decker, a red truck, a red Texaco sign, red paint on the walls of a building, a passing red car, a red telephone box, and red rear lights on cars and red traffic lights. All these might be said to indicate the blood that will soon be flowing.

After dropping Jessica off at her home (in Paulton's Square, SW3), Bob drives up to the adjoining King's Road, down which another red double-decker is traveling. At the same time, Van Helsing walks along the pavement on the *right*-hand side of the screen. Inside, Jessica calls upstairs for Mrs. Donnelly, forgetting that it is her night off, and Gibson puts his experience of filming in a narrow houseboat in *Goodbye Gemini* to good use in this confined space, placing the camera's POV upstairs looking down.

After dutifully knocking on the door of her grandfather's study, Jessica selects an appropriate book on the Black Mass for "a quiet bit of mind-blowing." A little later, and for the first and only time in a Hammer film, the newsagents W.H. Smith and Sons is mentioned, giving a further jolt to those who were hoping to be cocooned in the Victorian past. It is Van Helsing who says this, admonishing Jessica who is reading his copy of the "Tornhauser" *Treatise on the Black Mass* at his desk. He later delivers another of Houghton's splendid lines: "You seem to delight in deriding anything that is not on your particular wavelength," and then explains he has a lecture to prepare for the following day, which would make much more sense if the previous night's party had taken place on a Thursday. A university lecture on a Saturday seems unlikely; a Friday would be more likely.

Later that night, the friends arrive at St. Bartolph's. The establishing shot for the church shows the wooden fence that has been erected around it by the demolition firm, which goes by the somewhat inappropriate name of "H.L. Holderup." Jessica wonders about the "Ultima" inscription on her great-grandfather's gravestone, unaware of its vampiric significance. She also points out that the date of Van Helsing's death, September 12, 1872, was exactly 100 years ago to the day; but September 12, 1972, was actually a Monday, which doesn't fit in with the chronology at all. After being frightened by Joe in his skull mask, Jessica and Bob go inside and the ceremony soon begins.

Subtle details inspire subtle emotions: when Gibson cuts to a close-up of the tape recorder that is to provide the mood music for the ritual, he does so with a gentle Dutch angle. The only time Terence Fisher used this technique in a horror film was in *The Mummy*, where it certainly adds a considerable sense of unease to the shots of Felix Aylmer's Egyptologist, who can sense that the Mummy of Kharis is "coming" for him. Here, Gibson's Dutch angle is less extreme, but it nonetheless does its work as a signifier of unease. The tape deck is thus shown leaning to the *left*, and as the music begins, Anna and Gaynor, sitting around the pentagram with the others on the floor, smile at one another, so far unafraid. Johnny tells them to "dig the music, kids," while Laura lights a spliff. Joe is attracted to Laura's cleavage, and the handheld camera jerks from her close-up, to Bob, and then to Jessica. The drugs start to take effect as Johnny snarls, "Give yourself up to it."

Aldous Huxley, who had initiated the fashion for psychotropic drugs in the 1960s in his 1954 book, *The Doors of Perception*, had made far-reaching observations about the effects of mescalin when combined with music:

> And now someone produced a photograph and put a record on the turn-table. ...my body seemed to have dissociated itself almost completely from my mind—or, to be more accurate, though my awareness of the transfigured outer world was no longer accompanied by an awareness of my physical organism.... It was odd, of course, to feel that "I" was not the same as these arms and legs "out there," as this wholly objective trunk and neck and even head.[7]

Similar sensations begin to make themselves felt by the teenagers, and when Bob and Jessica kiss, Johnny is delighted, in the same way that Aleister Crowley regarded sex as a gateway to magical processes: "That's it," Johnny shouts. "That's it. Now you've got it together." His dialogue here is often criticized as being absurdly over the top, but all one has to do is compare it to Crowley's invocation of Pan to realize that, in this context, it isn't: "I rave; and I rape and I rip and I rend/Everlasting, world without end."[8] Nothing is too extreme when performing a Black Mass, not even "the silken shrouds of death."

As Johnny begins his invocation, Jessica beings to realize that something much more significant than a Friday night lark is taking place. Johnny is encircled by black candles, with the sacrificial goblet before him. The tape recorder then comes to the end of the spool. The tape clatters through the playback channel but, eerily, the music continues as the camera slowly zooms in to Johnny's face from below, which creates an almost abstract arrangement of triangular shadows. Jessica resists Johnny's invitation to help the demons, but Laura greedily asks to be taken in her place, as wind starts to blow dead leaves around the derelict building.

Echoing one of the publicity stills from *Taste the Blood of Dracula*, in which Lee and Linda Hayden are photographed before lights supposedly filtered through a stained glass window, the same colors are cast on the wall behind Johnny as he lifts Laura onto the altar. Another parallel with *Taste* occurs as Johnny raises the goblet and is surrounded by flashing orbs of light from the candles. (Sasdy always included flashing lights in his films for Hammer.) The orbs return when Johnny rotates the glass vial containing Dracula's ashes.

All the close-ups of the teenagers are on the *right* of the screen, while Johnny remains on the *left*. After Johnny slashes his wrist, Dracula's grave begins to pulsate and emit smoke, and as glutinous blood spills over Laura's neck and breast, everyone runs out. Johnny stands in the Gothic arch of the church door (again on the *left* side of the screen), watching the smoke rise from the grave. He pulls out the hundred-year-old wheel spoke (again on the *left*), and, like a genie let out of a bottle, Dracula gradually manifests from the cloud of dry ice in perhaps his most impressive Hammer resurrection. With his arrival, the natural order of things has been reversed, so Gibson films Lee on the *right* of the screen, with his first victim, Laura, on the *left*, which leads us to the famous shot of Dracula drinking her blood.

The following day, a No. 11 bus to Fulham makes its way down King's Road, past the Cavern coffee bar. Inside the Cavern, Greg, Gaynor, Anna, and Joe are discussing the previous night's events. Jessica and Bob turn up as well, followed by Johnny. Gibson then prefaces the imminent discovery of Laura's head with a shot of the Van Helsing gravestone before the camera pans out over the rubble of the churchyard. Four boys are playing football, while in the background we see a crane that is very like the one we saw in the main titles. The boys themselves foreshadow the ones often met with in the now notorious British Public Information films made later in the 1970s, such as *Lonely Water* (1973), *Play Safe* (1978), *Apaches* (1977), and *Children and Ponds* (1979). Shots of them are intercut with the conversation back in the Cavern, where Johnny has returned to his ironic Anton LaVey mode. He explains how he created the blood by means of a blood capsule: "they use them in TV and in the movies"—but obviously not the one he produces for his demonstration, because the result is more like weak cherry juice than the glutinous Kensington Gore that flowed the previous night. "Wait till Laura hears about it," Johnny says, smiling, upon which Gibson immediately cuts to a shot of her severed head in the churchyard. Two of the boys, filmed from below, stare down at what they have discovered, with another shot of the cruciform crane between them in the background. The use of children to discover a dead body had been used by Hammer before, notably in Peter Sasdy's *Countess Dracula* (1970). Here the idea is merely updated, and very effectively too.

Johnny hopes to entice Jessica with the offer of a ticket to the Jazz Spectacular at the Albert Hall, for which Gaynor says she would sell her soul. "No one has to sell their soul—not just yet, anyway," Johnny observes, but Bob informs him that he and Jessica have other plans, so Gaynor gets the ticket.

After the police discovery of Laura's body, we cut to a shot of the New Scotland Yard sign, which rotates before the then Met Police HQ on Broadway, This building had been opened in 1967, so was relatively new when Gibson filmed there. Edward Wright's rotating sign has since become world famous thanks to its many appearances in film and on television, and Gibson's shot of it was one of the first significant ones. An earlier sign had featured in the main titles of the London Weekend Television TV series *New Scotland Yard*, five of which were indeed scripted by Don Houghton between 1972 and '74. (Houghton wrote the very first episode, which also featured a bearded Barry Warren, who had played the clean-shaven vampire Carl Ravna in Hammer's *The Kiss of the Vampire* in 1964.) After showing us the spinning sign, Gibson cuts to a shot of Sergeant Pearson opening Murray's office door, which swings in the same direction as the sign outside, thus smoothing the edit into one continuous movement—another example of Gibson's fluid style. Murray discovers that Laura was part of a group that includes Jessica, and the name Van Helsing strikes a chord with him, as Lorrimer has helped the police once before in an extortion case connected to witchcraft. "He's a bit of a specialist in that sort of thing," Pearson explains. To enliven the scene, Gibson adds a shot of Pearson seen through the swinging spheres of the Newton's cradle, which Murray, lost in thought, sets in motion on his desk.

A largely black screen follows, which is in fact formed by the wall above the opening of the passageway through which Johnny is about to drive Gaynor on their return to his flat after the concert. We watch the car approach in the square of light, lower right, which eventually opens out to fill the screen as the car stops. After Johnny and Gaynor make themselves comfortable inside, we cut to Van Helsing's home, where Lorrimer, now wearing a cardigan, is shown pouring water into a glass of scotch. This is one of the ways in which the grammar of the film is so skillfully punctuated. We also see a clock, which informs us that it is quite late in the evening: 10:50 p.m. Murray and Cushing circle one another through their ensuing dialogue, adding movement to what could potentially be rather a static scene. They come to rest on opposite sides of the screen, permitting us a view of Sergeant Pearson in the background, who examines the Dracula woodcut and various anthropological artifacts hanging on the wall. A close-up of him confirms his interest in these unusual objects.

Back in Johnny's flat, things are becoming amorous. In a long shot from the far end of a corridor, Gaynor and Johnny are lying on the sofa. Gibson eventually zooms in to observe them kissing, and he keeps his camera moving when we return to Van Helsing's home. At first it moves gently to the left, as Lorrimer reaches out for a cigarette lighter before sitting down in the chair behind his desk. A close-up of him then emphasizes the significance of the information he gives Murray, that "the killer was trying to obliterate the real cause of death: vampirism."

Jessica now returns home to Paultons Square with Bob. For this scene, Gibson eschews Hammer's often-used "day-for-night" and films in actual darkness, further aiding the realism of his approach. After Jessica's interrogation by the police, Lorrimer asks Jessica about Johnny: "That name of his?" Another zoom pulls us closer to Cushing's face as Jessica replies, "Alucard?" The zoom informs us that Van Helsing is beginning to realize what this means, which is admittedly rather sluggish reasoning for a professor at London University.

Johnny now takes the distinctly stoned Gaynor to St. Bartolph's, but before her encounter with Dracula, Gibson cuts back to Lorrimer, who is filmed from behind, sitting at his desk, where he reverses the orthography of "Alucard" on a sheet of paper. One of the many "good ideas" Cushing credited Gibson with having appears a little contrived on a critical viewing, but it nonetheless works very well as a way of punctuating Van Helsing's line. He cups the paper in his hand, and after voicing his horrified realization that Johnny is "a disciple of Dracula," he crushes it, adding, "Oh my God!"

Gibson articulates Jessica's subsequent nightmare by cutting between her writhing on her bed and a gradual zoom shot of Dracula standing before the altar in St. Bartolph's. He stands within the magic circle, still left on the floor after the Black Mass, and growls, in a magnificent close-up, "She is not the one." Another zoom brings us closer to his face. "You have not learnt to obey," and closer still when he reiterates, "She is *not* the one." Assured by Johnny that he will secure Jessica for him later, Dracula accepts the offer of Gaynor, whom he wastes no time in biting. At this moment, we cut back to Jessica's bedroom, where she wakes up and screams. Van Helsing arrives to reassure her, just as did General Spielsdorf, whom Cushing played in *The Vampire Lovers* (1970), in which Pippa Steel's Laura had a similar kind of nightmare. Houghton also provides another memorable line for Jessica to say, after Van Helsing assures her, "The nightmare's over." "No," she replies, "I don't think it is."

We return to St. Bartolph's, where Dracula has drained Gaynor of her blood. One of Gibson's most fluid moments now occurs when Dracula descends the steps from the altar to accept Johnny's demand for immortality. The camera simultaneously pans to the left, behind Johnny's back, creating an appropriately anti-clockwise arc of movement. Dracula places his hand on Johnny's shoulder, looking down at him, as Johnny exposes his neck. We need see no more to realize what is going to happen next.

Back in the Paultons Square study, Gibson now has Van Helsing on the left of the screen, with the Dracula woodcut on the right, both illuminated by a dim beam of light. Again, the positioning indicates the reversal of the natural order of things. The divided screen also presents a powerful visual metaphor of the opposition of good and evil. In an extra domestic touch, Van Helsing has obviously made himself a mug of nighttime cocoa as he prepares to fight evil incarnate.

In the next scene, another of Gibson's parallels with the events of 1872 occurs when Johnny drives over Tykes Water Bridge in the fictional "Hyde Park" and bundles Gaynor's body out of his Triumph Stag. The body then rolls into the lake.

After the scene with the woman named Marjorie Baynes in the laundromat, we find ourselves, the following morning, in the church of Our Lady of Dolours, where Van Helsing fills his vial with holy water from the stoup. During the ensuing conversation between Van Helsing and Murray in his Scotland Yard office, Gibson largely relies on close-ups do the job, but one moment seems to echo a famous shot in Jacques Tourneur's 1943 film *I Walked with a Zombie*, in which the shadows of a Venetian blind are cast somewhat disconcertingly over the players, much as they are, very briefly, over Cushing's face when Murray stands up to close the blinds against the sunshine. Cushing also employs his cigarette to articulate the line: "100 years ago there was proof—positive proof" of a vampire living in London. (The cigarette proves a useful worry bead, as it would do in *The Satanic Rites of Dracula* and even in Michael Carreras's 1974 *Shatter*, Cushing's last film for Hammer.) The cigarette is soon replaced by the famous Cushing index finger: He stands up, and walks to the left. Then he turns to face Murray and, moving past him, eventually reaches the right of the screen. Such choreography articulates the information he is imparting, and makes the scene so much more interesting than it would be without it. One of his observations, however, is illogical. He suggests that if the stake were removed from Dracula's heart, he might walk again; however, the stake (or spoke) was obviously removed back in 1872, and Dracula wasn't resurrected then. Another "Cushing finger" underscores his concluding remarks: "This monster is strong again," he insists, slowly then stubs out his cigarette to create further tension when asking what Murray is going to do "unofficially" about the case. A close-up emphasizes the sincerity of his parting line after Murray says he hopes he's wrong about the entire affair: "I wish

I was, Inspector. I wish to God I was." A close-up of Murray's profile on the left of the screen ends the scene.

After we observe Bob return to the Cavern, Van Helsing is next seen through the window of his study, where he is preparing himself for the ordeal ahead by taking up his Bible, the vial of holy water, and a silver-bladed knife. We then cut to watch Bob climb over the fence of the Cavern just before a policeman appears in the background (another small but perfectly choreographed detail, which adds to the realism of Gibson's approach). Johnny is waiting for Bob inside.

With milk bottles caught in the moonlight behind him, Van Helsing later inspects the fence of St. Bartolph's. He then talks to Mrs. Donnelly from a phone box and discovers that Jessica has gone to the Cavern with Bob, whom Johnny has now initiated into the ranks of undead. Panicking, he runs down King's Road, which Gibson enlivens with a mirror image of him resting against a plate glass window. Yet another red double-decker passes him as he arrives at the Cavern, where a 180-degree pan reveals that it is now deserted—apart from Jessica's crucifix lying on the floor. As he realizes what has happened, a car horn serves as a scream. He runs down King's Road, passing the triangular Bass Charrington sign we saw first during the main titles. A shop dummy stares down impassively, and Van Helsing momentarily thinks this might be his granddaughter. Jessica will indeed resemble a shop dummy when hypnotized by Dracula later on. Yet another bus passes him, as we cut to a shot of the Essoldo cinema sign. Beneath this, he finally encounters Anna, who gives him Johnny's address. (The Essoldo, appropriately, became the venue for the stage version of *The Rocky Horror Show* in 1973. In *A.D. 1972* it appears that a horror film might be on the bill, as the film in question is advertised as having an "X" certificate. Either "Head" or "Dead" seems to be part of the title of another film advertised on the marquee.) Gibson takes care to reflect the Essoldo sign in the windshield of a car in the foreground.

Another 180-degree pan presents a Whistlerian panorama of sunrise on the Thames Embankment, with Battersea Power Station in the distance. Entering Johnny's flat, Van Helsing demands, "Where is she?" His stillness, and his position above Johnny, echoes the first appearance of Dracula at the top of the stairs in the 1958 film, only here the tables have been turned. The ensuing combat between Van Helsing and Johnny also has certain similarities with the culminating combat of 1958. Cushing is just as athletic as he was 14 years earlier, eventually forcing Neame's equally athletic Johnny into the bathroom. Johnny's subsequent demise in the shower also echoes Hitchcock's *Psycho* (1960) to some extent (particularly Gibson's repeated shots of the showerhead itself). He pulls the blind that shades the glass roof and is then filmed from above, reacting to the light. We then share his POV, and this alternation is repeated before he falls into the bath, where he perishes from the running water of the shower. In all there are ten shots and 24 cuts in this scene—15 cuts up to Van Helsing's appearance at the door, where he once again demands, "Where is she?" The *Psycho* shower sequence contains 78 shots and 52 cuts, so Gibson's scene is somewhat less complex, but it is still highly successful in its own terms, and light-years away from the style of Terence Fisher. The police arrive, and as they enter the flat we see Van Helsing reflected in the shaving mirror that has fallen on the floor after his use of it as a kind of light saber.

Essoldo Cinema A.D. 2024—King's Road, Chelsea (photograph by David Huckvale).

The final ten minutes of the film are introduced by a shot of Battersea Bridge, with two more red London buses driving over it in opposite directions, while smoke rises from the chimneys of Battersea Power Station. Maintaining the red leitmotif, Van Helsing walks down Cremorne Road, past a red pillar-box, and into Blantyre Street. Gibson here foreshadows Nicolas Roeg's more consistent inclusion of a red object in virtually every shot of *Don't Look Now* in 1973. In that film, redness foreshadows the scarlet raincoat of the dwarf killer who eventually slays Donald Sutherland's character. In *A.D. 1972*, it obviously refers to Dracula's sole nourishment. As he walks down Blantyre Street, Van Helsing passes two children playing patty-cake on a doorstep. This enhances the idea of the professor's vulnerability, and the idea of innocence being in great danger at this high point in the drama.

Van Helsing makes his way painfully through the gap in St. Bartolph's fence and immediately confronts the dead body of Bob lying by a tombstone, suggesting that Bob might have been trying to shelter from the sunlight. Entering the church, he then discovers Jessica lying on the altar. Unable to awaken her from the trance Dracula has induced in her, he attaches a crucifix around her neck before preparing his vampire trap in the graveyard. This is a technique Don Houghton would use again in *The Legend of the 7 Golden Vampires*, in which Lawrence Van Helsing uses sharpened bamboo stakes. In *A.D. 1972*, he resorts to the traditional variety, concealed in a specially dug pit. The work takes some time, and eventually the sun begins to set, which Gibson shows in a distinctly poetic shot of the Chelsea Embankment, which is aided immeasurably by Vickers's score.

Dracula now appears, foregrounded by cobwebs and black candles quivering in the supernatural breeze. Dracula continues to reverse the order of things, being filmed on the right of the screen as he awakens Jessica from her trance. Repelled by her crucifix, he pulls it off with evident discomfort, striking another classic pose as smoke rises from the undead flesh of his hand. As he prepares to bite Jessica, Van Helsing (who is now on the left-hand side of the screen) shouts his name and compels him to remember the events of 1872. Intercut with a zoom toward Dracula's face, Gibson reprises shots from the prologue. Just as he did in 1958, Dracula hurls a candlestick at his adversary, and is then shown confronting Van Helsing beneath a Gothic arch in a high-angle shot. It is at this moment that Lee inserted the modified line from Stoker's novel.

Ascending the spiral staircase to the choir gallery, we are reminded of the dangerous spiral staircase in Robert Wise's *The Haunting* (1963), as well as the ascent to the bell tower in Hitchcock's *Vertigo* (1958). Gibson might also have been thinking of Robert Siodmak's *The Spiral Staircase* (1946). Handheld camerawork (inevitable in such a confined space) aids the audience's involvement here. Instead of hurling Van Helsing to his death over the precipice of the broken balustrade, Dracula choses to throw him against the wall, whereupon Van Helsing produces his knife. Plunging this into the vampire's chest should destroy him, but, as happened in *Dracula Has Risen from the Grave*, Dracula survives. He doesn't pull the blade out by himself, however. That is a job for the hypnotized Jessica, who waits below. Gibson's impressive shot of the prone Count, taken from above, then zooms toward his face, again lending a dynamic energy to the scene.

Granted this temporary reprieve, Dracula pursues Van Helsing to the churchyard, where all that remains is for his nemesis to throw holy water into his face. This causes him to lose his footing and fall onto the sharpened wooden stakes, which a rapid zoom points out all too clearly. As soon as this happens, Van Helsing now reverts to the right-hand side of the screen, the proper order of things having been restored. Dracula gazes up at his adversary (from the left), and as Van Helsing thrusts his shovel onto the vampire's back, Gibson films him from below, echoing the imposing shot of Dracula's resurrection at the hands of Alucard only three days before.

With Dracula duly disintegrated, Van Helsing wraps his jacket around Jessica's shoulders, much as he had put his overcoat with its comforting fur collar around the little girl, Tanya, in the 1958 *Dracula*, and reiterates the inscription on Lawrence's gravestone, "Requiescat in Pace Ultima," which, for those who need a translation, is superimposed in red letters as "Rest in Final Peace."

Interlude 2: Cars, Locations and Costumes

THERE ARE VARIOUS DETAILS SPECIFIC to the period in which *Dracula A.D. 1972* was filmed that seem worth pursuing, especially as so many fans of the film regard it as an evocation of a time that never was. The early 1970s definitely did exist, even if they are now so clouded by fading memory or lack of experience that they might seem to have been an almost mythical period. In this interlude I want to address some of the realities of location, traffic, and costume.

Nothing dates a film quite so much as the forms of transport on display. Period dramas need to match cars with costumes, and sometimes the vehicles are stars of a film in their own right, as we see in *Genevieve* (dir. Henry Cornelius, 1953), *The Love Bug* (dir. Robert Stevenson, 1969), and *The Yellow Rolls-Royce* (dir. Anthony Asquith, 1964), not to mention James Bond's Aston Martin in *Goldfinger* (dir. Guy Hamilton, 1964). In the sphere of horror films, one thinks of the splendid 1930s vintage cars in *The Devil Rides Out*. In *A.D. 1972*, the modes of transport are less glamorous, perhaps, but no less evocative of the time. I have already mentioned the ubiquitous red London Routemaster buses we see traveling down King's Road, which, alongside the K2 telephone box, the Mini, and the London Underground map, are now considered to be one of Britain's most characteristic designs. As we have seen, Gibson exploits these vehicles not only to signal "London" but also to form part of his scarlet symbolism, which is so relevant to this story concerned with blood, but these, of course, are not the only vehicles.

During the main titles we are shown a crowded King's Road, in which taxi cabs and Minis jostle alongside a Ford Thames 10 cwt camper van. That vehicle would later often appear in *The Sweeney*, the TV series we have already identified as being foreshadowed by Gibson's film. We also see a Jaguar Mark X and a Hillman Avenger, which are both indicative of the fact that the U.K. still had a motor industry at this time. Inspector Murray and his sergeant are driven to Van Helsing's residence, and later to Johnny's flat, in a Hillman Hunter, where, nearby, a Hunter deluxe is parked. A still indicates that a subsequently unused scene was shot in which Van Helsing is driven there by Anna Bryant in her Hillman Imp, a less luxurious ride, no doubt, in contrast to the 1968 Mercedes 280 SL, which is also parked in Johnny's desirable street. A Super Imp is also to be seen. A brown Hillman Imp is parked opposite Van Helsing's front door in an earlier shot, sharing the frame with a Triumph Herald 1200 Saloon, a common sight in British fantasy television shows such as *Man in a*

Suitcase, *The Baron* and *The Champions*. When that period was re-created for *Heartbeat*, a police series set in the 1960s but made in the 1990s, the Triumph Herald was imported to help re-create the period.

Earlier in *A.D. 1972*, the police arrive to eject the gatecrashers at Charles's party in a Rover 3500, a car that was indeed used by the Met throughout the 1970s and '80s. As well as featuring in *The Sweeney*, the Rover 3500 is also to be seen in contemporaneous fantasy films such as *The Asphyx* (dir. Peter Newbrook, 1972), *The Mutations* (dir. Jack Cardiff, 1974), *The House that Vanished*, and *Vampyres* (both directed by José Ramón Larraz in 1973 and 1974).

Behind the bus that passes Johnny and friends as they enter the Cavern Coffee Bar after the Stoneground party, we see a Humber Hawk (Mark IV), another regular in British films during this period. In particular, it can be seen in *Scream and Scream Again* (dir. Gordon Hessler, 1970), in which Michael Gothard's "composite," Keith, is handcuffed to it, prior to pulling his hand off and leaving it dangling from the bumper. A Humber also appears in *The Magic Christian* (dir. Joseph McGrath, 1969), in which film Christopher Lee made a fleeting appearance as "Ship's Vampire."

We also see several Ford Anglia 105Es in *A.D. 1972*, notably when Johnny drives across Battersea Bridge toward his flat (in quite the wrong direction if we are being

Shot but not seen—Anna Briant (Janet Key) delivers Van Helsing (Peter Cushing) to Johnny Alucard's flat in her Hillman Imp in an unused scene.

literal with regard to the actual locations used). Anglia 105Es were first introduced in 1959, and with their American styling, including tailfins, chrome grille, and "eye" headlamps, they became very popular. Indeed, this car is the pride and joy of Richard Todd's John Cummings in John Guillermin's thriller, *Never Let Go* (1960). When his brand new but uninsured Anglia is stolen by Peter Sellers's unscrupulous villain, Lionel Meadows, Cummings is driven to distraction by the loss, and the rest of the film is devoted to his increasingly desperate attempts to retrieve his pride and joy. In *A.D. 1972*, we only see Anglias in the background. They ceased production in 1968 and so were already becoming old-fashioned, as was inevitable for such a self-consciously "stylish" design. The Citroën Dyane 6, in which Bob drives Jessica to and from her grandfather's house, was much more up to date, if less luxurious. Its green paintwork, adorned with purple and gold decoration, was how Gibson interpreted what Houghton had originally described as a "dazzle-coloured mini car."[1] Unsurprisingly, this car featured more often in continental productions, and its striking contrast to the more familiar British cars on display marks out its owners' hippie credentials. As Bob drives Jessica home after their visit to the carwash, they pass an Alfa Romeo 1750, a vehicle that was indicative of the rising popularity of foreign cars at the time, but British cars, like the Triumph 2000, which Bob passes, nonetheless remained ubiquitous.

Johnny drives a much flashier, saffron-yellow Triumph Stag, which model (and color) had previously appeared in *Diamonds Are Forever* (dir. Guy Hamilton, 1971), but there are other even sportier cars in the King's Road, such as a Marcos 3-Litre GT, which drives past a parked Ford Mustang. That highly unusual vehicle suggests the affluence and modernity of the location more eloquently than anything else in the shot, which Gibson obviously intended. Mini Coopers and Mini Minors are also as indicative of the period as Mary Quant's miniskirts, so we are bound to encounter them more often. The latter passes the Chelsea Male clothing store in King's Road. Van Helsing also walks past a green-topped Mini on his way home, an up-to-date model of which was, remarkably, parked a few doors down when I visited Paultons Square myself in 2024. This was such a coincidence, I was forced to wonder if a fan of the film, who realized the connotations of the street in which he lived, had bought this model in tribute to it.

The locations of *A.D. 1972* are as important as the cars to create the realism sought by Houghton and Gibson. Paultons Square had several notable former residents before Van Helsing took up residence at No. 12. Gavin Maxwell, author of *Ring of Bright Water*, lived at No. 9, while Jean Rhys, most famous for *The Wide Sargasso Sea*, her prequel to *Jane Eyre*, lived in Flat 22. Samuel Beckett also spent 11 years there at No. 48, and the artist Augustus John lived at No. 45. Built on the site of a farmer's market, the square has a central garden, enclosed by iron railings, and it is along the side of this garden that Van Helsing walks on his way home.

Paultons Square adjoins King's Road, so named as it was originally a private road for Charles II when he was traveling to Kew; it wasn't made into a public thoroughfare until 1830. Among the notable people who lived there are film director Sir Carol Reed and entertainer Sir Peter Ustinov. Johnny's flat, however, is further north at Hillgate Place in Notting Hill. With its passageway leading to Johnny's inner sanctum, it is ideally tucked away for such a secretive character.

Prior to his visit there, Van Helsing stops off to collect holy water from Our Lady of Dolours in Fulham Road. It is appropriate that he should have selected a Roman Catholic church, as the Anglican church has always been nervous with regard to superstitions, as Stoker points out in his novel when an old lady accosts Jonathan Harker in his room at the Golden Krone Hotel at Bistriz, imploring him on her knees not to venture to Castle Dracula:

> She then rose and dried her eyes, and taking a crucifix from her neck offering it to me. I did not know what to do, for, as an English Churchman, I have been taught to regard such things as in some measure idolatrous.[2]

Catholicism remained rather more in touch with superstition, and it is anyway much more difficult to steal holy water from an Anglican church. In the vestibule of Our Lady of Dolours it is there for the taking from the stoup. We see only a glimpse of the interior, but it is an important moment, and it requires acknowledgment.

There is also one short scene shot in a pub, in which Bob asks Jessica what film she would like to see that night. Houghton's original idea was to make a more specific reference to vampire films here, suggesting Bob takes Jessica to see either *Lust for a Vampire*, or a film that doesn't actually exist, called *The Monster Takes a Bride Bride*[3]; but this was wisely dropped, along with showing them emerging from an Odeon cinema. The pub scene is very short, which suggests that it may well have been filmed in a real pub. Caroline Munro recalls that the exterior of the Chelsea Potter pub in King's Road, once frequented by Mick Jagger, Jimi Hendrix, and David Bowie, was used.[4] The pub sign today shows the most famous Arts and Crafts Chelsea potter, William De Morgan, crafting one of his creations, though it was originally called the Commercial Tavern, and was renamed in 1958 due to David Rawnsley's nearby Chelsea Pottery. If shots of the exterior were filmed, they were cut from the finished print, though the interior shot featuring Bob and Jessica could indeed have been filmed there.

Chelsea Male, the boutique adjacent to the Cavern Coffee Bar, might well have provided some of the clothes worn by Johnny and his friends. Again, some of the costumes in the film foreshadow the glam-rock fashions that were yet to come with the likes of Slade, Mud, and the now disgraced Gary Glitter, who all jettisoned the intensity of '60s popular music, diving instead into hedonism and self-indulgent superficiality. Anna wears a sparkling silver creation covered in sequins, with matching headband and a butterfly brooch, and the go-go girl, played by Maureen Flanagan, wears silver leather hot pants, which had begun to replace miniskirts. Johnny, whom Houghton originally described as "a dark, Byronic-looking boy who wears extravagant Georgian style clothing,"[5] wears a frilled shirt, plum colored velvet jacket, and fedora at the party, changing the frilled shirt for a red one, thus conforming to Houghton's Byronic requirements. No one wears old military uniforms, which were in such vogue in the '60s, but Michael Kitchen's Greg does wear an Indian brocade jacket over his orange T-shirt, while Joe's monkish habit certainly reflects the fashion for caftans and flowing robes, a purple velvet example of which Jessica wears for the Black Mass, along with a matching head scarf. Caroline Munro wore her own thigh-length boots for the party scenes, but the fringed and leather clothes were "pulled from the wardrobe room." She explained, "Everybody wore a fringe! I owned a lot of fringe jackets and things."[6] Stephanie Beacham's clothes were specially made, however. Marsha Hunt wears large artificial poppies in her hair like enormous earrings, which is reminiscent of Alphonse Mucha's design "Moon and the Poppy," or the poppy girl in one of Carlos Schwabe's designs for Baudelaire's *Les fleurs du mal*. This is significant because the early 1970s saw a revival of interest in Art Nouveau and Symbolist artists, until then distinctly out of vogue. (A major exhibition of French Symbolist art opened at the Hayward Gallery in London on June 7, 1972.)

Peter Cushing, who often wore clothes in private in which he had appeared on film, manages to combine a contemporary style with references to the 19th century. The watch chain and fob on his waistcoat does not preclude a conventional turn-down collar and tie, raincoat, and, when digging his trap for Dracula, a suede sports jacket. When visited by the police at his home, he is found wearing a more comfortable beige cardigan, with the wings of his bow tie tucked neatly under his collar. Houghton described Michael Coles's Inspector Murray as "a new wave" policeman[7]; accordingly, he wears fairly long '70s hair with sideburns, and a fashionable striped jacket with high-cut lapel. When outside, he wears a suede overcoat with a luxurious fur-lined collar. David Andrews's sergeant is equally dapper in a dark three-piece suit, a tie decorated with the kind of pocket watch Van Helsing still uses, and an appropriately scarlet handkerchief in his top pocket. The collar of his shirt is fashionably wide but mercifully lacking in rounded corners.

Bob wears the outfit that has dated least, as denim has never gone out of fashion, though the cravat and sleeveless suede jerkin belong more properly to the '70s.

Nine

Décor and Music

AMONG THE MAIN ATTRACTIONS OF Hammer's Gothic horror films are the company's incredibly detailed sets. Bernard Robinson, Hammer's original art director, was famed for making silk purses out of many a sow's ear. Along with the many excellent composers who provided the accompanying music, he was essential to the success of the early films. Other designers took over after Robinson's demise, and Scott MacGregor's interiors for *Taste the Blood of Dracula* reveled in Victorian bric-a-brac above and beyond the demands of the story, particularly in the drawing room of Geoffrey Keen's William Hargood. Alas, MacGregor's sets for *Scars of Dracula*, which followed soon after, failed to live up to that standard. Dracula's fire-damaged castle in that film was as pantomimic as the script and performances, but Don Mingaye's ruined church set for *Dracula A.D. 1972* is surely one of Hammer's greatest Gothic achievements. There is nothing here to give away the fact that it is a fake, constructed at Elstree Studios, so convincing is the imitation of the church's derelict Gothic interior. Mingaye and his art department spared no trouble to create the other highly detailed sets and props, which give *Dracula A.D. 1972* such realism.

The opening party scene required a traditional upper-class setting, so the walls are covered with an ivory wallpaper with acanthus decoration, on which are hung oil paintings of landscapes and portraits in generous gilt frames. The ceiling cornice is decorated with dentils, while the windows are dressed with gold damask drapes, swagged with fringed and elaborately pleated pelmets. A mahogany buffet table is illuminated by a candelabra and decorated with a silver swan-necked dish. Chandeliers hang from the ceiling. A marble Adam-style fireplace, on the mantelpiece of which stand two large Chinese ginger jars, occupies the far wall. An even larger ginger jar can be seen behind Philip Stewart when he talks to the police. Classical columns and arched niches punctuate the architecture, and the doorways are topped with classical pediments. Traditional sofas, chairs, occasional tables, and lamps in the form of classical vases furnish the room. On top of the baby grand piano in the corner, not only does another go-go dancer cavort but there is also a selection of sheet music, one piece of which is a piano reduction of the principal themes of E. Thorne's simplified solo version of Rachmaninoff's Second Piano Concerto, published by Boosey & Hawkes, which the piano itself is presumably rather more accustomed to play than what Cory Lerios is performing on it. The bearded man painting a psychedelic decoration onto a mirror, leaving space for his own face to appear, seems to be referencing the hippie musical *Hair*, which premiered in 1967, four years before *A.D. 1972* started filming. The colors used are very similar to the red, greens, and yellows of the original *Hair* poster.

Mingaye has explained that his inspiration for the interior of the Cavern coffee bar came to him during a wander through a field one morning: "I walked through a load of lovely cobwebs and thought, 'what a good idea, I'll use that in the set.' I suggested it to Josephine [Douglas], and it was agreed. Then Josephine decided to put a jukebox in the middle of it, which seemed terribly wrong and didn't work. We made alcoves round and cobweb things and tried to link it to some sort of Dracula-type atmosphere."[1] Part of that atmosphere is helped by the red lamps, which illuminate the entrance sign outside. Inside, the screens behind Johnny reflect the suitably decadent violet light.

Johnny's flat, which later so impresses Gaynor ("It's really fantastic," she enthuses), features white walls and black fittings. The artwork is also predominantly white and black, with appropriately blood-red decorations. One of them is emblazoned with "SUS!" which is appropriate, implying something or someone suspicious. Johnny is most certainly that. Another large painting features Iranian imagery of massed turbaned warriors on horseback; but along with the black lampshades and chrome spotlights, Johnny also has a taste for the antique, like many a '60's hippie, so he also possesses an old grandfather clock, a Tiffany lamp hanging over his billiards table (with plenty of blood-red balls), a glass obelisk, and the head of an Indian Buddha. The poster behind the billiard table is for the short film *Muerte al invasor* ("Death to the Invader"), directed by Tomás Gutiérrez Alea and Santiago Álvarez in 1962. The title alone is sufficiently appropriate to accompany Johnny's thoughts when Van Helsing bursts in upon him. Of course, he also has his own coffin, but never has an opportunity to use it as a vampire. On top of the coffin is a pile of *Time Out* magazines, the uppermost one of which displays the image of a face that could well be from a horror film, while at the other end of the coffin is

Poster for *Hair*.

"Come in for a bite!"—Johnny Alucard's bachelor pad at 75 Hillgate Place, Notting Hill (photograph by David Huckvale).

a copy of Bevis Hillier's 1969 volume on Art Nouveau posters. Johnny decorates his Dracula shrine with two large spherical glass paperweights, and his purple curtains, edged with a Greek key motif, echo the decadent color scheme of the Cavern. The bathroom in which he meets his end is decorated with suitably black tiles.

Van Helsing's home in Paultons Square is a more homely version of the opening party set. In the hall, a kilim rug (always rather an expensive furnishing accessory indicative of middle-class surroundings) leads to the staircase. Potted plants and a brass gasolier add extra style. Similar wallpaper to that of the party house (carefully reprised in *The Satanic Rites of Dracula*) along with paintings (watercolors of maritime scenes) once more prevail. In the study, the wallpaper is darker, as is appropriate for a gentleman's private retreat, and the paintings (including the portrait of Laurence Van Helsing over the fireplace) are in oils, more elaborately framed. The crescent built-in bookcase, which would also be reprised in *The Satanic Rites of Dracula*, is in fact an echo of the similarly curved one in *Taste the Blood of Dracula*, which we see in the study of the equally scholarly Jonathan Secker. Antique furniture and white-painted woodwork effectively contrast with Johnny's black tiles and eclectic modern style.

Van Helsing's old-world comforts match his waistcoat, watch chain, and bow tie. On his main desk (he has two), in front of a sculpture of an eagle with spread wings, stand a microscope and magnifying glass, appropriate for an anthropologist.

"Bring them back to this mausoleum?"—the Van Helsing residence at 12 Paultons Square, Chelsea (photograph by David Huckvale).

Egyptian imagery has been pinned to the back wall, along with a large map of the world, and leaning against the wall are some anatomical diagrams. There is also an esoteric painting hanging over a tallboy on which stand two chunky inkwells with brass stoppers, and hanging next to several African masks and artifacts is the Dracula woodcut that so intrigues Sergeant Pearson. A medieval woodcut of the Devil surrounded by witches hangs below the woodcut, against which images of Assyrian and Egyptian artifacts have been placed. The study also displays a chess set, potted plants, and copies of two Renaissance engravings of the cosmos from Andreas Cellarius's 1660 *Celestial Atlas*.

A lamp, with classical column for a base, stands by the door, complementing the elaborate ormolu light fittings on the wall. It is also rather pleasing to notice that when Murray and his sergeant visit, a black cat can briefly be seen asleep on the sofa below the large allegorical oil painting by the door. When we later see Van Helsing sitting at his desk, reversing Alucard's name, a partially obscured typescript

Andreas Cellarius, *Celestial Atlas*, 1660.

(perhaps the lecture he mentions earlier) includes the words "[equi]torial Borneo" and "the afterlife," which do indeed suggest an anthropological subject—yet further evidence of the attention to detail in the production design department. The desk also displays a miniature skull, through the eye sockets of which a snake winds in occult fashion.

Inspector Murray's office is rather more sophisticated than those that will later appear in *The Sweeney*, complete with potted plants, executive toys, and of course the essential framed photograph of Queen Elizabeth II on the wall.

Music

Mike Vickers had originally worked with the pop group Manfred Mann before becoming a freelance arranger for the Beatles, the Scaffold, Tom Jones, and Cilla Black. With the arrival of the Moog synthesizer (he was probably the first person in England to own one in 1968), he became something of a pioneer, and electronic music (though not, ironically, by Vickers himself) does indeed rub shoulders with the jazz, pop, and more traditional idioms in the soundtrack of *Dracula A.D. 1972*.

Vickers is not credited as "Mike" (how he is usually known), but the rather more formal "Michael Vickers," and the style of the music he composed for *A.D. 1972* is not really the kind of thing spaced-out teenagers were listening to in the 1970s. The "rock" idiom here is more indebted to the big-band sound of Stan Kenton, with its punchy, syncopated brass punctuating a quartet of saxophones that "swing" the main theme during the opening credits.

As the words "A Hammer Production" appear on screen, a snare drum, soon joined by a tom-tom, sets up the galloping rhythm that helps create the momentum of the advancing horses. We are in the traditionally funereal (or tragic) key of C-minor, in which the cellos and horns then intone the main theme. The cellos play the first two notes and the horns play the triplet and beat of the second half of the opening phrase, while the cellos continue beneath it with a counterpoint motif. As this section is set in the 19th century, Vickers keeps the rhythmic element as foursquare as he can, restricting the instrumentation to traditional acoustic timbres, though the tom-toms do suggest that we are not in James Bernard territory here. The second half of the opening phrase is harmonized with a descending chromatic passage in the cellos, chromatic scales always providing a sense of increased anxiety, as they distort the sense of tonality. The theme is then intoned again, this time the horns playing the complete phase, the bass guitar and piano joining in with the cellos. The narration now begins. When it reaches "…the final confrontation between Lawrence Van Helsing…." Vickers repeats the theme, adding the sepulchral timbre of the electric organ playing the two-chord accompaniment. A shot of the spinning wheels of the coach is emphasized by a shiver on the suspended cymbal and a fortissimo chord in the trombones, which slide, somewhat jazzily, down a tone. The trombone slide is repeated as we see the leather traces that are soon to snap. When this happens, the horns glissando through an octave and the cymbals shiver once again, and as the horses gallop away, the piano, trombones, bass guitar move through an ascending scale which is decorated with triplet figuration in the cellos, reaching a climax as Dracula puts his hand before his face and the coach crashes into a tree. A fortissimo chord for all brass and organ, along with plenty of percussion, underscores the impact of the crash. The wheel rolls into the lake and we cut to Alucard's ancestor riding toward the scene of the crash on his horse. He has his own theme, rising up five notes, and to contrast with all the preceding mayhem, Vickers scores this for two horns and the wind section, rather quieter.

The camera now zooms slowly in to Van Helsing, lying on the ground. For this, the organ and piano again play the two chords that support the main theme, which, after some syncopation, are punctuated by trills from the wind section as we zoom in and out of focus on the spinning wheel of the crashed coach, toward which Van Helsing crawls. As we catch our first sight of Dracula's cape behind the wheel, a semitone trombone glissando, supported by a timpani roll, begins its association with Dracula throughout the score. A snare drum triplet then introduces a reprise of the main theme as Van Helsing makes his way further toward the coach.

Suddenly, Dracula appears, pierced by the spoke of one of the coach wheels, which Vickers emphasizes with fortississimo glissando from the brass. (This is an effect often used in big-band orchestrations, such as those by Stan Kenton, but perhaps the most famous use of it effect, albeit for very different purposes, occurs at the end of Henry Mancini's *Pink Panther* theme.) As Dracula staggers around, this glissando is repeated two more times. The triplet agitation that began this cue continues, as Dracula reaches out his hand to grab Van Helsing, and as he pushes his face away from him, yet another glissando effect occurs.

We now cut to Alucard Senior galloping toward the action, his theme again on horn and wind, and the dynamic mezzo forte. The contest between Dracula and Van Helsing now reaches its peak, the falling semitone that symbolizes the vampire being repeated four times, gradually growing louder until slower triplets and trills on the wind emphasize Van Helsing's struggle to stake Dracula through the heart. As he achieves this, a fortississimo chord for full orchestra exploits the tritone harmony James Bernard had used for his "Dra-Cu-La" chord. The tritone (which is notated as either an augmented fourth or diminished fifth), is also known as "diabolus in musica" ("the devil in music,") and is a prerequisite for all horror film composers. Bernard's "Dra-Cu-La" chord can of course be played in any pitch, but if we think of it as G-D flat, we can compare it to Vickers's chord. Bernard slips in an added discord against the upper D (a clashing C). Vickers, however, inverts that relationship, clashing an A against the G. This seems to be a homage to the composer who preceded him. The chord is cut abruptly off in the brass and wind but allowed to dwindle very effectively in piano cello and bass guitar as Dracula gasps, and is repeated as he expires.

Philip Martell recorded all of Vickers's score as written, which can be heard on the GDI CD release of the score, but there are certain changes made in the final edit on the actual soundtrack of the film. The first of these changes now occurs when Alucard dismounts and walks toward Dracula's corpse. Vickers scored this with a lonely restatement of Alucard's theme on flute, but during the recording session it was decided to accompany the theme with quiet chords on the organ. (These chords aren't in the MS score.) Instead of this much more effective scoring, a rather obvious, almost cartoon-like section for piano, introduced by a string tremolo, has been inserted. This lasts only seven seconds before we return to what Vickers intended for Dracula's disintegration, which consists of his falling semitone in the brass, with threatening percussion punctuated by the two chords that accompanied the main theme, played on piano.

Another interpolation on the soundtrack occurs after Van Helsing collapses and Johnny pulls the wheel spoke from Dracula's ashes before putting on Dracula's ring. Again, Vickers's original music can be heard on the CD, where we again hear Alucard's theme on flute, accompanied by chords in the organ. On the soundtrack, however, different music replaces this: a low trombone with harp interjection, that in fact interrupts the thematic unity of the score without adding anything significant to the action. This interpolation lasts 21 seconds, but then returns to Vickers's score, as Alucard produces the glass vial into which he will scoop the ashes. To accompany this, the electric guitar, which plays Dracula's falling semitone, is instructed to "use foot volume pedal with silent attacks—*pp*—*f*." This is repeated four times. The pitch is raised by a semitone for the fifth time before a quietly snarling brass chord brings the cue to an end.

There is no music in the next scene depicting Van Helsing's funeral, Vickers sensibly leaving the sound effects of the tolling bell and the eloquent words of the burial service to speak for themselves. The main title sequence is introduced with a roll on timpani and bongos, which rises through a crescendo until the jet plane appears in the sky, when the introductory chords of the main theme are played by bass, cello, percussion, organ, piano, trombones, and trumpets. Vickers dispenses with violins and violas throughout his score, replacing them with a quartet of saxophones, which soon join in with the syncopated statement of the main theme, previously heard in foursquare rhythm in the prologue. The syncopation, along with the timbre, signifies modernity. After repeating the theme, a subsidiary theme arrives, following classic "song" form, followed by a reprise of the opening theme, after which we cut to the Stoneground number. The two punchy chords that open the main title music might be regarded as a modernization of the effect created by Wagner in his Siegfried Funeral March in the third act of *Götterdämmerung*. Two peremptory chords of C-minor punctuate this march and provide a musical equivalent to the shock of death itself.

The next cue accompanies Johnny back in his flat, as he examines the vial of Dracula's ashes and Dracula's ring. An electric organ, cellos, and basses play a C-minor chord with an added seventh, which is similar to the so-called "spy" chord (much used in James Bond music). The latter is constructed in the same way, but has an extra major ninth on top. Vickers's chord nonetheless adds a further sense of modernity and "coolness" to the scene, while the electric guitar plays the falling semitone that is by now already associated with Dracula. Vickers marks this "Use foot volume pedal. Silent attacks"—though in the recording the first note is more audible than he perhaps intended. A bass clarinet adds to the mysterious texture, before horns and flutes bring this short cue to a close.

The rest of reel two requires no music (apart from the radio music heard in Bob's Citroën). It returns in reel three, as Van Helsing contemplates his grandfather's book and the woodcut of Dracula in his study. A bass clarinet (always useful for the invocation of mystery) begins this cue with a descending scale (again in C-minor), which is followed by the "Dracula" semitone on piano, cellos, and basses. When Van Helsing looks at the Dracula woodcut, a muted solo horn snarls out a three-note motif, which significantly encompasses the tritone, without which no horror film score would be complete. As Van Helsing rubs the temples of his forehead, horns inject more rhythmic movement with two repeated chords, before a breathy flute adds more "spy" texture with its upwardly ascending fragment. The final chord is sustained until Bob's car drives up outside St. Bartolph's in the next scene, thus joining the two scenes together. Philip Martell, always sensitive to the mechanics of this sort of thing, noted on the score "out under car"—i.e., fade out the music out under the sound of the car engine.

Vickers's most avant-garde music is reserved for the Black Mass scene in reel four, but before this begins, the opening stages of Johnny's ceremony are accompanied by a track from *An Electric Storm*, by the David Vorhaus group, the White Noise, first released in 1969. The track chosen was, appropriately, "Black Mass: An Electric Storm in Hell," which was something of a landmark in electronic music at the time, predating the Moog synthesizer, when the creation of so-called "radiophonic" music was a laborious process requiring tape editing and sound filtering. Inspired by one of the Unit Delta Plus lectures given by Delia Derbyshire (who had electronically realized Ron Grainer's famous *Dr. Who* theme at the BBC Radiophonic Workshop), Vorhaus, himself a electronics engineer, invited Derbyshire and her BBC colleague Brian Hodgson to collaborate with him. The resulting album has been described by Matthew Murphy as a mélange of "musique concrète effects, weird bits of radio theater, and long stretches of gothic horror."[2] "Electric Storm in Hell" is "a spirited cacophony layered thick with percussion, funereal chanting, and the tormented screams of the damned."[3] As the sleeve notes continued, "MANY SOUNDS HAVE NEVER BEEN HEARD—BY HUMANS: SOME SOUND WAVES YOU DON'T HEAR—BUT THEY REACH YOU. 'STORM STEREO' TECHNIQUES COMBINE SINGERS, INSTRUMENTALISTS AND COMPLEX ELECTRONIC SOUND. THE EMOTIONAL INTENSITY IS AT A MAXIMUM." Vorhaus himself explained: "I use voices a lot too, but not as conventional vocals. I always use a lot of voices, and if somebody having an orgasm in the background is used as part of one of the waveforms, it makes the sound more interesting, without the listener actually knowing what they're hearing."[4] Internet fans of such psychedelia inevitably employ the rhetoric of the period in which it was released:

> This is no ordinary album. An Electric Storm will take you to outer space, into the future, tear your brain apart and then give it back; stimulants should be taken with caution guys. It's electronic and psychedelic yet still slots in nicely into any psyche, kraut or space rock fans collection. ... After a while it feels like a boulder rolling around and around in a trashcan, it's pan-tastic (sorry) and gets pretty weird in there. Piercing screams cry out as lost souls implode and lasers blast as we witness the destruction of all space and life.[5]

It is thus the perfect way to start off the satanic ceremony in *Dracula A.D. 1972*, where it is ostensibly played on a portable reel-to-reel tape recorder that Joe switches on, but when the tape runs out, the electric storm continues to rage, suggesting that demonic forces have now taken control of the proceedings. It is only when Johnny says, "I call on Jessica Van Helsing," that Vickers brings in his own music under the electric storm.

Here, he requires the improvisatory skills of his musicians. Again in C-minor, the organ and Moog synthesizer are given specific chords (those seventh, proto-"spy" chords, already discussed) but the saxophones are given the ad lib instruction to follow the notes in the organ chords but "stay in high register. Start fairly sparsely, gradually play more." Similarly, the percussion and vibraphone perform "ad lib rolls, rattles and tremolos." Gradually, the electric storm is faded out, and when Johnny picks up the glass vial, the electric guitar returns to play the falling "Dracula" semitones (Vickers carefully indicates the flashes the vial makes). By this time, all we hear is Vickers's improvised sax and percussion track, which is "fairly busy by now" when Johnny is seen pouring Dracula's ashes into the goblet. While this improvised cue continues, Vickers superimposes another cue over it, which articulates the action. Timpani thunder out a rhythm with the bass guitar accompanied by conga drums and tam-tam as we cut to Dracula's grave, which is now beginning to emit smoke. The action is accompanied by a repeated falling semitone, this time sliding down on sinister trombones. Vickers then builds up to the shock of Johnny's flick knife with fortissimo chords in the horns and brass, and a note from the horns underscores his line "by the six thousand terrors of hell…" after which syncopated and fortissimo brass and horns underscore the shock of Johnny slashing his wrist. We alternate between the ceremony indoors and the grave outside; each time we cut to the latter, the semitone motif accompanies it.

An up-tempo riff based on the opening chords of the main title music then accompanies the hurried exit of the horrified onlookers, as the goblet of blood spills onto Laura's breast.

Now begins the most experimental aspect of the entire score with the materialization of Dracula from his grave. For this sequence, Vickers employs a vast tone cluster, which gradually rises in pitch and volume (the final three bars in the cellos and basses slithering down through a serpentine glissando) in the manner of Krzysztof Penderecki's *Kosmogonia*, which had been composed only two years earlier in 1970. What better way to announce the arrival of the arch-vampire in a swinging Chelsea graveyard than with this tribute to musical modernism? Vickers instructs his players to "START FROM LOWEST NOTE POSSIBLE, GRADUALLY ASCEND OVER 12 BARS ENDING ON WRITTEN NOTE," which results in a gigantic C-minor chord for full orchestra. All that remains (in this cue at least) is for Dracula to bite Laura, which he does to note clusters on the organ oscillating semitones and a repeated descending figure on the electric guitar, to remind Dracula that he is now in the 20th century. As Dracula sinks in his fangs, the horns and brass intone a macabre fanfare, and the scene ends abruptly.

I've been unable to identify the saxophone and piano music that Johnny plays on a record in his flat while entertaining Gaynor, but it does rather resemble "The Great Gig in the Sky" on Pink Floyd's *Dark Side of the Moon* album, which, in 1972, was yet to be released (it came out the following year), but is suggestive of the kind of thing modish teenagers like Johnny would have been listening to at the time. It could well have been an improvised track performed by Vickers's players during the recording session, which he never bothered to write down in the score, or it could be a library track.

When Van Helsing is shown in his study working out that "Alucard" spells "Dracula" backward, the decision was made to include another short example of music by James Bernard—specifically some of the vibraphone tremolo and two-note horn motif that accompanies the operation scenes in *Frankenstein Must Be Destroyed*. This may have been at the insistence of Michael Carreras, or of Josephine Douglas. Philip Martell recorded the cue as Vickers wrote it on the master tape, so presumably felt satisfied with it as it stands there. Vickers's music for these few bars, which one can hear on the GDI CD of the score, is just as effective from a dramatic point of view, but it was perhaps felt that a taste of the old sound-world of Hammer was necessary to reassure more traditional fans, despite the fact that it was rather late in the day for that. The Bernard quotation lasts only 16 seconds before the falling semitone on electric guitar, associated with the glass vial, takes over, as Van Helsing underlines the word "Dracula."

Jessica's subsequent dream, which turns out not to be a dream at all, involves

Gaynor being attacked by Dracula in St. Bartolph's. The "Dracula" falling semitone appropriately underscores this, over a syncopated quaver rhythm in percussion and electric bass, while the organ alternates two chords (C-minor with added sixth, and F major with added sixth). When Dracula intones his dialogue ("She is not the one.... You have not learnt to obey"), Vickers interjects a saxophone figure in the pauses in between each line, which interestingly involves three notes, the last two falling an octave, which has certain things in common with James Bernard's "Dra-Cu-La" theme—not its rhythm and harmony, but certainly its octave and syllabic value. It also reminds one of the operatic nature of Lee's portrayal of Dracula. Although he is speaking, the musical setting turns this into a kind of recitative section—an approach Bernard had used in *Taste the Blood of Dracula* when Dracula says, "They have destroyed my servant. They shall be destroyed." The semitone figuration returns as Dracula advances to attack, with a note cluster in the organ and tremolos in the saxophones also forming a cluster. The descending scalic motif on electric guitar ("WITH FUZZ") has also been heard before. The brass fanfare returns too, all building up to climax as the fangs sink in and Jessica wakes up screaming.

During the subsequent "conversation" between Dracula and Johnny on the steps of the altar in St. Bartolph's, the electric guitar returns with the so-called "wah-wah" effect that had been made popular by Isaac Hayes in his score for Gordon Parks's blaxploitation police drama *Shaft*, made in the same year. It was therefore distinctly modish at the time, and would be used again by John Cacavas when scoring *The Satanic Rites of Dracula* in 1973. As Dracula descends the steps to place his hand on Johnny's shoulder, the camera rotating to follow him, Vickers articulates the moment with an interjection on drums, while alto sax reaches up to a high B natural, imitating a wailing scream. This, and the underlying chord, carry on into the next scene showing Van Helsing in silhouette, lighting a cigarette in his study—another beautifully composed shot in Gibson's succession of painterly images. A bass clarinet takes over, quietly meandering until Van Helsing opens a small box on his desk, which contains a crucifix. Vickers now has the two flutes and alto flute, accompanied by horn chords, play the "sacred" theme reminiscent of a chorale. "God grant I can find your strength," Van Helsing prays, looking at the portrait of his grandfather. The tranquil mood then segues into the return of the "wah-wah" guitar and heavy percussion as saxophone sextuplets rise over punctuating horn and brass chords as Johnny drives off to find his first victim, his neck marked with the kiss of the vampire. The music on his radio, which plays as he observes Marjorie Baynes leaving the laundromat, is again unidentified, presumably a library track, or improvised by Vickers's musicians.

Later that evening, Van Helsing returns to his home after his meeting with Inspector Murray at Scotland Yard. We observe him through the window of his study, as the bass clarinet introduces a return of the chorale theme, later taken up by the flutes and alto flute, and accompanied by two alternating chords on the horns and the appropriately sacred connotation of the organ. Van Helsing takes out his silver-bladed knife and prepares for the ordeal ahead. A nice touch in the score of a crescendo in suspended cymbal at the very end of this cue sadly can't be heard in the film or the CD.

By now, Bob has been vampirized as well, and has persuaded Jessica to go with him to the Cavern, where Johnny is waiting for them. The piano and cellos create a sense of apprehension with two semitones in a low register, while syncopated chords on the electric organ prepare us for a return of the "wah-wah" guitar and Johnny's three-note rising theme on saxophones. As he appears from the shadows, cellos and doubles basses perform a low tremolo glissando to great effect. After Johnny has his hand singed by Jessica's crucifix, Bob prepares to sink his fangs into her neck, and rising chords in full orchestra suggest that he'll succeed, but Johnny pulls him back, leaving the orchestra cut off at the height of its climax (a kind of musical coitus interruptus) before falling semitones associated with Dracula's ashes and glissando in brass, cello, and basses. "She's not for us," Johnny explains. "She belongs to the Master. He commands." (Referring to Dracula as "the Master" is Don Houghton's sly way of referencing his past as a scriptwriter for *Dr. Who*.)

Van Helsing's frantic dash down King's Road after his phone call to Mrs. Donnelly calls for a reprise of the main title theme, which segues into a contrasting musical hiatus as he enters the Cavern. Here the organ plays its familiar chords, while a rising flute leads up to a fortissimo chord, accompanied by "sizzle" cymbal, glockenspiel, and vibraphone when he spots Jessica's crucifix lying in a pool of light on the floor. The main theme returns as he continues to run before bumping into Anna Bryant.

Before we follow him to Johnny's flat, we are shown a panorama of the Thames, accompanied by vibraphone, maracas, and a cymbal (played on the bell of the instrument). Over a held chord the organ and flutes answer one another, with Vickers helpfully suggesting the players might like to "take a breath if necessary" during their sustained notes. Then we are with Johnny, who is preparing for his encounter with Dracula. The "wah-wah" effect returns, along with his theme on saxophones. Van Helsing climbs the steps to the flat's entrance, accompanied by a meandering piano line, played in octaves. During the dialogue between them, cellos and basses sustain first a G, then a C, which latter moves through a crescendo as Van Helsing grabs Johnny's hand and reveals the mark of Jessica's crucifix on his flesh. Vickers articulates this with a rising semitone on the horn. As Van Helsing asks further questions, the bass guitar sets up a threatening rhythm, echoed by snare drum, which leads into the music for the fight that will end in Johnny's death. More "wah-wah" accompanies this. Saxophones wail, punctuated by staccato chords in horns and brass, for which Vickers was again indebted to Stan Kenton's style, which he much admired. Van Helsing throws a Bible into Johnny's coffin, which action the piano and brass echo with a descending staccato phrase, accompanied by timpani, cymbals, and a fortissimo roll on the tam-tam. Then, during the dialogue, Vickers sustains a quiet chord in the horns before the struggle continues again, with a lead-in from the drums and a return of the "wah-wah" guitar and those Kentonesque brass punctuations. To emphasize the significance of the light, which Van Helsing sees being reflected by a shaving mirror onto the wall, Vickers uses a glockenspiel and vibraphone to color the trills on saxophone, which he makes sure coincide with the image. A key change then increases the excitement as Johnny is pushed back by the light, which Van Helsing reflects at him from the rising sun. Vickers originally intended the cue to continue during Johnny's death agonies up to and including the arrival of the police outside the flat, but it was obviously thought to be more effective to let the sound effects and dialogue do the job by themselves. The whole cue can be heard on the CD. A very Kentonesque *fortissimo* for full orchestra accompanies the final shot of Johnny's corpse, as the sergeant looks in the bathroom. The brass and wind and saxophones are instructed to swoop up to the notes from an indefinite pitch to begin with, which, combined with the subsequent discord, provides a fitting end for Johnny's admittedly rather brief reign of terror.

The mood changes with the following shot of Chelsea Bridge at sunrise. An alto flute gently intones the main theme, accompanied by counterpoint in the piano, cellos, and basses. The alto flute creates a sense of apprehension and loneliness as Van Helsing makes his way to St. Bartolph's. As he struggles through the gap in the fence, an ordinary flute then plaintively joins in with two rising notes in a higher register, but as we discover Bob's corpse in the graveyard, the brass join in with chords that begin forte, then suddenly become much softer before immediately moving through a crescendo. This happens twice, followed by a rhythmic punctuation as Van Helsing turns Bob's head and reveals the puncture marks on his neck.

There is no time to be lost, however, so Van Helsing makes his way inside the church, where Jessica is found lying in a trance on the altar. The mood becomes much more tender with the return of the chorale theme on flute, organ, and cello, with quiet interjections from the vibraphone. When he discovers that Jessica is still alive, he gasps, "Thank God!" and horns join in to help articulate the play of emotions here. As he leaves her, having fixed a crucifix around her neck, glockenspiel and vibraphones, imitating a chiming clock, suggest that time is of the essence.

After we seen Van Helsing begin to dig the trench in which he hopes to ensnare Dracula, one of the film's most poetic moments occurs. By this time, the day is well past and the sun has begun to set once more. As Van Helsing turns the silver-bladed knife, it catches the light, at which a bell-tree shimmers, leading to a chord in vibraphone, organ, and horns as we cut to a shot of a London plane tree. Gibson zooms toward this, and then pans down to the setting sun behind it. Flutes play a descending triplet pattern to match the movement and the crepuscular mood, aided by muted horns, and as Van Helsing catches sight of the setting sun itself, the bell-tree returns with another shiver of sound. The descending triplets recur in the wind section as we cut back to Van Helsing at his labors, sharpening his stakes for the ensuing confrontation.

An eerie wind accompanies Dracula's entrance, to which Vickers only adds only quiet, slowly paced octaves on the piano, outlining the previous sections harmonic contour. As Jessica opens her eyes, another Kentonesque brass sting enhances the shock, followed by a tremolo glissando on cellos and basses. With the ordeal of snatching off Jessica's crucifix over, the agony of which is suggested musically by dotted rhythms in the brass, Dracula prepares to bite his victim to triplet repetitions in the horns, which move through a crescendo, creating anxiety. The mood then changes to one of surprise and then recollection as Van Helsing shouts Dracula's name. "Look on me, Dracula. Look on me and remember," he says. A glockenspiel occupies Van Helsing's pauses, again rather like a clock chiming, the tension raised by bongo drums. As we see Dracula do just that with flashbacks to the film's 1872 prologue, his descending semitone motif returns. As this reaches a climax with the memory of his death, he stares malevolently at his opponent, accompanied by yet another tremolo glissando in the cellos and basses. As if to remind him that he is now in 1972, the electric bass plays a syncopated beat below the equally syncopated brass. Lee then delivers his slightly adapted quotation from Stoker's novel before a drum lead-in begins the final fight with a reprise of the main title theme. A chromatic scale in triplets leads up to Van Helsing's silver-bladed knife being plunged into Dracula's chest. Extra impact is provided by the horns and brass, which create musical "punches"—chords that indefinitely slide down in pitch from their original note.

After Dracula falls over the edge of the choir loft, the tempo changes to reflect the dramatic hiatus. Piano and trombones intone a motif that is in fact identical to the opening three notes of Schubert's "Unfinished" Symphony, but for the fact that the symphony is in B minor and this section of *Dracula A.D. 1972* is in C-minor (most of the score is in C-minor, in fact). The similarity to Schubert's famously sinister theme is appropriate, as Dracula now lies on his back, stabbed through the heart and soon to die, unless he can compel Jessica to pull the knife out. This he does by will power alone, and as she advances toward him, the saxophones and bass clarinet trill away on F-sharps and C-sharps, while the piano, cellos, and basses oscillate slow quaver patterns in semitones, providing the perfect sense of unease and anxiety as Van Helsing shouts down below, "Jessica! Don't go near him!" She does, of course, and to increase the anxiety, Vickers raises the trills on the saxophones and the oscillating quavers below by a semitone. "In God's name, don't touch him!" Van Helsing shouts again before rushing down to ground level. As we focus on the bloody knife, which Jessica holds in her hands, a sinister horn call, punctuated by stabbing chords from the brass, announces Dracula's triumph.

This leads to another reprise of the main theme as Dracula chases Van Helsing outside into the graveyard and, blinded by the holy water that is thrown into his face, he slips and falls into the specially dug trap at his feet. Trombones, so often used by composers over the ages to announce death, now come into their own with solemn gravity as Van Helsing finishes off the job by pushing Dracula onto the stakes with his spade. Reiterated C-minor seventh chords for full orchestra accompany each of Dracula's dying agonies. He then begins to disintegrate, with a repetition of the music that accompanied his original disintegration in the prologue.

Taking Jessica in his arms, Van Helsing leads her away as the organ takes up the chorale theme and delivers the last line of the film: "Requiescat in Pace Ultima." Vickers's original idea, as recorded on the CD, was not to end on a reprise of the main theme but to accompany the final credits with a more introspective continuation of the chorale theme, but this must have been considered too downbeat a mood with which to send the audience home, so the main theme plays us out.

Epilogue: Requiescat in Pace Ultima

I HAVE ALREADY FLOATED SOME OF the reasons why *Dracula A.D. 1972* has been loved and loathed, but before we leave this particular film to continue its progress under its own steam, it might be useful to explore a few more general reasons why the horror genre should have exerted such a perennial appeal virtually from the invention of the cinema itself. While other genres explore the horrors of war, poverty, and violent crime, the horror genre is perhaps the most direct expression of the unremembered horror of being born, the unknown horror of dying, the anxieties of living, the complexities of sex, and the grotesque disorders of old age. Of course, life offers many pleasures as well, and horror also has room for comedy, as we see in films such as *Abbott and Costello Meet Frankenstein* and Mel Brooks's *Young Frankenstein* (1974).

As we have seen, "Horror" was not a term much liked by either Lee or Cushing, both of whom pointed out that they were entertainers and had no wish to repel their audiences, as the word implies. Steven King identified three types of horror: "The Grossout: the sight of a severed head tumbling down a flight of stairs ... The Horror: the unnatural, spiders the size of bears ... And the last and worst one: Terror ... it's when the lights go out and you feel something behind you ... but when you turn around there's nothing there."[1] Both actors suggested various alternatives, such as "fantasy," "macabre," "fantastic," and "graveyard"; but "horror" has stuck as the defining word of the genre, thanks mainly to the creation of the notorious "H" Certificate in 1932 by the British Board of Film Censors in the wake of the Universal horror films that were causing so much concern among the guardians of conventional morality at the time.

This brings us to the crux of the matter, which is indeed one of morality. Most horror films are all about morality—both an exposure of the flimsiness of morality itself and a flirtation with its denial before a restoration of the status quo, which the defeat of such a flirtation only strengthens. A friend of mine once claimed that Hammer films offered the allure of the forbidden before snatching it away from you, and she definitely had a point. It was, after all, the entire sales technique of Dennis Wheatley's occult novels—the "wonderful come on" described by Robert Irwin. British and American horror films are therefore largely about religion in general and Christianity in particular, and it should not surprise us to know that both Cushing and Lee were committed Christians, which beliefs doubtless informed their performances in the intensely religious films they both found themselves making for

Hammer and other companies who benefited from the horror boom Hammer created. Philosophically speaking, these films are ultimately reactionary, which is probably why so many Marxist intellectuals, who regard religion as the opium of the people, have dismissed them over the years.

(Cushing kept his political views to himself. Christopher James Stone, a Labour Party member, recalled: "I did canvass him once. This was when I was the election agent for the Labour Party candidate for the County Council elections in—I think—1985. I knocked on his door not knowing it was his house. He was polite but firm, telling me that, as an actor, he didn't get involved in politics."[2] Lee, however, was obviously right wing, once lamenting "the almost complete breakdown of discipline in this country" as well as continually reminding his audiences of the danger of black magic: "you will not only lose your mind you will lose your soul."[3] The conservative M.P. Michael Gove, who appeared with Lee in *A Feast at Midnight* (dir. Justin Hardy, 1996), admired him as "a traditional British Conservative" and Eurosceptic "deeply attached to our democracy and deeply suspicious of what he saw as the anti-democratic tide of European immigration."[4] Lee also regarded David Cameron as the best Conservative prime minister of his lifetime.)

Two years before Bram Stoker published *Dracula*, that great philosophical anti-Christ, Friedrich Nietzsche, employed the imagery that novel would make world-famous as a way of attacking Christian morality itself, which he regarded as the main ailment of humanity as a species and the bane of all our history. In his fascinating if sometimes rather hysterical polemic, *The Anti-Christ*, he laid into traditional morality with an intriguing metaphor:

> The concept of guilt and punishment, the entire "moral world-order," was invented *in opposition to* science—in *opposition to* the detaching of man from the priest.... Man shall *not* look around him, he shall look down deep into himself; he shall *not* look prudently and cautiously into things in order to learn, he shall not look at all: he shall *suffer*.... And he shall suffer in such a way that he has need of a priest at all times.—Away with physicians! *One has need of a Saviour.*—The concept of guilt and punishment, including the doctrine of "grace," or "redemption," or "forgiveness"—*lies* through and through and without ay psychological reality—they were invented to destroy the *causal sense* of man: they are an outrage on the concept of cause and effect!—And *not* an outrage with the fist, with the knife, with honest hatred and love! But one from the most cowardly, cunning, lowest instincts! An *outrage of the priest*! An *outrage of the parasite!* A vampirising of pale subterranean bloodsuckers![5]

For Nietzsche, Christian morality was the greatest crime against humanity, as it opposed scientific enquiry and our impulse for self-determination: "the priest *rules* through the invention of sin."[6] In *Dracula A.D. 1972*, however, Nietzsche's imagery is reversed. It is Van Helsing who is the priest (and hence the moral bloodsucker) in opposition to the "truth" of what Dracula represents: among other things, the amoral sex drive and the Will to Power, which Nietzsche regarded as the vital, life-enhancing attributes of the species. The destruction of Dracula by Van Helsing personifies what Nietzsche regarded as the deadening, life-denying morality of Christianity.

We see, in all of Hammer's vampire films, the triumph of this morality after the audience has been titillated by the possibility of its defeat. As Nietzsche explains, "The passions become evil and malicious if they are regarded as evil and malicious.

Thus Christianity has succeeded in transforming Eros and Aphrodite ... into diabolical kobolds and phantoms by means of the torments it introduces into the consciences of believers whenever they are excited sexually."[7] Consequently, the body itself becomes evil:

> Whatever proceeds from the stomach, the intestines, the beatings of the heart, the nerves, the bile, the semen—all those distempers, debilitations, excitations, the whole chance operation of the machine of which we still know so little!—had to be seen by a Christian such as Pascal as a moral and religious phenomenon, and he had to ask whether God or Devil, good or evil, salvation of damnation was to be discovered in them! Oh what an unhappy interpreter! How he had to twist and torment his system. How he had to twist and torment himself so as to be in the right![8]

The bloody destruction of Dracula at the end of *A.D. 1972*, in which we hear his bodily fluids gurgle as Van Helsing drives condemnatory stakes through his heart before the body disintegrates to dust, is just such a purging of the instincts that Dracula releases in his victims. Van Helsing's moral zeal, demonstrated so passionately in the office of Inspector Murray, is exactly the kind of attitude Nietzsche attacked throughout his philosophical career.

Noël Carroll, however, takes the view that while we crave conventional moral—even genetic—order, we are nonetheless attracted by what opposes it:

> Recall again that the objects of art-horror are, by definition, impure. This is to be understood in terms of their being anomalous. Obviously, the anomalous nature of these beings is what makes them disturbing, distressing and disgusting. They are violations of our ways of classifying things and such frustrations of a world-picture are bound to be disturbing.
>
> However, anomalies are also interesting. The very fact that they are anomalies fascinates us. Their deviation from the paradigms of our classificatory scheme captures our attention immediately. It holds us spellbound. It commands and retains our attention. It is an attracting force; it attracts curiosity, i.e., it makes us curious; it invites inquisitiveness about its surprising properties. One wants to gaze upon the unusual, even when it is simultaneously repelling.
>
> Monsters ... are repelling because they violate standing categories. But for the self-same reason, they are also compelling of our attention. They are attracted, in the sense that they elicit interest, and they are the cause of, for many, irresistible attention again, just because they violate standing categories. They are curiosities. They can rivet attention and thrill for the self-same reason that they disturb, distress, and disgust.[9]

Carroll references Steven King's belief that

> ...horror fiction is really as Republican as a banker in a three-piece suit. The story is always the same in terms of its development. There's an incursion into taboo lands, there's a place where you shouldn't go, but you do, the same way that your mother would tell you that the freak tent is a place you shouldn't go, but you do. And the same thing happens inside: you look at the guy with three eyes or you look at the fat lady or you look at the skeleton man or Mr. Electrical or whatever it happens to be. And when you come out, well, you say, "Hey, I'm not so bad. I'm all right. A lot better than I thought." It has that effect of reconfirming values, or reconfirming self-image and our good feelings about ourselves.... Monstrosity fascinates us because it appeals to the conservative Republican in a three-piece suit who resides with all of us. We love and need the concept of monstrosity because it is a reaffirmation of the order we all crave as human beings.[10]

It would therefore seem that the Nietzschean feels sorry for Dracula, while the followers of Carroll and King are ultimately grateful to Van Helsing, but both are fascinated by what Dracula offers them.

Horror films' preoccupation with the irrational impulses of the unconscious of course has much in common with the program of Surrealism, which was encapsulated in André Breton's 1924 *Surrealistic Manifesto*:

> We are still living under the rule of logic ... the absolute rationalism which remains in fashion permits the consideration of facts only narrowly relevant to our experience. Under the banner of civilization, under the pretext of progress we have managed to banish from the mind anything which ... could be pointed to as superstition or fantasy.... *Perhaps the imagination is on the verge of recovering its rights.* If the depths of the mind harbour strange forces capable either of reinforcing or of combating and overwhelming those on the surface *then it is our greatest interest to capture them.*[11]

It is no surprise to realize that this manifesto appeared only two years after Murnau's *Nosferatu* and two years before Henrik Galeen's *The Student of Prague*. Horror films are the most immediate way of exploring these otherwise often unexplored regions of daily existence.

There are, however, other aspects of the psyche at work. All drama requires conflict to work at all. Even Samuel Beckett's *Waiting for Godot* offers the conflict of a desire for meaning in a world totally lacking it. Why else should we be attracted to Westerns and war films? Heroism and bravery justify violence in those genres, but horror films expose the instincts that the Marquis de Sade was always ready to acknowledge. Sade was a realist. He did not necessarily advocate what became known as sadism, but he saw little point in an idealism that denied the instincts that led to it. These instincts exist and might as well be faced rather than moralized away. Nietzsche also recognized that "to practice cruelty is to enjoy the highest gratification of the feeling of power" and power is the ultimate "good"[12]: "What is happiness?—The feeling that power increases—that a resistance is overcome.... What is more harmful than any vice?—Active sympathy for the ill-constituted and weak—Christianity...."[13] He also recognized that morality encouraged the evil of voluntary suffering:

> In the act of cruelty the community refreshes itself and for once throws off the gloom of constant fear and caution. Cruelty is one of the oldest festive joys on mankind. Consequently it is imagined that the gods too are refreshed and in festive mood when they are offered the spectacle of cruelty—and thus there creeps into the world the idea of *voluntary suffering*, self-chosen torture, is meaningful and valuable.[14]

While we may not take up the mantle of voluntary suffering ourselves while watching a horror film, there is no denial that the instinct for cruelty is to a greater or lesser extent catered to by the genre.

But overriding all this is perhaps the greatest of all our fears: that of death itself. This anxiety, which is the fount of all the other anxieties explored in horror films, is the bedrock on which we construct our illusory certainties. Arthur Schopenhauer was fully aware of this:

> The fear of death is, in fact, independent of knowledge, for the animal has it, although it does not know death. Therefore in every animal the fear of its own destruction, like the care for its maintenance, is inborn.... The greatest of evils, the worst thing that can threaten anywhere, is death; the greatest anxiety is the anxiety of death. Nothing excites us so irresistibly to the most lively interest as does danger to the lives of others; nothing is more dreadful

than execution. Now the boundless attachment to life which appears here cannot have sprung from knowledge and reflection. To these, on the contrary, it appears foolish, for the objective value of life is very uncertain, and it remains at least doubtful whether existence is to be preferred to non-existence.... Consequently, this powerful attachment to life is irrational and blind; it can be explained only from the fact that our whole being-in-itself is the will-to-live, to which life therefore must appear as the highest good, however embittered, short, and uncertain it may be.[15]

Our fascination with Dracula's death and disintegration negotiates the incomprehensible awareness we have of our own. It is the most fascinating of all the fascinations of horror. In his book on the subject of Death, Maurice Maeterlinck draws our attention to lines from a play by Marie Lenéru called *Les Affranchis*:

Death and death alone is what we must consult about life; and not some vague future or survival, in which we shall not be present. It is our own end; and everything happens in the interval between death and now. Do not talk to me of those imaginary prolongations which wield over us the childish spell of number; do not talk to me—to me who am to die outright—of societies and people! There is no reality, there is no true duration, save that between the cradle and the grave. The rest is mere bombast, show, delusion![16]

Maeterlinck, who unlike Cushing and Lee lost his faith, remarked:

The more our thoughts struggle to turn away from it, the closer do they press around it. The more we dread it, the more dreadful it becomes, for it battens but on our fears. He [who] seeks to forget it burdens his memory with it; he who tries to shun it meets naught else.[17]

Horror films are obviously about death, which is why so many of them feature funerals, just as *A.D. 1972* begins with one. The Service for the Burial of the Dead has provided perhaps the most quoted lines in the genre. They were forged from our fear of death, an afterlife being imagined, according to the likes of Nietzsche, because we find it hard, if not impossible, to accept the impermanence and insignificance of our own egos and the assembly of tissue from which they are created. (Cushing himself once somewhat illogically argued that there has to be an afterlife because life would be altogether "too ironic" without it. But why shouldn't life be ironic?) The burial service surely contains some of the most beautiful lines ever written about the stark reality of our inevitable dissolution:

Man that is born of a woman hath but a short time to live, and is full of misery. He cometh up, and is cut down, like a flower; he fleeth as it were a shadow, and never continueth in one day.
In the midst of life we are in death.

But overlaying such realism is its simultaneous denial. The body is described as "foul" and "vile," and despite "ashes to ashes, dust to dust" we have the "sure and certain hope of the Resurrection to eternal life." That *Dracula A.D. 1972* begins with these words and ends with the superimposition of "Rest in Final Peace" over a shot of the triumphant Van Helsing, leading the traumatized and reformed Jessica back to his "mausoleum" of conventional morality, encapsulates its deeply Christian and ultimately reactionary message. Despite all the horror it depicts, the film ultimately reassures us that all will be well, that there is meaning in our suffering and salvation for our souls. Hammer films were never existentialist.

Which brings me to an existential vampire film I haven't mentioned yet. In many ways, it has much in common with *Dracula A.D. 1972*, being a vampire story in modern dress, made the year before Gibson's film. It too features a sports car, long-haired men wearing cravats, purple shirts, and flared velvet trousers, goblets of blood, sex scenes, electric guitars on the soundtrack, ruined Gothic architecture, and a predominantly young cast. It was filmed in France, however, and is a very different affair from Hammer's approach to youth culture. Instead of being viewed from the middle-aged perspective of Don Houghton, Jean Rollin's *Les frisson des vampires* is a rather more engaged hippie-eyed vision. Even more significantly, it dispenses with the moral structure of *A.D. 1972*. *Les frissons* is perhaps the most existentialist vampire film ever made, if we take Anthony Thorlby's definition of existentialism as an unmasking of "men's false ideas about the world, the life-lies (as they came to be called) that they cling to and drown without."[18] Vampirism is obviously a false idea, but Rollin uses it as a metaphor for presenting some uncomfortable truths about the human condition: that sexuality is endlessly polymorphous, that it often involves cruelty, that we must all die, and that none of it makes any moral or metaphysical sense. Indeed, one of the characters says at one point, "I really don't know what's going on." Another says, "These days everything is unbelievable." Rollin's surreal imagery, often flooded with vivid red and blue light and shrouded in billowing dry ice, is very different from the stylish realism of Gibson, and aids Rollin's other important message, that the weird is quite normal, because everything about life is weird—and ultimately meaningless and irrational.

A brilliant metaphor of such meaninglessness occurs in the castle's library, which one might compare with Van Helsing's rather more modest bookshelves. For Van Helsing, books contain the vital knowledge to keep the spiritual status quo in place. In *Les frissons*, the books themselves become irrationally and inexplicably malevolent, flying off their shelves and badly injuring the bemused hero of the story. Knowledge here is meaningless and cannot save us from the existential dilemma in which we all find ourselves. The book-battered young man a newlywed whose bride wants to visit her two curious cousins in their Gothic chateau before going on honeymoon to Italy. But the cousins have been made into vampires by one of cinema's most extraordinary female vampires, with the Wagnerian name of Isolde, played by Dominique. She manifests herself in a grandfather clock, and later emerges down a chimney stack through an elaborate fireplace. She seduces the bride, as well as piercing the breasts of another victim with two razor sharp cones attached to her own nipples. In the end, as David Pirie describes it, "Isolde is reduced to sucking the blood from her own veins, a precise and evocative image of the circularity and futility of physical appetite and excretion."[19] Isolde criticizes the two cousins for complaining about their undead lot, calling them "bourgeois vampires," which they are, for all their hippie clothing. After all, they live in a huge castle and all their needs are met by two servants; in this they certainly resemble the highly privileged "teenagers" in Gibson's film. Ultimately, they feed on the young bride before dying on a beach as the sun rises. The final shot of the film captures the newlywed husband running in despair along the shoreline, wildly firing his revolver at nothing. Thorlby's metaphor of how we drown without a life-lie seems to be the unfortunate young man's fate here: the sea will probably wash him away.

Dracula's Demise—Christopher Lee in *Dracula A.D. 1972*.

There is no redemption for him or anyone else—and certainly no *requiem in pace ultima*.

Dracula A.D. 1972 and *Les frisson des vampires* really belong together as two sides of the same coin. They are both fascinating responses to their time, with different moral values and very different aesthetics, but curiously complementary.

Appendix: Alan Gibson's "Notes on Directing (1987)"

Tackling the Script

There is always something a director can bring to the project. Oddly enough, the challenge in improving and making entertaining a mediocre script can be very good for one.

But it mustn't become a habit! Nothing beats doing a good script.

Read it through once quickly. First impressions, for mood and style, are important and should be fairly potent immediately. Second time around try reading it ignoring the stage directions. (In some pieces this will make the script almost incomprehensible, but it is useful for discovering how much of the story and characterization come across solely on what the people say to each other and to other people…)

Read again and again and keep the storyline forefront. Telling the story is of prime importance. Do not get sidetracked.

Where there is action and development through behavior consider how you wish to convey it through your visuals and pacing. What unspoken dialogue is there between the characters? What do the characters do when they are alone? Is their behavior different?

Design

Doubtless by now you will have "seen" a good measure of the script in your head and a few compositions and camera angles will have become quite clear. So, before meeting with the designer, have several key elements you require to achieve these visuals jotted down. In the way of a sketch or ground plan layout. Many a good set has been constructed to facilitate *one* particular angle.

Bowlered Over—Alan Gibson on location for *Dracula A.D. 1972.*

Usually, it turns out to be excellent for the rest of the scenes as well. Also have a clear picture of how you want the film to look. Colours. Textures. The more detail you can bring to the first meeting with the designer ... the quicker you both are going to understand where each other is coming from ... and they will be anxious to agree and convey your thoughts if you feel strongly and have conviction. Listen to them carefully as well. You will find that some of their ideas will spark off more from you, and so on.

Casting

Make sure you cast well. It not only is important for the obvious reasons of performance ... but a true professional will save a lot of time and trouble. Apart from looking for someone with talent ... the range they can cope with is vital. Be aware, as well, that you cast with variety. There is nothing worse than having two or three people who look even vaguely similar. (It happens so much in the U.S. imports: the young actresses always seem to be dark-haired and bony; completely interchangeable.) It helps to maintain a clear line through the plot if you have instant recognition of your characters from scene to scene.

During casting sessions be aware of how natural the actor/actress is. Take great cognizance of the fact that they are more than likely quite nervous. Talk to yourself for a moment or two while they gather themselves. Sometimes one can tell a lot from a reading ... other times it is quite meaningless. After a goodly time directing one can usually glean something from a few pages read for you.... It is something intangible, but a good actress/actor will find a way of letting it be known. Even a few minutes of just listening and observing the applicant will give you a quality of the person ... and with a reasonable CV that might be enough. Very often after seeing people for days ... if you recall one or two of them a few days later it is extraordinary how much more relaxed they are and how much more of their true self appears.

The READ-THRU is a nerve-wracking time for most everyone. The cast don't know what to expect, usually don't know anyone and are convinced that they will be the only one to make a fool of themselves. If you, the director, appear relaxed and calm, and make sure it all seems very informal and that, apart from some hard work, it will be fun.

You can't beat a pub lunch on the first day's rehearsal; it breaks down barriers, creates an atmosphere, and starts the whole project off with a relaxed and easy feeling of togetherness.

Thespians

Try never to correct or tick off an actor in the general hearing range of the *whole* cast. During a scene the other performers may be privy to what you are saying, as it may bear some relevance to the scene in general. A gentle word aside has much more effect ... they can take it in without feeling embarrassed or their confidence weakened. It may seem unnecessary but for the first few days in rehearsal you will find that the cast are quite vulnerable. Patience is a good quality to possess. Later after you start doing more runs and everyone has got to know each other and feels more comfortable with their characters then open notes to the cast are fine and this stage better. In the time given for rehearsing a TV play, and the often disjointed pattern of rehearsals, a good notion is, just before breaking...(to go to the Studio or out to location) a speed word run is a very beneficial exercise. Have the cast sit around in a circle and speak the whole play/film. The cast will balk at first and find it odd, but in my experience, they have all found it useful. For everyone, too. The ASM can read in *brief* scene setting before the dialogue of each new scene but other than that just the words ... and as quick as they can ... fixes the plot and through line in everyone's head.

Camera Script

This is such a personal thing there isn't much I can say....
Everyone has a different way of working.
Some directors arrive at rehearsal with the script fully worked out as far as plotting and

shots are concerned. Others have some key shapes and relationships worked out and still there is another breed that arrives with a blank page in their head and sketch it out as they go. They are all valid, but they all have disadvantages.

Personally, I like to have a specific shape, but don't write anything down except perhaps a few notes for myself, and give a short rundown to the first AD.

I find that to keep an open mind is essential, especially on exterior locations. The whole exercise alters in a VT studio piece. A Camera script is essential. Though more and more one finds oneself putting "as directed" over some scenes.

It is surprising how easy it is to make the change from multi-camera to single camera-working.

On a VT [videotape] location two camera set up is very time saving. Though the absence of the third camera can be frustrating at times. On the last shoot I did "The Charmer" for [London Weekend Television]; we started the series with 11 days' location work with the two-camera unit. And within a day I was fully in tune with the concept.

It means that one wasn't falling into the two-shot … close-up … close-up routine. And when one is working at speed one begins to value the developing shot. It also saves a great deal of time.

—Alan Gibson, 1987

Chapter Notes

Introduction

1. David Pirie, *The Vampire Cinema*, London: Quarto, 1977, 93.
2. *Ibid.*, 94.
3. *Ibid.*, 93.
4. *Ibid.*, 94.
5. *Ibid.*, 93.
6. *Ibid.*, 95.
7. Alan Frank, *Horror Movies*, London: Octopus, 1974, 133.
8. Roger Ebert, "*Dracula A.D. 1972*," review, rogerebert.com, December 13, 1972, https://www.rogerebert.com/reviews/dracula-a-d-1972-1972.
9. David Miller, *The Peter Cushing Companion*, London: Reynolds & Hearn, 2000, 134–135.
10. Alan Frank, *Monsters and Vampires*, London: Octopus, 1976, 34.
11. Leslie Halliwell, *The Dead That Walk*, London: Palladin, 1988, 68.
12. *Ibid.*, 69.
13. Jonathan Rigby, *Christopher Lee—The Authorised Screen History*, London: Reynolds & Hearn, 2001, 146.
14. Dez Skinn (ed.), *Hammer's Halls of Hammer Magazine 21*, vol. 2, no. 9, June 1978, London: Top Sellers, 9 ("Christopher Lee Speaks Out").
15. Christopher Lee, *Lord of Misrule—The Autobiography of Christopher Lee*, London: Orion, 2003, 301.
16. Sinclair McKay, *A Thing of Unspeakable Horror—The History of Hammer Films*, London: Aurum Press, 2007, 140.
17. *Ibid.*, 51.
18. Lee, *Lord of Misrule*, 301.
19. Simon J. Ballard, *Scream* Magazine, November/December 2023, 9–10 ("'He's Waiting to Freak You Out!'—Hammer's Modern-Day Dracula Movies Explored…").
20. "*Dracula A.D. 1972* Reviews," Rotten Tomatoes, https://www.rottentomatoes.com/m/dracula_ad_1972/reviews.
21. Friedrich Nietzsche (trans. R.J. Hollingdale), *Untimely Meditations*, Cambridge: Cambridge University Press, 1983, 60–61 ("On the uses and disadvantages of history for life").
22. Susan Sontag, *On Photography*, London: Penguin, 1979, 15.
23. *Fortean Times*, No. 354, June 2017 (Bob Fisher, "Hauntology").

Chapter One

1. Christopher Lee, *Lord of Misrule—The Autobiography of Christopher Lee*, London: Orion, 2003, 301.
2. Bram Stoker (ed. Leonard Wolf), *The Annotated Dracula*, London: New English Library, 1976, 266.
3. Dez Skinn (ed.), *Hammer's Halls of Hammer Magazine 21*, vol. 2, no. 9, June 1978, London: Top Sellers, 8 ("Christopher Lee Speaks Out").
4. Stoker, *The Annotated Dracula*, 214.
5. *The Nineteenth Century*, vol. 18, London, July–December 1885, 136 (Emily Gerard, "Transylvanian Superstitions").
6. Wilkie Collins (ed. Peter Haining), *Sensation Fiction*, London: Peter Owen, 2004, 7.
7. Wilkie Collins (ed. Dorothy Goldman), *Basil*, Oxford: Oxford University Press, 1990, 48.
8. *Ibid.*, 130.
9. *Ibid.*, 147.
10. Stoker, *The Annotated Dracula*, 1976, 20.
11. Collins, *Basil*, 174.
12. *Ibid.*, 215.
13. *Ibid.*, 303.
14. *Ibid.*, 304.
15. *Ibid.*, 326.
16. John Burke, *The Second Hammer Film Omnibus*, London: Pan, 1967, 181 ("Dracula—Prince of Darkness").
17. Stoker, *The Annotated Dracula*, 30.
18. *Ibid.*, 22.
19. *Ibid.*, 23.
20. *Ibid.*, 54.
21. Richard Wagner (trans. Edwin Evans), *Judaism in Music*, London: William Reeves, 1910, 9.
22. Richard Wagner (trans. William Ashton Ellis), "Judaism in Music," Internet Archive, https://archive.org/details/judaisminmusic/page/n1/mode/2up, 2.
23. Stoker, *The Annotated Dracula*, 306.
24. Charles Maturin, *Melmoth the Wanderer*, London: Folio, 1993, 366.
25. Stoker, *The Annotated Dracula*, 189.

26. *Ibid.*, 178.
27. *Ibid.*, 59.
28. *Ibid.*, 204.
29. *Ibid.*, 62.
30. *Ibid.*, 169.
31. *Ibid.*, 156.
32. *Ibid.*, 236.
33. *Ibid.*, 177.
34. Wilkie Collins, *The Moonstone*, London: Collins, 1973, 419.
35. Stoker, *The Annotated Dracula*, 233.
36. *Ibid.*, 300.
37. Kenneth Clarke, *The Gothic Revival—An Essay on the History of Taste*, London: John Murray, 1974, 2.
38. John Betjeman (ed. Stephen Games), *Trains and Buttered Toast*, London: John Murray, 2006, 39 ("A Hundred Years of Architecture in Wessex").
39. Sinclair McKay, *A Thing of Unspeakable Horror—The History of Hammer Films*, London: Aurum Press, 2007, 140.
40. Terence Towles Canote, "Mama Told Me Not to Come: The Sixties Party Scene on Film," A Shroud of Thoughts, February 2, 2010, http://mercurie.blogspot.com/2010/02/mama-told-me-not-to-come-sixties-party.html.
41. Richard Klemensen (ed.), *Little Shoppe of Horrors—The Journal of Classic British Horror Films*, Issue 22, Des Moines, IA: Elmer Valo Appreciation Society, March 2009, 58 (Bruce G. Hallenbeck, "The Making of *Dracula A.D. 1972*").

Chapter Two

1. Friedrich Nietzsche (trans. R.J. Hollingdale), *Untimely Meditations*, Cambridge: Cambridge University Press, 1983, 83 ("On the uses & disadvantages of history for life").
2. Susan Sontag, *Against Interpretation*, London: Vintage, 2001, 224–225 ("The Imagination of Disaster").
3. *Ibid.*, 278–283 ("On Camp").
4. Christopher Lee, *Lord of Misrule—The Autobiography of Christopher Lee*, London: Orion, 2003, 177.
5. Sontag, *Against Interpretation*, 20 ("On Style").
6. Lee, *Lord of Misrule*, 178.
7. "Hitchcock at the NFT," BBC, 1969, https://www.bbc.co.uk/iplayer/episode/m00226pd/hitchcock-at-the-nft.
8. Richard Klemensen (ed.), *Little Shoppe of Horrors—The Journal of Classic British Horror Films*, Issue 47, Des Moines, IA: Elmer Valo Appreciation Society, October 2021, 60 (David Gee, "Dracula and the Modern Age").
9. Umberto Eco (trans. William Weaver), *Travels in Hyperreality*, London: Picador, 1987, 198 ("Reading Things").
10. *Ibid.*, 208 ("Reading Things").
11. *Ibid.*, 198 ("Reading Things").
12. *Ibid.*, 200 ("Reading Things").
13. Edward Buscombe, *Making* Legend of the Werewolf, London: British Film Institute, 1976, 23.
14. S.S. Prawer, *Caligari's Children—The Film as Tale of Terror*, Oxford: Oxford University Press, 1980, 204.
15. Eco, *Travels in Hyperreality*, 209 ("Reading Things").
16. Ibid.

Chapter Three

1. Alexandre Dumas, *The Count of Monte Cristo*, London: Routledge, no date, 239.
2. *Ibid.*, 75.
3. Bram Stoker, *The Jewel of Seven Stars*, Far Thrupp: Alan Sutton, 1996, 128.
4. James Malcolm Rymer, *Varney, the Vampire*, London: Wordsworth, 2010, 372.
5. Dez Skinn (ed.), *Hammer's Halls of Hammer Magazine 21*, vol. 2, no. 9, June 1978, London: Top Sellers, 8 ("Christopher Lee Speaks Out").
6. Stephen Wischusen (ed.), *The Hour of One—Six Gothic Melodramas*, London: Gordon Fraser, 1975, 99 (J.R. Planché, "The Vampire, or The Bride of the Isles").
7. Peter Cushing, *Past Forgetting—Memoirs of the Hammer Years*, London: Weidenfeld & Nicolson, 1988, 25.
8. Hoob, "The Truth About Factory Entertainment's Ring of Dracula," YBMW, September 3, 2010, https://youbentmywookie.com/news/the-truth-about-factory-entertainments-ring-of-dracula-9924.
9. Thomas Kyd (ed. J.R. Mulryne), *The Spanish Tragedy*, London: Ernest Benn, 1970, xx.
10. *Ibid.*, 123.
11. *Ibid.*
12. Gamini Salgado (ed.), *Three Jacobean Tragedies*, Harmondsworth: Penguin, 1969, 45 (Tourneur: "The Revenger's Tragedy").
13. *Ibid.*, 95–96 (Tourneur: "The Revenger's Tragedy").
14. Sylvan Barnet, Monty Berman, and William Burto (eds.), *Classic Theatre—the Humanities in Drama*, Boston: Little, Brown, 1975, 165 (Webster: "The Duchess of Malfi").
15. *Ibid.*, 168 (Webster: "The Duchess of Malfi").
16. *Ibid.*, 185 (Webster: "The Duchess of Malfi").
17. Umberto Eco (trans. William Weaver), *Travels in Hyperreality*, London: Picador, 1987, 202–203 ("Reading Things").
18. *Ibid.*, 201 ("Reading Things").
19. *Ibid.*, 198 ("Reading Things").
20. Richard Wagner (trans. Stewart Spencer), *Selected Letters of Richard Wagner*, London: J.M. Dent, 1987, 309 (Letter to August Röckel, 25/26 Jan. 1854).
21. Dante (trans. Henry Wadsworth Longfellow), *The Divine Comedy: Inferno*, Canto 34, https://www.gutenberg.org/cache/epub/1004/pg1004-images.html#CantoI.XXXIV.
22. John Milton, *The Poetical Works of John*

Milton, London: Frederick Warne, 1896, 106–107 ("Paradise Lost").
  23. *Ibid.*, 135 ("Paradise Lost").
  24. Wischusen (ed.), *The Hour of One*, 99 (J. R. Planché ("The Vampire, or The Bride of the Isles").

Chapter Four

  1. Peter Hutchings, *Dracula—The British Film Guide 7*, London: I.B. Tauris, 2003, 8.
  2. S.S. Prawer, *Caligari's Children—The Film as Tale of Terror*, Oxford: Oxford University Press, 1980, 246.
  3. *Hollywood U.K.* (prod. Charles Chabot, 1992), Episode 2, YouTube, https://www.youtube.com/watch?v=Mb7O0QgnGL4.
  4. Robert Murphy, *Sixties British Cinema*, London: British Film Institute, 1992, 124.
  5. *Hollywood U.K.*, Episode 2.
  6. Murphy, *Sixties British Cinema*, 143–144.
  7. *Hollywood U.K.* Episode 4, YouTube, https://www.youtube.com/watch?v=KuBWbAuntkk.
  8. Murphy, *Sixties British Cinema*, 171.
  9. *Hollywood U.K.*, Episode 3, YouTube, https://www.youtube.com/watch?v=bDILotHd7A8.
  10. Robert Irwin, *Satan Wants Me*, Sawtry: Dedalus, 1999, 317.
  11. Sinclair McKay, *Thing of Unspeakable Horror—The History of Hammer Films*, London: Aurum Press, 2007, 141.
  12. https://en.wikipedia.org/wiki/Alexander_Walker_(critic).
  13. Peter Cushing, *Past Forgetting—Memories of the Hammer Years*, London: Weidenfeld & Nicolson, 1988, 27.
  14. Marcus Hearn (ed.), *Hammer Horror Magazine 1*, no. 1, 1995, 6.
  15. Campbell Dixon, review of *The Curse of Frankenstein* in *The Daily Telegraph*, May 4, 1957: "But when the screen gives us severed heads and hands, eyeballs dropped in a wine glass and magnified, and brains dished up on a plate like spaghetti, I can only suggest a new certificate—'SO' perhaps; for Sadists Only."

Interlude 1

  1. Thomas Carlyle, *The French Revolution*, London: Chapman and Hall, 1912, 45.
  2. *Ibid.*, 91.
  3. Hall Caine, *Recollections of Rossetti*, London: Century, 1990, 30.
  4. *Ibid.*, 42–44.
  5. Arthur Ransome, *Bohemia in London*, New York: Dodd, Mead, 1907, 58.
  6. William Hope Hodgson, *Carnacki the Ghost-Finder* (Dennis Wheatley Library of the Occult) London: Sphere, 1974, 83.
  7. Aleister Crowley (ed. John Symonds and Kenneth Grant), *Confessions of Aleister Crowley*, Harmondsworth: Penguin Arkana, 1989, 889–890.

  8. Christopher Lee, *Lord of Misrule—The Autobiography of Christopher Lee*, London: Orion, 2003, 219.
  9. *Ibid.*, 294.
  10. Cyril Scott, *My Years of Indiscretion*, London: Mills & Boon, 1924, 146–147.
  11. *Ibid.*, 180.
  12. *Ibid.*, 154.
  13. James McNeil Whistler, *Ten O'Clock—A Lecture*, Portland, ME: Thomas Bird Mosher, 1916, 13.
  14. "Who was Peter Warlock? The mysterious circumstances surrounding the composer's sudden death," ClassicFM, February 18, 2020, https://www.classicfm.com/discover-music/who-was-peter-warlock/
  15. David Huckvale, *James Bernard—Composer to Count Dracula*, Jefferson, NC: McFarland, 2002, 77.

Chapter Five

  1. Robert Irwin, *Satan Wants Me*, Sawtry: Dedalus, 1999, 88.
  2. Roman Polanski, *Roman by Polanski*, London: Heinemann, 1984, 278.
  3. Christopher Lee, *Lord of Misrule—The Autobiography of Christopher Lee*, London: Orion, 2003, 227.
  4. Irwin, *Satan Wants Me*, 54.
  5. John Milton, *The Poetical Works of John Milton*, London: Frederick Warne, 1896, 265 ("Paradise Lost").
  6. Victoria Hyatt and Joseph W. Charles, *The Book of Demons*, London: Lorrimer, 1974, 41.
  7. Milton, *The Poetical Works of John Milton*, 106 ("Paradise Lost").
  8. Arthur Edward Waite, *The Brotherhood of the Rosy Cross*, New York: Barnes and Noble, 1993, 495.
  9. Bernard Bromage, *The Occult Arts of Ancient Egypt*, Wellingborough: Aquarian, 1960, 143.
  10. Irwin, *Satan Wants Me*, 77.
  11. "Consulting the Experts: Rollo Ahmed," Dennis Wheatley website, n.d., http://www.denniswheatley.info/museum/room.asp?id=7&exhib=3.
  12. Colin Wilson, *The Occult*, London: Granada/Mayflower, 1973, 580.
  13. *Ibid.*, 592.
  14. Dennis Wheatley (ed.), *Satanism and Witches*, London: Sphere, 1974, 10.
  15. *Ibid.*, 184 ("The Secret Grimoire of Turiel").
  16. Alan Richardson and Marcus Claridge, *The Old Sod: The Odd Life and Inner Work of William G. Gray*, Ignotus Press, 2003, 58–59.
  17. Richard Klemensen (ed.), *Little Shoppe of Horrors—The Journal of Classic British Horror Films*, Issue 22, Des Moines, IA: Elmer Valo Appreciation Society, March 2009, 46 (Bruce G. Hallenbeck, "The Making of *Dracula A.D. 1972*").
  18. "'You'll not only lose your mind, but you'll lose your soul'-Christopher Lee on the occult,"

YouTube, https://www.youtube.com/watch?v=vRVQD4FKPrY .

19. "Highgate Vampire Bishop Sean Manchester," YouTube, https://www.youtube.com/watch?v=AlFjtc1Wij4 .

Chapter Six

1. Christopher Lee, *Tall, Dark and Gruesome*, London: Victor Gollanez, 1997, 234.
2. Gordon Burn, "Ghoul of the Month," in *The Sunday Times Magazine*, August 14, 1977, 37.
3. Kenneth Williams (ed. Russell Davies), *The Diaries of Kenneth Williams*, London: HarperCollins, 1993, 483 (Entry for November 10, 1974).
4. S. S. Prawer, *Caligari's Children—The Film as Tale of Terror*, Oxford: Oxford University Press, 1980, 267.
5. Richard Klemensen (ed.), *Little Shoppe of Horrors* Magazine, Des Moines, IA: Elmer Valo Appreciation Society, issue 22, March 2009, 57 (Bruce G. Hallenbeck, "The Making of *Dracula A.D. 1972*").
6. "NBC Network - Tomorrow with Tom Snyder – 'Monsters & The Movies' (Complete Broadcast, 6/18/1976)," YouTube, https://www.youtube.com/watch?v=c4Pjsw0ELoI .
7. Barbara Belford, *Bram Stoker—A Biography of the Author of Dracula*, London: Weidenfeld & Nicolson, 1996, 312.
8. Hallenbeck, "The Making of *Dracula A.D. 1972*," 57.
9. Roland Barthes (trans. Annette Lavers), *Mythologies*, London: Paladin, 1973, 56.
10. *Wogan*, BBC TV, February 24, 1988,
11. "Peter Cushing Interview 1973," YouTube, https://www.youtube.com/watch?v=Bh96B1zJ1FA .
12. Peter Cushing, *An Autobiography*, London: Weidenfeld & Nicolson, 1987, 134.
13. *Ibid.*, 77.
14. *Ibid.*, 128.
15. Dez Skinn (ed.), *The House of Hammer Magazine 18*, vol. 2, no. 6, March 1978, London: Top Sellers, 28 (Alan Frank, "The Life and Times of Peter Cushing").
16. Prawer, *Caligari's Children*, 203.
17. Christopher Lee, *Lord of Misrule—The Autobiography of Christopher Lee*, London: Orion, 2003, 301.
18. Prawer, *Caligari's Children*, 204.
19. Peter Cushing, *Past Forgetting—Memories of the Hammer Years*, 28.
20. *Ibid.*, 27.
21. Bram Stoker (ed. Leonard Wolf), *The Annotated Dracula*, London: New English Library, 1976, 109.
22. Montague Summers, *The Vampire in Europe*, Wellingborough: Aquarian Press, 1980, ix.
23. *Ibid.*, 115.
24. J. Sheridan Le Fanu, *In a Glass Darkly*, London: John Lehmann, 1957, 15.
25. *Ibid.*, 16.
26. Renée Hayes, *The Society for Psychical Research*, London: Macdonald, 1982, 101.
27. *Ibid.*, 112.
28. *Ibid.*, 47.
29. Lee, *Lord of Misrule*, 302.
30. *Ibid.*, 143.
31. *Ibid.*, 119.
32. *Ibid.*, 118.
33. Stoker, *The Annotated Dracula*, 20.
34. Lee, *Lord of Misrule*, 176.
35. Stoker, *The Annotated Dracula*, 21–22.
36. *Ibid.*, 37.
37. Lee, *Lord of Misrule*, 326.
38. Dez Skinn (ed.), *Hammer's Hall of Horror Magazine 2*, no. 9, June 1978, London: Top Sellers, 8 (Alan Frank, "Christopher Lee Speaks Out").
39. Richard Klemensen (ed.), *Little Shoppe of Horrors—The Journal of Classic British Horror Films*, Issue 47, Des Moines, IA: Elmer Valo Appreciation Society, October 2021, 63 (David Gee, "Dracula and the Modern Age").
40. Tim Stout (ed.), *Supernatural Horror Filming*, No. 1, Westcliffe-on-Sea: Dorset Publishing, 1969, 18–19 (Tim Stout, "Dracula Has Risen from the Grave").
41. Richard Klemensen (ed.), *Little Shoppe of Horrors—The Journal of Classic British Horror Films*, Issue 47, Des Moines, IA: Elmer Valo Appreciation Society, October 2021, 60 (David Gee, "Dracula and the Modern Age").
42. "Christopher Lee Speaks Out."
43. Jonathan Rigby, *Christopher Lee, The Authorised Screen History*, Richmond: Reynolds & Hearn, 2001, 146.
44. Lee, *Lord of Misrule*, 181.
45. Hallenbeck, "The Making of *Dracula A.D. 1972*," 58.
46. Lee, *Lord of Misrule*, 182.
47. Richard Klemensen (ed.), *Little Shoppe of Horrors Magazine*, Issue 22, March 2009, 57 (Denis Meikle, "Introduction to *Dracula A.D. 1972*").

Chapter Seven

1. Richard Klemensen (ed.), *Little Shoppe of Horrors—The Journal of Classic British Horror Films*, Issue 47, Des Moines, IA: Elmer Valo Appreciation Society, October 2021, 65 (David Gee, "Dracula and the Modern Age").
2. Gee, "Dracula and the Modern Age," 69.
3. Richard Klemensen (ed.), *Little Shoppe of Horrors—The Journal of Classic British Horror Films*, Issue 22, Des Moines, IA: Elmer Valo Appreciation Society March 2009, 57 (Bruce G. Hallenbeck, "The Making of *Dracula A.D. 1972*").
4. Gee, "Dracula and the Modern Age," 60–61.
5. *Ibid.*, 61.
6. Richard Klemensen (ed.), *Little Shoppe of Horrors Magazine*, Issue 22, March 2009, 54 (Denis Meikle, "Introduction to *Dracula A.D. 1972*").
7. Bram Stoker (ed. Leonard Wolf), *The Annotated Dracula*, London: New English Library, 1976, 247.

8. Gee, "Dracula and the Modern Age," 61.
9. Marilyn Rodrigues, "Hitting the High Seas with a Heavy Heart," *Catholic Weekly*, October 2, 2018, https://www.catholicweekly.com.au/hitting-the-high-seas-with-a-heavy-heart/.
10. Gee, "Dracula and the Modern Age," 61.
11. *Ibid.*, 70.
12. Richard Klemensen (ed.), *Little Shoppe of Horrors Magazine*, Issue 22, March 2009, 60 (Bruce G. Hallenbeck, "Stoneground Unearthed").
13. *Ibid.*

Chapter Eight

1. Richard Klemensen (ed.), *Little Shoppe of Horrors—The Journal of Classic British Horror Films*, Issue 47, Des Moines, IA: Elmer Valo Appreciation Society, October 2021, 62 (David Gee, "Dracula and the Modern Age").
2. *Ibid.*
3. Richard Klemensen (ed.), *Little Shoppe of Horrors—The Journal of Classic British Horror Films*, Issue 22, Des Moines, IA: Elmer Valo Appreciation Society, March 2009, 92 (Richard Klemensen, "Alan Gibson").
4. *Ibid.*, 91.
5. Nigel Havers, *Playing with Fire*, London: Headline Review, 2006, 279–230.
6. Richard Klemensen (ed.), *Little Shoppe of Horrors—The Journal of Classic British Horror Films*, Issue 22, March 2009, 46 (Bruce G. Hallenbeck, "The Making of *Dracula A.D. 1972*").
7. Aldous Huxley, *The Doors of Perception*, Harmondsworth: Penguin, 1959, 43–44.
8. Aleister Crowley, *Magick Book Four*, San Francisco: Weiser Books, 1994, 122 ("Hymn to Pan").

Interlude 2

1. Richard Klemensen (ed.), *Little Shoppe of Horrors—The Journal of Classic British Horror Films*, Issue 47, Des Moines, IA: Elmer Valo Appreciation Society, October 2021, 60 (David Gee, "Dracula and the Modern Age").
2. Bram Stoker (ed. Leonard Wolf), *The Annotated Dracula*, London: New English Library, 1976, 7.
3. Gee, "Dracula and the Modern Age."
4. Richard Klemensen (ed.), *Little Shoppe of Horrors—The Journal of Classic British Horror Films*, Issue 22, Des Moines, IA: Elmer Valo Appreciation Society March 2009, 54 (Bruce G. Hallenbeck, "The Making of *Dracula A.D. 1972*").
5. Gee, "Dracula and the Modern Age."
6. Hallenbeck, "The Making of *Dracula A.D. 1972*," 54.
7. Gee, "Dracula and the Modern Age."

Chapter Nine

1. Hallenbeck, "The Making of *Dracula A.D. 1972*," 59.

2. https://pitchfork.com/reviews/albums/10482-an-electric-storm/.
3. *Ibid.*
4. https://www.readersdigest.co.uk/culture/music/forgotten-album-white-noise-an-electric-storm.
5. https://www.headheritage.co.uk/unsung/review.php/1143.

Epilogue

1. https://www.goodreads.com/quotes/84666.
2. Christopher James Stone, "Whitstable People: Peter Cushing," Whitstable Views, n.d., https://whitstableviews.com/2017/04/09/town-was-the-perfect-place-for-an-actor-who-sought-obscurity/.
3. "'You'll not only lose your mind, but you'll lose your soul' | Christopher Lee on the occult," YouTube, https://www.youtube.com/watch?v=vRVQD4FKPrY.
4. Serina Sanhu, "Christopher Lee was a 'traditional British Conservative' says Michael Gove," *The Independent*, June 15, 2015, https://www.independent.co.uk/news/people/christopher-lee-was-a-traditional-british-conservative-says-michael-gove-a26026.html.
5. Friedrich Nietzsche (trans. R.J. Hollingdale), *The Twilight of the Idols and the Anti-Christ*, Harmondsworth: Penguin, 1968, 165 ("The Anti-Christ").
6. *Ibid.*, 166.
7. Friedrich Nietzsche (trans. R.J. Hollingdale), *Daybreak*, Cambridge: Cambridge University Press, 1997, 45.
8. *Ibid.*, 50.
9. Noël Carroll, *The Philosophy of Horror*, New York: Routledge, 1990, 188.
10. *Ibid.*, 199.
11. Simon Wilson, *Salvador Dali*, London: Tate Gallery, 1980, 9.
12. Nietzsche, *Daybreak*, 16.
13. Nietzsche, *The Twilight of the Idols and Anti-Christ*, 115–116 ("The Anti-Christ").
14. Nietzsche, *Daybreak*, 16.
15. Arthur Schopenhauer (trans. E.F.J. Payne), *The World as Will and Representation*, vol. 2, New York: Dover, 1958, 465–466.
16. Maurice Maeterlinck (trans. Alexander Teixeira de Mattos), *Death*, London: Methuen, 1912, 1–2.
17. *Ibid.*, 3–4.
18. David Daiches and Anthony Thorlby, *Literature and Western Civilization—The Modern World II: Realities*, London: Aldus Books, 1972, 144 (Anthony Thorlby, "Irrationalism").
19. David Pirie, *The Vampire Cinema*, London: Quarto, 1977, 106.

BIBLIOGRAPHY

Books

Barnet, Sylvan, Monty Berman, and William Burto (eds.), *Classic Theatre—The Humanities in Drama*, Boston: Little, Brown, 1975.
Barthes, Roland (trans. Annette Lavers), *Mythologies*, London: Paladin, 1973.
Belford, Barbara, *Bram Stoker—A Biography of the Author of Dracula*, London: Weidenfeld & Nicolson, 1996.
Betjeman, John (ed. Stephen Games), *Trains and Buttered Toast*, London: John Murray, 2006.
Brommage, Bernard, *The Occult Arts of Ancient Egypt*, Wellingborough: Aquarian, 1960.
Burke, John, *The Second Hammer Film Omnibus*, London: Pan, 1967.
Buscombe, Edward, *Making Legend of the Werewolf*, London: British Film Institute, 1976.
Caine, Hall, *Recollections of Rossetti*, London: Century, 1990.
Carlyle, Thomas, *The French Revolution*, London: Chapman and Hall, 1912.
Carroll, Noël, *The Philosophy of Horror—or Paradoxes of the Heart*, New York: Routledge, 1990.
Clarke, Kenneth, *The Gothic Revival—An Essay on the History of Taste*, London: John Murray, 1974.
Collins, Wilkie, *The Moonstone*, London: Collins, 1973.
Collins, Wilkie (ed. Dorothy Goldman), *Basil*, Oxford: Oxford University Press, 1990.
Collins, Wilkie (ed. Peter Haining), *Sensation Fiction*, London: Peter Owen, 2004.
Crowley, Aleister, *Magick Book Four*, San Francisco: Weiser Books, 1994.
Crowley, Aleister (eds. John Symonds and Kenneth Grant), *Confessions of Aleister Crowley*, Harmondsworth: Penguin Arkana, 1989.
Cushing, Peter, *An Autobiography*, London: Weidenfeld & Nicolson, 1987.
Cushing, Peter, *Past Forgetting—Memoirs of the Hammer Years*, London: Weidenfeld & Nicolson, 1988.
Daiches, David, and Anthony Thorlby, *Literature and Western Civilization—the Modern World II: Realities*, London: Aldus Books, 1972.
Dante (trans. Henry Wadsworth Longfellow), *The Divine Comedy: Inferno*, Canto 34, https://www.gutenberg.org/cache/epub/1004/pg1004-images.html#CantoI.XXXIV.
Dumas, Alexandre, *The Count of Monte Cristo*, London: Routledge, n.d.
Eco, Umberto (trans. William Weaver), *Travels in Hyperreality*, London: Picador, 1987.
Frank, Alan, *Horror Movies*, London: Octopus, 1974.
Frank, Alan, *Monsters and Vampires*, London: Octopus, 1976.
Halliwell, Leslie, *The Dead that Walk*, London: Palladin, 1988.
Havers, Nigel, *Playing with Fire*, London: Headline Review, 2006.
Hayes, Renée, *The Society for Psychical Research*, London: Macdonald, 1982.
Hodgson, William Hope, *Carnacki the Ghost-Finder* (Dennis Wheatley Library of the Occult, Vol. 5), London: Sphere, 1974.
Huckvale, David, *James Bernard: Composer to Count Dracula*, Jefferson, NC: McFarland, 2002.
Hutchings, Peter, *Dracula* (The British Film Guide 7), London: I.B. Tauris, 2003.
Huxley, Aldous, *The Doors of Perception*, Harmondsworth: Penguin, 1959.
Hyatt, Victoria, and Joseph W. Charles, *The Book of Demons*, London: Lorrimer, 1974.
Irwin, Robert, *Satan Wants Me*, Sawtry: Dedalus, 1999.
Kyd, Thomas (ed. J.R. Mulryne), *The Spanish Tragedy*, London: Ernest Benn, 1970.
Lee, Christopher, *Lord of Misrule—The Autobiography of Christopher Lee*, London: Orion, 2003.
Le Fanu, J. Sheridan, *In a Glass Darkly*, London: John Lehmann, 1957.
Maeterlinck, Maurice (trans. Alexander Teixeira de Mattos), *Death*, London: Methuen, 1912.
Maturin, Charles, *Melmoth the Wanderer*, London: Folio, 1993.
McKay, Sinclair, *A Thing of Unspeakable Horror—The History of Hammer Films*, London: Aurum Press, 2007.
Miller, David, *The Peter Cushing Companion*, London: Reynolds & Hearn, 2000.
Milton, John, *The Poetical Works of John Milton*, London: Frederick Warne, 1896.

Murphy, Robert, *Sixties British Cinema*, London: British Film Institute, 1992.
Nietzsche, Friedrich (trans. R.J. Hollingdale), *Daybreak*, Cambridge: Cambridge University Press, 1997.
Nietzsche, Friedrich (trans. R.J. Hollingdale), *The Twilight of the Idols and the Anti-Christ*, Harmondsworth: Penguin, 1968.
Nietzsche, Friedrich (trans. R.J. Hollingdale), *Untimely Meditations*, Cambridge: Cambridge University Press, 1983.
Pirie, David, *The Vampire Cinema*, London: Quarto, 1977.
Polanski, Roman, *Roman by Polanski*, London: Heinemann, 1984.
Prawer, S.S., *Caligari's Children—The Film as Tale of Terror*, Oxford: Oxford University Press, 1980.
Ransome, Arthur, *Bohemia in London*, New York: Dodd, Mead, 1907.
Richardson, Alan, and Marcus Claridge, *The Old Sod: The Odd Life and Inner Work of William G. Gray*, Ignotus Press, 2003.
Rigby, Jonathan, *Christopher Lee—The Authorised Screen History*, London: Reynolds & Hearn, 2001.
Rymer, James Michael, *Varney, the Vampire*, London: Wordsworth, 2010.
Salgado, Gamini (ed.), *Three Jacobean Tragedies*, Harmondsworth: Penguin, 1969.
Schopenhauer, Arthur (trans. E.F.J. Payne), *The World as Will and Representation*, Vol. 2, New York: Dover, 1958.
Scott, Cyril, *My Years of Indiscretion*, London: Mills & Boon, 1924.
Sontag, Susan, *Against Interpretation*, London: Vintage, 2001.
Sontag, Susan, *On Photography*, London: Penguin, 1979.
Stoker, Bram, *The Jewel of Seven Stars*, Far Thrupp: Alan Sutton, 1996.
Stoker, Bram (ed. Leonard Wolf), *The Annotated Dracula*, London: New English Library, 1976.
Summers, Montague, *The Vampire in Europe*, Wellingborough: Aquarian Press, 1980.
Wagner, Richard (trans. Edwin Evans), *Judaism in Music*, London: William Reeves, 1910.
Wagner, Richard (trans. Stewart Spencer), *Selected Letters of Richard Wagner*, London: J.M. Dent, 1987.
Waite, Arthur Edward, *The Brotherhood of the Rosy Cross*, New York: Barnes and Noble, 1993.
Wheatley, Dennis (ed.), *Satanism and Witches* (Dennis Wheatley Library of the Occult, Vol. 21), London: Sphere, 1974.
Whistler, James McNeil, *Ten O'Clock: A Lecture*, Portland, ME: Thomas Bird Mosher, 1916.
Williams, Kenneth (ed. Russell Davies), *The Diaries of Kenneth Williams*, London: HarperCollins, 1993.
Wilson, Colin, *The Occult*, London: Granada/Mayflower, 1973.
Wilson, Simon, *Salvador Dali*, London: Tate Gallery, 1980.
Wischusen, Stephen (ed.), *The Hour of One—Six Gothic Melodramas*, London: Gordon Fraser, 1975.

Magazines and Newspapers

Ballard, Simon J., "'He's Waiting to Freak You Out—Hammer's Modern-Day Dracula Movies Explored," *Scream Magazine*, Nov./Dec .2023, 9–10.
Burn, Gordon, "Ghoul of the Month," *The Sunday Times Magazine*, August 14, 1978.
Dixon, Campell, review of *The Curse of Frankenstein*, *The Daily Telegraph*, May 4, 1957.
Fisher, Bob, "Hauntology," *Fortean Times*, No. 354, June 2017.
Frank, Alan, "Christopher Lee Speaks Out," *Hammer's Halls of Hammer Magazine 21*, vol. 2, no. 9, June 1978, 8.
Frank, Alan, "The Life and Times of Peter Cushing," *The House of Hammer 18*, vol. 2, no. 6, March 1978, 28.
Gee, David, "Dracula and the Modern Age," *Little Shoppe of Horrors—The Journal of Classic British Horror Films*, Issue 47, October 2021, 60.
Gerard, Emily, "Transylvanian Superstitions," *The Nineteenth Century*, vol. 18, July–December 1885, 136.
Hallenbeck, Bruce G., "The Making of *Dracula A.D. 1972*," *Little Shoppe of Horrors—The Journal of Classic British Horror Films*, Issue 22, March 2009, 58.
Hallenbeck, Bruce, G., "Stoneground Unearthed," *Little Shoppe of Horrors—The Journal of Classic British Horror Films*, Issue 22, March 2009, 60.
Hearn, Marcus (ed.), *Hammer Horror Magazine*, vol. 1, no. 1, 1995, 6.
Klemensen, Richard, "Alan Gibson," *Little Shoppe of Horrors—The Journal of Classic British Horror Films*, Issue 22, March 2009, 92.
Sandhu, Serina, "Christopher Lee was a 'traditional British Conservative' says Michael Gove," *The Independent*, June 15, 2015, https://www.independent.co.uk/news/people/christopher-lee-was-a-traditional-british-conservative-says-michael-gove-a26026.html.

Websites

Canote, Terence Towles, "Mama Told Me Not to Come: The Sixties Party Scene on Film," A Shroud of Thoughts, February 2, 2010, http://mercurie.blogspot.com/2010/02/mama-told-me-not-to-come-sixties-party.html.

"Consulting the Experts: Rollo Ahmed," Dennis Wheatley, n.d., http://www.denniswheatley.info/museum/room.asp?id=7&exhib=3.
"*Dracula A.D. 1972* Reviews," Rotten Tomatoes, https://www.rottentomatoes.com/m/dracula_ad_1972/reviews?page=7&type=user.
"Highgate Vampire Bishop Sean Manchester," YouTube, https://www.youtube.com/watch?v=AlFjtc1Wij4.
"Hitchcock at the NFT," BBC, 1969, https://www.bbc.co.uk/iplayer/episode/m00226pd/hitchcock-at-the-nft.
"Hollywood UK Part 2: Making It in London. British Cinema In The 60s. BBC 1993. Edit," YouTube, https://www.youtube.com/watch?v=Mb7O0QgnGL4.
"Hollywood UK Part 3 (British Cinema In The 60s BBC 1993 Documentary)," YouTube, https://www.youtube.com/watch?v=bDILotHd7A8.
"Hollywood UK Part 4 (British Cinema In The 60s BBC 1993 Documentary)," YouTube, https://www.youtube.com/watch?v=KuBWbAuntkk.
Hoob, "The Truth About Factory Entertainment's Ring of Dracula," YBMW, September 3, 2010, https://youbentmywookie.com/news/the-truth-about-factory-entertainments-ring-of-dracula-9924.
Murphy, Matthew, "An Electric Storm (review)," Pitchfork, August 3, 2007, https://pitchfork.com/reviews/albums/10482-an-electric-storm/.
"NBC Network—Tomorrow with Tom Snyder—'Monsters & The Movies' (Complete Broadcast, 6/18/1976)," YouTube, https://www.youtube.com/watch?v=c4Pjsw0ELoI.
"Peter Cushing Interview 1973," YouTube, https://www.youtube.com/watch?v=Bh96B1zJ1FA.
Rodrigues, Marilyn, "Hitting the High Seas with a Heavy Heart," *Catholic Weekly*, October 2, 2018, https://www.catholicweekly.com.au/hitting-the-high-seas-with-a-heavy-heart/.
Stone, Christopher James, "Whitstable People: Peter Cushing," Whitstable Views, n.d., https://whitstableviews.com/2017/04/09/town-was-the-perfect-place-for-an-actor-who-sought-obscurity/.
Wagner, Richard (trans. William Ashton Ellis), "Judaism in Music," Internet Archive, https://archive.org/details/judaisminmusic/page/n1/mode/2up.
Waite, Arthur Edward, "The Brotherhood of the Rosy Cross," Internet Archive, https://archive.org/stream/A.EWaiteTheBrotherhoodOfTheRosyCross/A.+E+Waite+-+The+Brotherhood+of+the+Rosy+Cross_djvu.txt.
"'You'll not only lose your mind, but you'll lose your soul' | Christopher Lee on the occult," YouTube, https://www.youtube.com/watch?v=vRVQD4FKPrY.

Television

Hollywood U.K. (prod. Charles Chabot, 1992), Episode 2.
Wogan, BBC TV, February 24, 1988.

INDEX

Numbers in **_bold italics_** indicate pages with illustrations

Abbott and Costello Meet Frankenstein (dir. Charles Barton) 45, 165
The Abominable Dr. Phibes (dir. Robert Fuest) 42, 58
Ace of Wands (TV series) 81–82
Ackermann, Forrest J 45
Adamson, Al 18
Aeschlyus 44, 49
Les Affranchis (Marie Lenféru) 169
Ahmed, Rollo 86–87
Alda, Alan 83
Alea, Tomás Gutiérrez 152
Alexander, Lewis 123–124
Alfie (dir. Lewis Gilbert) 54
Alf's Button Afloat (dir. Marcel Varnel) 123
Alice's Adventures in Wonderland (dir. William Sterling) 115, 129
Allen, Glenda 21, ***114***, 125, ***126***
Álvarez, Santiago 152
An American Werewolf in London (dir. John Landis) 124
And Now the Screaming Starts (dir. Roy Ward Baker) 115
Anderson, Lindsay 55
Anderson, Michael 110
Andrews, Barry 106
Andrews, Dana 123
Andrews, David 66, 120, 150
Andrews, Eamonn 110
Anger, Kenneth 80, 113
Anne of a Thousand Days (dir. Charles Jarrott) 59
The Anniversary (dir. Roy Ward Baker) 63
Anthony, Jane 113
The Anti-Christ (Friedrich Nietzsche) 79, 166
Antonioni, Michelangelo 23, 27, 54, 116
Apaches (Public Information Film; dir. John MacKenzie) 139

Armstrong, Michael 26
Asher, Jack 109
Ask Agamemnon (Jenni Hall) 26
The Asphyx (dir. Peter Newbrook) 147
Asquith, Anthony 73, 146
Asquith, Robin 63
Assault (dir. Sydney Hayer) 59
Atkins, Susan 34
Attenborough, Richard 57
Austin, Ray 60
Aylmer, Felix 123, 138

Bacharach, Bert 26
Badham, John 32
Bailey, Alice A. 89
Bain, Bill 61
Baker, Roy Ward 3, 4, 23, 31, 33, 59, 63, 87, 115
Ballard, J.G. 136
Ballard, Simon J. 7
Bannen, Ian 60, 62
Barnes, Tim ***114***, 125
The Baron (TV series) 147
Barr, Patrick 63
Barrett, Sir William Fletcher 101, 102
Barry, Charles 28
Barthes, Roland 96
Basil (Wilkie Collins) 14–15, 19
Bates, Ralph 3, 9, 63, 77, 119
Baudelaire, Charles 150
Bava, Mario 42
Beacham, Stephanie 1, 10, ***24***, 61, 112, 113, ***114***, ***118***, ***124***, 125, 150
Beardmore, Colin 125
The Beatles 11, 23, 35, 53, 55, 71, 79, 81, 155
Beatty, Robert 3
Beausoleil, Bobby 80–81
Beck, Jeff 81
Beckett, Samuel 148, 168
Beethoven, Ludwig van 80
Benjamin, Walter 97
Berger, Helmut 77

Bergman, Ingrid 128
Bernard, James 28, 37, 48, 53, 72–73, ***74***, 75, 131, 134, 156, 157, 160, 161
Berova, Olinka 82
Betjeman, John 23, 28
Beyond the Valley of the Dolls (dir. Russ Meyer) 27
Bilbow, Marjorie 5
Björling, Jussi 103
Black, Cilla 155
Black, Isobel 57
The Black Art (Rollo Ahmed) 86–87
The Black Cat (dir. Edgar J. Ulmer) 41
"Black Mass: An Electric Storm in Hell" (*An Electric Storm, the White Noise*) 65, 158–159
Blackwood, Algernon 78
Blakeley, John 125, 127, 135
Blakely, Colin 63
Blavatsky, Helena Petrovna 78
Blood from the Mummy's Tomb (dir. Seth Holt) 42, 59, 63, 93
Blood of Dracula's Castle (dir. Al Adamson) 18
Blood on Satan's Claw (dir. Piers Haggard) 59, 112
Blow Up (dir. Michelangelo Antonini) 23–24, 27, 54, 116
The Blue Lamp (dir. Basil Dearden) 119
Blue Peter (TV show) 52
Blyth, Ernest ***114***, 123, 124
Bogarde, Dirk 55, 75, 119
Bogart, Humphrey 38
Bohemia in London (Arthur Ransome) 70
Bolan, Marc 116
Book of Thoth (trans. Ernest Alfred Wallis Budge) 89
Booth, Anthony 27
Bowers, Lally 17, 123
Bowie, David 81, 149
Bown, Andy 81
Brahms, Penny 125

187

Index

Bramall, Richard 81
Brando, Marlon 61
Branson, Richard 55
Breton, André 168
The Brides of Dracula (dir. Terence Fisher) 3, 32, 45, 58, 132
Broderick, Susan 23
Brodie-Innes, John William 78
Bromage, Bernard 86
Brookes, Mel 165
The Brotherhood of the Rosy Cross (Arthur Edward Waite) 85
Brown, Pamela 58
Browning, Tod 15, 16
Bryan, Dora 61
Budge, Ernest Alfred Wallis 89
Burgess, Anthony 59
Burke, John 15
Burke and Hare (dir. Vernon Sewell) 59
Burton, Richard 59
Busby, Charles Augustin 28
Busby, Thomas 28
Bush, Dick 109, 112, 129
Bushell, Anthony 123
Byrne, Eddie 119

Cabanne, Christie 104
The Cabinet of Dr. Caligari (dir. Robert Wiene) 38
Cacavas, John 161
Caine, Hall 69
Caine, Michael 54, 61
Cameron, Baron David 166
Canote, Terence Towles 27
Cardiff, Jack 75, 147
Cargill, Patrick 25, 76, 116
Carlson, Veronica 43
Carlyle, Thomas 67
"Carmilla" (J. Sheridan Le Fanu) 18, 101
Carradine, John 17, 18, 45
Carreras, Sir James 110
Carreras, Michael 106, 128, 141, 160
Carroll, Noël 167
Carson, John 10
Carus, Paul 89
Casablanca (dir. Michael Curtiz) 10, 38, 49
Cellarius, Andreas 154, **154**
Chaffey, Don 3
Chambers, Vikki 81
The Champions (TV series) 147
Chaney, Lon, Jr. 13, 18, 113
Charles II, King 148
The Charmer (TV series; dir. Alan Gibson) 128, 175
"Chelsea Reach" from *London Pieces* (John Ireland) 71–72
Children and Ponds (Public Information Film) 139
Children Shouldn't Play with Death Things (dir. Bob Clark) 64–65
Chopin, Frédéric François 29
Christie, John 57
Christie, Julie 53–54
Churchill and the Generals (dir. Alan Gibson) 128
City of the Dead (dir. John Moxey) 42
Clark, Bob 64
Clark, Jim 124
Clarke, Gage 18
Clarke, Baron Kenneth 23
Clay, Nicholas 58
Clayton, Jack 61
Clegg, Tom 120
A Clockwork Orange (dir. Stanley Kubrick) 4, 59
Clouzot, Henri-Georges 63
Colditz (TV series) 113
Cole, George 60
Coles, Michael 1, 10, 21, 66, 120, 121, 130, 150
Collins, Joan 62, 63, 77
Collins, Wilkie 14, 19, 21, 22
Collinson, Madeleine 60
Collinson, Mary 60
Collinson, Peter 59, 60
Colmes, Walter 42
Comfort, Lance 123
El Conde Dracula (dir. Jess Franco) 18, 104
Connor, Kevin 90
Cooper, George A. 123
Coote, Robert 77
Corlan, Anthony 120
Corman, Roger 26, 42
Corruption (dir. Robert Hartford-Davis) 26–27
Cossins, James 63
Cotton, Joseph 128
Count Dracula (dir. Philip Saville) 18
The Count of Monte Cristo (Alexandre Dumas) 41
Count Yorga—Vampire (dir. Bob Kelljan) 32, 106
Countess Dracula (dir. Peter Sasdy) 59, 139
Coward, Noël 103
Crash (dir. David Cronenberg) 136–137
The Creature from the Black Lagoon (dir. Jack Arnold) 41
The Creeping Flesh (dir. Freddie Francis) 124
Crescendo (dir. Alan Gibson) 128, 129, 130
The Crimson Cult (dir. Vernon Sewell) see *The Curse of the Crimson Altar*
Cronenberg, David 136
Crossroads (TV series) 112, 122–123

Crow, William Bernard 87
Crowley, Aleister 70, 72, 78, 79, 80, 81, 88, 138
Crucible of Terror (dir. Ted Hooker) 59
Cunningham, John 28
The Curse of Frankenstein (dir. Terence Fisher) 2, 48, 52, 97, 110
The Curse of the Crimson Altar (dir. Vernon Sewell) 26, 35
Curtiz, Michael 10, 38, 49
Cushing, Helen 50, 93
Cushing, Peter 1, 7, 25, 27, 37, **37**, 39, 40, 42, 44, 45, 50, 52, 58, 61, 62, 63, 65, 66, 85, 92–104, **93**, **95**, **99**, 106, 109, 110, 113, 121–12, 122, 123, 126–127, 128, 130, 132, 142, **147**, 150, 165, 166, 169
Cutts, Graham 123

Dahl, Roald 58
Daleks' Invasion Earth 2051 A.D. (dir. Gordon Flemyng) 125
Dallamano, Massimo 77
Daly, Michael 24
The Dance of the Vampires (dir. Roman Polanski) 34
Dante Alighieri 50
Dark Side of the Moon (Pink Floyd) 160
Darling (dir. John Schlesinger) 53
Darwin, Charles 78
Davies, Rupert 43
Davis, Sammy, Jr. 40
Dead of Night (TV series) 82
Dearden, Basil 55, 75, 119
Death Line, (dir. Gary Sherman) 63–64
"The Death Watcher" (dir. John Duguid) 57
Defence of the Realm (dir. David Drury) 119
Dehn, Paul 72–73
Delaney, Shelagh 52
Delgado, Roger 117
De Morgan, William 149
Dent, Malcolm 80
Derbyshire, Delia 52, 65, 159
The Devil Rides Out (dir. Terence Fisher) 9, 73, 80, 83, 86, 146
The Devils (dir. Ken Russell) 59
The Devils of Loudon (Aldous Huxley) 59
De Woolf, Francis 3
Les diaboliques (dir. Henri-George Clouzot) 63
Diamonds Are Forever (dir. Guy Hamilton) 148
Dickie, Olga 125

Dicks, Ted 60
Dicks, Terence 117
Die Screaming, Marianne (dir. Pete Walker) 60, 76
Dieren, Bernard van 72
Disney, Walt 29, 117
Disraeli, Benjamin 21
Dixon of Dock Green (TV series) 119, 121
Dr. Jekyll and Mr. Hyde (Robert Louis Stevenson) 61
Dr. Jekyll and Sister Hyde (dir. Roy Ward Baker) 3, 23, 59, 119, 120
Dr. Who (TV series) 52, 81, 112, 117, 159, 162
Dr. Who and the Daleks (dir. Gordon Flemyng) 121
Dominique 170
Don Giovanni (Wolfgang Amadeus Mozart) 103
Don't Look Now (dir. Nicolas Roeg) 143
Doomwatch (dir. Peter Sasdy) 61, 62
The Doors of Perception (Aldous Huxley) 80, 138
Dors, Diana 77
Douglas, Josephine 89, 110–*111*, 134, 152 160
Dracula (Bram Stoker) 4, 6, 7, 8, 9, 13–15 18–22, 32, 42–43, 68, 94, 95, 101, 106, 107, 125, 144, 149, 164, 165
Dracula (dir. John Badham) 32
Dracula (dir. Terence Fisher) 5, 6, 7, 30, 33, 38, 43, 45, 52–53, 100, 106, 107–108, 109, 119–120, 134, 142, 144, 145
Dracula (dir. Tod Browning) 15–16, 17
Dracula Has Risen from the Grave (dir. Freddie Francis) 3, 8, 15, 31–32, 43, 45, 51, 90–91, 105, 106, 120, 123, 132, 144
Dracula: Prince of Darkness (dir. Terence Fisher) 3, 7–8, 15, 31, 43, 50, 54, 90, 120
Dracula's Daughter (dir. Lambert Hillyer) 16, 73
Dragoti, Stan 32
Dreyer, Carl 18
Drury, David 119
The Duchess of Malfi (John Webster) 48
Dukas, Paul 117
Dumas, Alexandre 41
Durden, Richard 120
Dyson, Noel 116

Easy Rider (dir. Dennis Hopper) 27
Eberhardt, Norma 18
Ebert, Roger 4
Eco, Umberto 38–39, 49
Eden, Mark 35
Edna the Inebriate Woman (dir. Ted Kotcheff) 56
Edwards, Vince 76
The Egyptian Book of the Dead (trans. Ernest Alfred Wallis Budge) 89
Eh, Joe (TV series; dir. Alan Gibson) 129
Eisner, Lotte H. 38
Elder, John (aka Anthony Hinds) 43
Elektra (Hofmannsthal/Strauss) 46
Elès, Sandor 59
Eliot, T.S. 49, 70, 90
Éliphas Lévi 9
Elizabeth II, Queen 155
Ellis, William 1, *24*, 65, 112, 113, *114*, 115
Emergency Ward 10 (TV series) 111, 112
Emery, Gilbert 16
Escape into Night (dir. Richard Bramall) 81
Et mourir de plaisir (dir. Roger Vadim) 18
The Eumenides (Aeschylus) 46
The Evil of Frankenstein (dir. Freddie Francis) 92
Ewen, Cecil L'Strange 89
Ewers, Hanns-Heinz 78
Ewing, Barbara 43
The Exorcist (dir. William Friedkin) 83
Eye of the Devil (dir. J. Lee Thompson) 33, 82

The Faces 125
Faithful, Marianne 81
Fantasia (dir. Ben Sharpsteen, et al.) 117
Farmer, Suzan 43
Farrant, David 90
A Fascinating History of Magic, Witchcraft and Occultism (William Bernard Crow) 87
Father, Dear Father (dir. William G. Stewart) 25–26, 76, 115–116, 127
Fear in the Night (dir. Jimmy Sangster) 57, 62, 63
A Feast at Midnight (dir. Justin Hardy) 166
Fiander, Lewis 119
Finch, Peter 63
Find the Link (TV series) 110
Fine, Harry 60
Fisher, Bob 11
Fisher, Terence 3, 5, 9, 31, 41, 53, 54, 58, 109, 110, 123, 130, 131, 134, 137, 142

Flanagan, Maureen *114*, 125, 149
Fleming, Ian 70, 73
Flemyng, Gordon 121, 125
The Flesh and Blood Show (dir. Pete Walker) 62, 63, 64
Les fleurs du mal (Charles Baudelaire) 150
Floyd, Calvin 104
Foch, Nina 17
Fonda, Peter 26
Fontaine, Joan 82
Forbes, Bryan 34
Ford, Derek 113
Fortune, Dion 78, 87, 88
Four-Sided Triangle (dir. Terence Fisher) 3
Fox, James 75
Francis, Freddie 3, 8, 26, 31, 39, 58, 61, 84, 92, 123–124
Franco, Jess 18, 104
Frank, Alan 4, 5
Frankel, Cyril 82, 123
Frankenstein (Mary Shelley) 15
Frankenstein and the Monster from Hell (dir. Terence Fisher) 45
Frankenstein Must Be Destroyed (dir. Terence Fisher) 58, 92, 160
Frankenstein—The True Story (dir. Jack Smight) 124
Franklyn-Robbins, John 125
Freda, Riccardo 17
Frenzy (dir. Alfred Hitchcock) 59
Fright (dir. Peter Collinson) 59–60, 66
Le frisson des vampires (dir. Jean Rollin) 18, 170, 171
From Beyond the Grave (dir. Kevin Connor) 90
Fuest, Robert 42, 58

Galeen, Henrik 168
Gallagher, Ken 87
Garbo, Greta *94*, 96
Gardner, Gerald 89
Garner, Alan 82
Gaster, Moses 88
Gates, Tudor 60
Gaunt, Valerie 106
Gee, David 114
Gee, Grant 11
Geeson, Judy 26, 57, 63, 75, 129
Genevieve (dir. Henry Cornelius) 146
George, Susan 59, 60, 66
Gerard, Emily 14
Get Carter (dir. Mike Hodges) 61
Ghost Story for Christmas (TV series) 82

Index

The Ghoul (dir. Freddie Francis) 26, 58
Gibson, Alan 3, 4, 5, 7, *24*, 25, 35, *37*, 38, 50, 59, 64, 72, 73, 76, 77, 81, *99*, 106, 107, 109, 112, 120, 121, 122, 123, 125, 126, 128–134, 136–144, 146, 148, 161, 165, 170, *171*
Gibson, Jessica 128
Gibson, Sarah 128
Gilbert, Lewis 54
Gilbert, William Schwenck 26
Gillen, Jeff 65
Gilliat, Sidney 110
Giordano Bruno and the Hermetic Tradition (Francis A. Yates) 87
Glendenning, Candace 63
Glitter, Gary 149
The Godfather (dir. Francis Ford Coppola) 96
Godula, Brian 125
Goethe, Johann Wolfgang von 117
Goldfinger (dir. Guy Hamilton) 146
Goodbye Gemini (dir. Alan Gibson) 26, 73, 128, 129–130, 137
Gorey, Edward 32
Gothard, Michael 147
Götterdämmerung (Richard Wagner) 103, 158
Gough, Michael 85
Gove, Michael 166
Grainer, Ron 52, 159
Gray, Charles 73, 83
Gray, William 88
Green, Celia 102
Green, Guy 123
Greene, Richard 62
Grimm Brothers 8, 15
Grundy, Bill 66
Guest, Val 119
Guillermin, John 148
Gunning, Christopher 26
Gurney, Sharon 64
Gwynne, Michael 120

Haggard, H. Rider 102
Haggard, Piers 59, 112
Haining, Peter 14
Hair (Gerome Ragni/James Rado/Galt MacDermot) 116, 151–152
Hall, Jenni 26
Hall, Stewart 60
Hallet, Neil 60
Halliwell, Leslie 5
Hamilton, Guy 74, 146, 148
Hamlet (William Shakespeare) 16, 46, 49
Hammer Presents Dracula with Christopher Lee (LP; prod. Don Norman) 108, *108*, 130
Hammerhead (dir. David Miller) 75–76
Hands of the Ripper (dir. Peter Sasdy) 61, 120, 124
Hanley, Jenny 43, 63
Hardy, Oliver 96
Harlow, Hugh 128
Harris, Rolf 60
Harryhausen, Ray 70
Hartford-Davis, Robert 26, 61
Hartley, Mariette 33
Hastings, Michael 61
The Haunted House of Horror (dir. Michael Armstrong) 26
The Haunted Palace (dir. Roger Corman) 42
The Haunting (dir. Robert Wise) 144
Havers, Nigel 128
Hawkins, Jack 77
Hayden, Linda 63, 138
Hayer, Sydney 59
Hayes, Isaac 161
Haynes, Patricia 60
Haynes, Renée 102
Hayter, James 3, 110
Heartbeat (TV series) 147
Heath, Edward 57
Helen Keller: The Miracle Continues (dir. Alan Gibson) 129
Helwing, Georg Andreas 101
Hemmings, David 23
Hemmingway, Ernest 38
Hendrix, Jimmy 149
Hendry, Ian 62
Herrmann, Bernard 34
Heseltine, Philip 72
Hessler, Gordon 124
Hickox, Douglas 42, 73, 76
Hillier, Bevis 153
Hillyer, Lambert 16
Hinds, Anthony 110
Hiralal, R.C. 71
His Dark Materials (Philip Pullman) 87
The History of the Devil and the Idea of Evil (Paul Carus) 89
Hitchcock, Alfred 34, 59, 110, 142
Hitler, Adolf 28, 30, 78
Hodgson, Brian 159
Hodgson, William Hope 70, 101
Hofmannsthal, Hugo von 46
Holcroft, Thomas 28
Holden, Gloria 73
Holloway, Ann 25
Holmes, Arthur Hill 28
Holmes, Robert 117
Holt, Seth 42, 93
Hooker, Ted 59
Hooper, Ewan 43
Horror of Dracula (dir. Terence Fisher) see *Dracula* (dir. Terence Fisher)
The Horror of Frankenstein (dir. Jimmy Sangster) 123
HorroRitual (promo-reel for *Dracula A.D. 1972*) *36*, 37
Hough, John 58, 60, *95*, 112
Houghton, Don 4, 16, 17, 24, 35, 46, 66, 90, 101, 105, 110, 111, 112, 114, 116–117, 119, 121–122, 123, 131, *132*, 135, 137, 139, 141, 144, 148, 149, 150, 162, 170
The Hound of the Baskervilles (dir. Terence Fisher) 3
House of Dracula (dir. Erle C. Kenton) 17
House of Frankenstein (dir. Erle C. Kenton) 17, 45
The House That Vanished (dir. José Ramón Larraz) 147
House (TV show; prod. Josephine Douglas) 110
Howard, Vanessa 62
Hughes, Lynne *114*, 125
Hunky Dory (LP; David Bowie) 81
Hunt, Marsha 1, *24*, 35, *37*, 81, 88, 116, 150
Hunt, William Holman 67
Huntley, Raymond 123
Hurt, John 58, 123
Huson, Paul 89
Hutchings, Peter 53
Huxley, Aldous 59, 80, 138
Huysmans, Joris-Karl 78

I Ching (Richard Wilhelm/C.G. Jung) 87
I Don't Want to be Born (dir. Peter Sasdy) 77, 115
I, Monster (dir. Stephen Weeks) 61, 124
I Walked with a Zombie (dir. Jacques Tourneur) 141
If (dir. Lindsay Anderson) 55
I'll Never Forget Whatshisname (dir. Michael Winner) 73
In a Glass Darkly (J. Sheridan Le Fanu) 101
In the Devil's Garden (dir. Sydney Hayer) see *Assault*
Incense for the Damned (dir. Robert Hartford-Davies) 61
Inescourt, Frieda 16
Inferno (Dante Alighieri) 50
Inner Traditions of Magic (William Gray) 88
The Innocents (dir. Jack Clayton) 61
Ireland, John 71–72
Irving, Sir Henry 71, 104
Irwin, Robert 56, 79, 81, 83, 86, 165

Index

Jacobs, W.W. 62
Jagger, Chris 81, 113
Jagger, Mick 81, 113, 116, 149
James, Henry 61, 70
James, Montague Rhodes 82, 112
Jane Eyre (Charlotte Brontë) 148
Jarrott, Charles 59
Jarvis, Martin 10
Jefferson Airplane 81
Jeffries, Peter 130
Jekyll's Inferno (dir. Terence Fisher) see *The Two Faces of Dr. Jekyll*
The Jewel of Seven Stars (Bram Stoker) 42, 82
John, Augustus 148
Johnson, Arte 32
Jones, Freddie 129
Jones, Steven 81
Jones, Tom 155
Jourdan, Louis 18, 104
Journey to the Unknown (TV series) 128
Journey's End (Robert Cedric Sherriff) 96
Jung, Carl Gustav 79–80, 87
Jurgens, Curt 83

Kanner, Alexis 26, 129
Karloff, Boris 30, 35, 37, 41, 70–71, 97
Keen, Geoffrey 151
Keir, Andrew 3, 43
Kennedy, Ian 66
Kennedy, Troy 66
Kenton, Erle C. 17, 45
Kenton, Stan 156, 162–163
Key, Janet **24**, 50, 113, 114, 115, 127, **147**
Kieling, Wolfgang 34
King, Steven 165, 167
Kinnear, Roy 24
Kipling, Rudyard 55
The Kiss of the Vampire (dir. Don Sharp) 34, 57, 82, 83, 139
Kitchen, Michael 7, **24**, 113, 149
Klee, Paul 78
Kneele, Nigel 82
Koestler, Arthur 102
Kosmogomia (Krzysztof Penderecki) 160
Koteas, Elias 136
Kray brothers 53
Kubrick, Stanley 4, 5, 59
Kupka, František 78
Kyd, Thomas 46

The Lair of the White Worm (Bram Stoker) 70
Lallemond, Claude François 19
Landers, Lew 16
Landis, John 124

Landres, Paul 17
Lang, Fritz 38
Lang, Judy 34
Langella, Frank 32
LaPorte, Deirdre 125
Larraz, José Ramón 147
Latham, Philip 31
Laurel, Stan 96
LaVey, Anton 79, 136, 139
Led Zeppelin 80
Lederer, Francis 17–18
Lee, Birgit 38
Lee, Christina 38
Lee, Sir Christopher 1, 5, 6, 7, 8, **8**, 9, 13, 16, 17, 18, 30, 33, 34, 37–40, 42–44, 45, 46, 50, **51**, 52, 61, 64, 65, 70–71, 82, 83, 85, 89, 90, 92, **93**, 96, 97, 103–109, **107**, **111**, 122, 125, 126–127, 130, 132, 138, 139, 147, 161, 164, 165, 166, 169, **171**
Le Fanu, J. Sheridan 18, 101
Left, Right and Centre (dir. Sidney Gilliat) 110
The Legend of the Seven Golden Vampires (dir. Roy Ward Baker) 87, 144
The Legend of the Werewolf (dir. Freddie Francis) 39
Leland, David 120
Lenéru, Marie 169
Leon, Valerie 42
Lerios, Cory **114**, 125, **126**, 151
Lesley-Anne Down 59
Lester, Richard 55
Let's Make a Night of It (dir. Graham Cutts) 123
Letts, Barry 117
Lewis, Jerry 40
Liberace, Władziu Valentino 29–30
Lim, Pik-Sen 112
Lindsay, Jack 89
Lippert, Robert 82
Liszt, Franz 29, 30
Littler, Richard 11
Lloyd, Sue 27
Lodge, Sir Oliver 101
Lombroso, Cesare 22
Lonely Water (Public Information Film; dir. Jeff Grant) 139
Lorrain, Jean 78
Lorre, Peter 38
Losey, Joseph 75
Love at First Bite (dir. Stan Dragoti) 32
The Love Bug (dir. Robert Stevenson) 146
The Loved One (dir. Tony Richardson) 30
Lucifer Rising—A Love Vision (dir. Kenneth Anger, 1972) 80, 113
Ludwig II of Bavaria, King 29

Lugosi, Bela 13, 15, 16, 17, 18, 31, 41, 45, 104
Lumley, Joanna 57
Lust for a Vampire (dir. Jimmy Sangster) 35, 60, 63, 113, 149
Luttrell, Constance **124**, 125

The Mabinogion 82
MacGregor, Scott 151
Machen, Arthur 71, 78, 101
MacKenzie, Michael 82
Macmillan, Harold 23, 52
MacTaggart, James 82
Madhouse (dir. Jim Clark) 124
Maeterlinck, Maurice 169
The Magic Christian (dir. Joseph McGrath) 147
The Magician (W. Somerset Maugham) 70
Maharishi Mahesh Yogi 71
Malchus, Marius 88
The Mamas and the Papas 80
Mamoulian, Rouben **94**, 96
Man in a Suitcase (TV series) 146–147
The Man Who Laughs (dir. Paul Leni) 107
The Man with the Golden Gun (dir. Guy Hamilton) 97
Manchester, Sean 89–90
Mancini, Henry 157
Mander, Miles 16
Mann, Manfred 155
Manson, Charles 33–34, 55, 56, 65, 80
Mantovani, Annuzio Paolo 25
Marianne Dreams (Catherine Storr) 81
Mark of the Vampire (dir. Tod Browning) 16
Marla, Norma 123
Marschner, Heinrich 42
Martell, Philip 112, 157, 158, 160
Marx, Karl 55
The Mask of Satan (dir. Mario Bava) see *Black Sunday*
The Masque of the Red Death (dir. Roger Corman) 26
Mastering Witchcraft (Paul Huson) 89
Matheson, Judy 63
Maturin, Charles 20
Maugham, W. Somerset 70
Maxwell, Gavin 148
McCartney, Paul 55
McGrath, Joseph 147
McKay, Sinclair 6, 7, 25, 29, 57
Meade-Faulkner, John 82
The Meaning of Witchcraft (Gerald Gardner) 89
Melmoth the Wanderer (Charles Maturin) 20
The Mephisto Waltz (dir. Paul Wendkos) 83

Merritt, George 119
Meyrink, Gustav 78
Miller, David 75
Miller, Sir Jonathan 112
Miller, Philip "Pip" 2, 10, *24*, 35, 113, ***114***, ***118***, ***124***
Mills, Sir John 128
Milton, John 13, 33, 50, 84–85
"The Mind of Evil" (*Dr. Who* TV serial) 117
Mingaye, Don *24*, 129, 151, 152
Mitchell, Bill 35
Modesty Blaise (dir. Joseph Losey) 75
Mondrian, Piet 78
"The Monkey's Paw" (W.W. Jacobs) 62
The Moonstone (Wilkie Collins) 14, 22
Moreno, Lydia 125
Morris, Artro 121
Morris, Christopher 125
Morrison, Jim 80
Moxey, John 42
Mucha, Alphonse 150
Mud 149
Muerte la invasor (dir. Tomás Gutiérrez Alea & Santiago Álvarez) 151
Mulryn, J.R. 46
The Mummy (dir. Terence Fisher) 5, 10, 119, 123, 137
The Mummy's Hand (dir. Christie Cabanne) 104
Mundle, Clement Williams Kennedy 102
Mungo Jerry 116
Munro, Caroline 1, 9, *24*, 58, 65, 77, 106, ***107***, 108, 112, 116, ***117***, 125, 149–150
Munt, Peter 130
Murnau, F.W. 18, 168
Murphy, Matthew 159
Murphy, Robert 54
Murray, Pete 110
The Mutations (dir. Jack Cardiff) 75, 147
Myers, Frederick William Henry 101
Mystery and Imagination (TV series) 82

Nádasy, Countess Elisabeth 59
The Name's the Same (TV show) 110
Neal, Patricia 58
Neame, Christopher 1, 4, 45, ***83***, 94, 96, 106, 107, 108–109, 112, 113, ***114***, 117, ***118***, 125, 131, 142
Neuberg, Victor 88
Never Let Go (dir. John Guillermin) 148

Never Takes Sweets from a Stranger (dir. Cyril Frankel) 123
Neville, John 57
New Scotland Yard (TV series) 139
Newbrook, Peter 147
Newman, Paul 34
Nicholas, Paul 62
Nicholls, Anthony 55
Nietzsche, Friedrich 10, 29, 56, 79, 166–167, 169
The Night Digger (dir. Alasdair Reid) 58
Night of the Demon (dir. Jacques Tourneur) 123
The Nightcomers (dir. Michael Winner) 61
Niven, David 82
Nordau, Max 22
Norman, Don 108
Nosferatu (dir. F.W. Murnau) 18, 168
Nothing but the Night (dir. Peter Sasdy) 103

"O, Whistle and I'll Come to You, My Lad" (dir. Jonathan Miller) 112
The Oblong Box (dir. Gordon Hessler) 124
The Occult (Colin Wilson) 87
The Occult Arts of Ancient Egypt (Bernard Bromage) 86
O'Connolly, Jim 63
Olivier, Laurence 46, 96
The Omen (dir. Richard Donner) 83, 91
199 Park Lane (TV series; dir. Alan Gibson) 129
One Million Years B.C. (dir. Don Chaffey) 3
One More Time (dir. Jerry Lewis) 40
"Operation Safecrack" (episode of *Tales of the Unexpected*, TV series; dir. Alan Gibson) 128
The Oresteia (Aeschylus) 44, 49
Oriental Magic (Indries Shah) 87
The Origin of Species (Charles Darwin) 78
The Origins of Alchemy in Graeco-Roman Egypt (Jack Lindsay) 89
Ormsby, Alan 64, 65
Ormsby, Anya 65
Ornadel, Cyril 60
Ost, Valerie van 58
O'Sullivan, Richard 25
The Owl Service (TV series; dir. Peter Plummer) 82

Page, Jimmy 80–81
Paladino, Eusapia 102
Paradise Lost (John Milton) 50, 83
Parfitt, Judy 57
Parks, Gordon 161
Parsifal (Richard Wagner) 103
The Party's Over (dir. Guy Hamilton) 74–75
Past Forgetting—Memoirs of the Hammer Years (Peter Cushing) 97
Patience (After Sebald) (dir. Grant Gee) 11
Patrick, Nigel 62
Pearce, Jacqueline 94
Peckinpah, Sam 60
Péladan, Joséphin 78
Penderecki, Krzysztof 160
Pertwee, Jon 112
Peters, Luan 63
Phillips, Adam 11
Phillips, John 80
Phillips, Michelle 80
The Picture of Dorian Gray (Oscar Wilde) 77
Pink Floyd 81, 160
Pink Panther theme (Henry Mancini) 157
Pirie, David 4, 5, 170
Pitt, Ingrid 59
The Plague of the Zombies (dir. John Gilling) 120
Planché, J.R. 42, 44, 51
Play Safe (Public Information Film; dir. David Eady) 59, 139
Pleasence, Donald 64, 66
Plummer, Peter 82
Polanski, Roman 33–34, 55, 75, 80, 83, 123
Polidori, John 42
Portabella, Pere 103
Porter, Eric 61
Potter, Martin 26, 129
Powell, Eddie 130
Prawer, S.S. 39, 53, 94, 97
Presley, Elvis 52
Price, Alan 81
Price, Steve 125, 127, 134
Price, Vincent 42, 58
Prince of Terror, promo-reel for *Dracula A.D. 1972* 37
Procul Harem 81
Profumo, John 53
Psychic Self-Defense (Dion Fortune) 87
Psycho (dir. Alfred Hitchcock) 142
Psychomania (dir. Don Sharp) 62
Pullman, Philip 87
Pyne, Natasha 25

Quant, Mary 67, 148
Quarry, Robert 32, 106
The Quatermass Experiment (dir. Val Guest) 119
Quatro, Suzi 64
Queen Christina (dir. Rouben Mamoulian) **94**, 96

Rachmaninoff, Sergei 151
Radcliffe, Ann 15
Ransome, Arthur 70
Raven, Mike 59
Rawnsley, David 149
Redgrave, Sir Michael 128
Reed, Sir Carol 148
Reed, Oliver 74
Reeves, Michael 75
Reid, Alasdair 58, 62, 63
Repulsion (dir. Roman Polanski) 75, 123
Requiem pour un vampire (dir. Jean Rollin) 18
The Return of Count Yorga (dir. Bob Kelljan) 32–35, 106
The Return of Dracula (dir. Paul Landres) 17–18
Return of the Vampire (dir. Lew Landers) 16–17
Retz, Giles de 85
The Revenge of Frankenstein (dir. Terence Fisher) 41–42, 123
Revenge of the Creature (dir. Jack Arnold) 41
The Revenger's Tragedy (Thomas Middleton) 47
Rhys, Jean 148
Richard, Cliff 52
Richardson, Jo 122
Richardson, John 82
Richardson, Tony 30
Richet, Charles 102
Rigby, Jonathan 5, 106
Der Ring des Nibelungen (Richard Wagner) 49, 113
Ring of Bright Water (Gavin Maxwell) 148
Ripper, Michael 10, 120
Robin Redbreast (dir. James MacTaggart) 82
Robins, John 123
Robinson, Bernard 7, 151
Robinson, Harry 60
Robles, Gérman 17
Röckel, August 49
The Rocky Horror Show 142
Roeg, Nicolas 143
Rogers, Eric 59
Rollin, Jean 18, 170
The Rolling Stones 81
Rosemary's Baby (dir. Roman Polanski) 80, 83
Rossetti, Dante Gabriel 67–69, **68**

Rover, Abigail 18
Rushton, William Albert Hugh 102
Ruskin, John 23
Russell, Bertrand 52
Russell, Ken 59
Rymer, James Malcolm 42

The Sacred Magic of Abra-Melin the Mage 80
Sade, Marquis de 85, 168
Sampson, Annie **114**, 125, 126–127
Sanders, Alex 113
Sandford, Jeremy 56
Sangster, Jimmy 7, 57, 60, 61, 63
Sapphire (dir. Basil Dearden) 75
Sasdy, Peter 5, **8**, 9, 59, 61, 62, 77, 103, 115, 138, 139
Satan Wants Me (Robert Irwin) 56, 79, 81, 83, 86
The Satanic Rites of Dracula (dir. Alan Gibson) 4, 6, 8, 16, 19, 27, 33, 42, 44, 45, 50, 52, 57, 58, 63, 91, 105, 109, 121–122, 129, 141, 153, 161
Savile, Jimmy 60
Saville, Philip 18
The Scaffold 155
"The Scarlet Ceremonies" from *Decorations* (John Ireland) 71
Scars of Dracula (dir. Roy Ward Baker) 4, 6, 18, 31, 35, 43, 59, 63, 91, 110, 120, 151
Schlesinger, John 53
Schopenhauer, Arthur 168
Schreck, Max 18
Schubert, Franz 164
Schwabe, Carlos 150
Scott, Cyril 71, 78
Scott, Giles Gilbert 23
Scream and Scream Again (dir. Gordon Hessler) 147
Scriabin, Alexander 78
Sebald, G.W. 12
Sebring, Jay 34
Secret Grimoire of Turiel (trans. Marius Malchus) 88
The Secret of Dorian Gray (dir. Massimo Dallamano) 77
Secret Rites (dir. Derek Ford) 113
Sellers, Peter 148
Sgt. Pepper's Lonely Hearts Club Band (the Beatles) 11, 23, 79, 80
The Servant (dir. Joseph Losey) 75
Sewell, Brian 72
Sewell, Vernon 26, 59
Sex Pistols 66
Shadows of Fear (TV series) 57

Shaft (dir. Gordon Parks) 161
Shah, Indres 87
Shakespeare, William 42, 46, 49, 69, 96
Sharp, Don 34, 42, 62, 82
Shatter (dir. Michael Carreras) 141
Shaughnessy, Alfred 110
Shaw, Richard Norman 28
Shelley, Barbara 43, 54, 94
Shelley, Mary 15
Shelley, Percy Bysshe 79
Sherman, Gary 63
Sherriff, Robert Cedric 96
Shirley, Hon. Ralph 101
Siddal, Elizabeth 67
Sidgwick, Henry 101
"The Silent Scream" (episode of *The Hammer House of Horror*, TV series; dir. Alan Gibson) 129
Siodmak, Robert 16, 113, 144
Six-Five Special (dir. Alfred Shaughnessy) 110
Six-Five Special (TV show) 110
Skeggs, Roy 128
Skripal, Sergei 100
The Skull (dir. Freddie Francis) 85, 123
Slade 149
Smight, Jack 124
Smith, Brian John 125
Smith, Pamela Colman 70
The Snorkel (dir. Guy Green) 123
Snyder, Tom 94
Something to Hide (dir. Alasdair Reid) 62, 63
Son of Dracula (dir. Robert Siodmak) 16, 17, 113
A Song to Remember (dir. Charles Vidor) 29
Sontag, Susan 11, 30–31, 35
The Sorcerers (dir. Michael Reeves) 75
The Spanish Tragedy (Thomas Kyd) 46–47
The Spiral Staircase (dir. Robert Siodmak) 144
Stage Fight (dir. Alfred Hitchcock) 110
Star Wars Episode II—Attack of the Clones (dir. George Lucas) 105
Star Wars Episode IV—A New Hope (dir. George Lucas) 97
Star Wars Episode VI—The Return of the Jedi (dir. Richard Marquand) 119
Steele, Barbara 26
Steele, Pippa 141
Sterling, William 115
Stevenson, Robert Louis 59
Stewart, Philip 123, 124, 151

Stewart, Rod 125
Stewart, William G. 25
Stockhausen, Karlheinz 80
Stoker, Bram 4, 6, 7, 9, 13–15, 18–22, 30, 42, 68, **69**, 70, 71, 82, 94, 95, 100, 101, 104, 105, 106, 116, 125, 132, 144, 149, 164, 165
Stone, Christopher James 166
The Stone Tape (dir. Peter Sasdy) 82
Stoneground 1, 24, **114**, 123, 125–127, 134–135, 147, 158
Storr, Catherine 81
Strange Conflict (Dennis Wheatley) 87
Strauss, Richard 46
Straw Dogs (dir. Sam Peckinpah) 60
Stricklyn, Ray 18
The Student of Prague (dir. Henrik Galeen) 168
Style, Michael 60
Subotsky, Milton 62
Summers, Montague 101
Surrealisic Manifesto (André Breton) 168
Sutherland, Donald 143
Swami Abhedananda 71
Sweeney! (dir. David Wickes, 1977) 121, 124
The Sweeney (TV series) 66, 120, 121, 132, 146, 147, 154
Sweeney 2 (dir. Tom Clegg) 120
Swindell, Robert 82
The Sword of Moses—An Ancient Book of Magic (Moses Gaster) 88
Sykes, Peter 28

Tales from the Crypt (dir. Freddie Francis) 61, 62, 90, 93
Tales of the Unexpected (TV series) 128
A Taste of Honey (Shelagh Delaney) 52
Taste the Blood of Dracula (dir. Peter Sasdy) 5, 7, **8**, 9, 10, 18–19, 22, 24, 32, 35, 39, 43, 44, 84, 89, 90, 91, 105, 120, 130, 138, 151, 153, 161
Tate, Sharon 33, 34, 80
Tayman, Robert 46
10 Rillington Place (dir. Richard Fleischer) 57–58, 123
"Terror of the Autons" (*Dr. Who* TV serial) 117
The Terror of the Tongs (dir. Anthony Bushell) 123
Terry, Ellen 71
Thatcher, Margaret 55
That's Your Funeral (dir. John Robins) 123

Thaw, John 66, 120
Theatre of Blood (dir. Douglas Hickox) 42, 73, 76–77
Thomason, Reg 124
Thompson, J. Lee 33, 82
Thorlby, Anthony 170
Thorne, E. 151
To Have and To Have Not (dir. Howard Hawks) 38
To the Devil a Daughter (dir. Peter Sykes) 28
Todd, Bob 31
Todd, Richard 148
Toone, Geoffrey 123
Torn Curtain (dir. Alfred Hitchcock) 34
Torture Garden (dir. Freddie Francis) 123
Tourneur, Jacques 123, 141
Tower of Evil (dir. Jim O'Connelly) 63
Tower of London (dir. Rowland V. Lee) 97
Toynbee, Philip 87
A Treatise on Cosmic Fire (Alice A. Bailey) 89
The Trip (dir. Roger Corman) 26
Trog (dir. Freddie Francis) 124
Troughton, Patrick 43
The Turn of the Screw (Henry James) 61
Twilight of the Idols (Friedrich Nietzsche) 79
Twins of Evil (dir. John Hough) 57, 60, 63, 83, 93, **95**, 96, 112
Twinsanity (dir. Alan Gibson) see *Goodbye Gemini*
The Two Faces of Dr. Jekyll (dir. Terence Fisher) 123
"The Two Faces of Evil" (episode of *The Hammer House of Horror*; TV series; dir. Alan Gibson) 129
Tyler, Tom 104
Tynan, Kenneth 66

The Ugly Duckling (dir. Lance Comfort) 123
Ulmer, Edgar J. 41
Umbracle (dir. Pere Portabella) 103
Underground (dir. Anthony Asquith) 73
Unger, Kara 137
The Unquenchable Thirst of Dracula (screenplay by Anthony Hinds) 110
Ustinov, Sir Peter 148

Vadim, Roger 18
Valentino, Sal **114**, 125, **126**, 127, 135
Vambery, Arminius 101

Vampire Circus (dir. Robert Young) 46, 61, 62
The Vampire in Europe (Montague Summers) 101
The Vampire Lovers (dir. Roy Ward Baker) 33, 35, 60, 115, 141
La vampire nue (dir. Jean Rollin) 18
I Vampiri (dir. Riccardo Freda) 17
El Vampiro (dir. Fernando Méndez) 17
Vampyr (dir. Carl Dreyer) 18
"The Vampyre" (John Polidori) 42
Vampyres (dir. José Ramón Larraz) 147
Varnel, Marcel 123
Varney the Vampire (James Malcolm Rymer) 42–43
Veidt, Conrad 38, 107
The Vengeance of She (dir. Cliff Owen) 42, 82
Vickers, Mike 59, 131, 134, 144, 155
Victim (dir. Basil Dearden) 55, 75
Vidor, Charles 29
Le viol du vampire (dir. Jean Rollin) 18
Virgin Witch (dir. Ray Austin) 60
Vlad Tepes (the Impaler) 89, 101, 104
Vorhaus, David 158–159

Wagner, Richard 19, 49, 113, 158
Waite, Arthur Edward 70, 85–86
Waiting for Godot (Samuel Beckett) 168
Walker, Alexander 59
Walker, Pete 60, 62, 63, 76
Walsh, Kay 82
Warlock, Peter *see* Heseltine, Philip
Warner, Jack 119
Warren, Barry 139
Washbourne, Mona 62
Waterman, Dennis 59, 66, 120
Watson, Charles "Tex" 34
Waugh, Evelyn 30
Webster, John 48
Weglowski, Adam 101
Wendkos Paul 83
What Became of Jack and Jill (dir. Bill Bain) 61, 62
Wheatley, Dennis 28, 60, 70, 78, 79, 83, 86–87, 88, 89, 165
Whistler, James McNeill 67, 72, 142
Whitaker, David 76
The White Noise 65, 158

The Wicker Man (dir. Robin Hardy) 62, 103
Wicking, Christopher 127
Wide Sargasso Sea (Jean Rhys) 148
Wilde, Oscar 67, 72, **73**, 77
Wilhelm, Richard 87
Will Any Gentleman...? (dir. Michael Anderson) 110
Williams, Kenneth 93–94
Willis, Matt 16
Wilmer, Douglas 3, 75
Wilson, Colin 70, 87, 88
Wilson, Harold 52
Winner, Michael 61, 73
Winters, Shelley 63
Wise, Robert 144
Witchcraft (dir. Don Sharp) 42, 82
Witchcraft and Demonianism (Cecil L'Strange Ewen) 89
The Witches (dir. Cyril Frankel) 82
Wolf, Leonard 19, 94
A Woman Called Golda (dir. Alan Gibson, 1982) 128
The Woman in White (Wilkie Collins) 14
The Woman Who Came Back (dir. Walter Colmes) 42
Wright, Edward 139
Wymark, Patrick 85

Yarbro, Cheslea Quinn 67
Yates, Francis A. 87
Yeats, William Butler 78
The Yellow Rolls-Royce (dir. Anthony Asquith) 146
Young, Robert 46, 61
Young Frankenstein (dir. Mel Brooks) 165

Z-Cars (TV series) 119, 121
Zittrer, Carl 65

www.ingramcontent.com/pod-product-compliance
Lightning Source LLC
Chambersburg PA
CBHW060344010526
44117CB00017B/2958